"An impressive collection of remarkable and varied voices that ranges from one end of the prairie to the other like a cyclone, stirring up new ideas and putting the kibosh on the view held by some that 'flyover country' lacks important voices in contemporary literature."
—David Zimmerman, author, *Caring is Creepy* and *The Sandbox*

"This anthology turns the earth of a too-often stereotyped Midwest, and startling, beautiful things grow. From its provocative introductions by well-known writers, to its works by many writers new to print, this is a collection to take seriously."
—Stephen Pett, author, *Sirens* and *Pulpit of Bones*

"As a recent transplant to the Midwest from the Southwest, I gobbled up the poems, stories, and essays in this anthology as if they were farmers' market produce—fresh, sweet, ripe, spicier than you expect, good for you yet deliciously decadent. These authors—some lauded veterans, many emerging, all of them stunning in their talent—brood vividly, comically, mournfully, complexly on what it means to be from, to live in, and to leave the Midwest. This wondrous, energizing anthology evokes what it feels like to be rooted in and to write out of a specific sense of place and why such an endeavor matters in an age of globalization. *Prairie Gold* fills me with gratitude for the literary variety and richness of my new home."
—K. L. Cook, author, *Love Songs for the Quarantined* and *Last Call*

"For those who think that between New York and California there's nothing but three time zones, this anthology fills in a full continent's worth of great writing. In the spirit of William Gass, 'in the heart of the heart of the country,' the word is etched a little deeper, the colors fade and spark with tan internal luminosity, and the poems and stories in *Prairie Gold* speak in a defining vernacular of Real Life, Real People, Real Literature."
—Bob Holman, Bowery Poetry Club, Bowery Arts & Science, Co-Director, Endangered Language Alliance

"*Prairie Gold* offers a respectful nod to the traditional agrarian based identity of the Midwest, then gathers it's collective voice to challenge those comfortable notions of what defines the Midwest and what it means to be a Midwesterner."
—J. Harley McIlrath, author, *Possum Trot*

"Once again, Ice Cube Press steps up to the plate and hits home to us a book of creative writing—fiction, essays, and poems—that help us to hear the heartbeat of the American prairie. The selections, mostly by up-and-coming writers, provide a feast of words, ideas, and feelings not to be missed."
—Jonathan Andelson, Professor of Anthropology and Director, Center for Prairie Studies, Grinnell College

"I grew up in the South, where we were told early and often that the South was America's great literary soul. But the South is still trapped in its history of race and violence. The strength of *Prairie Gold* is how its writers show the evolution of the Midwest, how it grapples with a changing relationship with the land, the natural environment, and the late twentieth century dismantling of American industry. The Midwest captured in these works is truly the heartland of American experience."
—Larry Baker, author, *A Good Man* and *The Education of Nancy Adams*

Prairie Gold

An Anthology of the
American Heartland

Lance M. Sacknoff
Xavier Cavazos
Stefanie Brook Trout

Ice Cube Press, Est. 1993
North Liberty, Iowa

Prairie Gold:
An Anthology of the American Heartland

Copyright © 2014 Lance M. Sacknoff,
Xavier Cavazos, Stefanie Brook Trout, Editors

ISBN 9781888160819

Library of Congress Control Number: 2014933258

Ice Cube Press, LLC (Est.1993)
205 North Front Street
North Liberty, Iowa 52317-9302
www.icecubepress.com
e: steve@icecubepress.com
twitter: @icecubepress

Manufactured in the USA using acid-free, recycled
paper. The paper used in this publication meets the
minimum requirements of the American National
Standard for Information Sciences—Permanence of
Paper for Printed Library Materials, ANSI Z39.48-1992

Cover design: Jamie Campbell
Consulting Editor: Elizabeth Stranahan

Dedication:

Lance: For my family, Lloyd, Gloria, and Devan Sacknoff, who have continually given me new and exciting perspectives on my life, my work, and myself.

Xavier: For my wife, Shelly, who endures and celebrates with me my passion for the Arts!

Stefanie: For the people I call family and the places I call home.

And for the sustenance of the Midwestern wildernesses and prairies that nourish and fortify our lives, our thoughts, and our creativity.

To Susan,

a fellow Hamline-ite

& CNFer.

Lovely to meet you.

Warm wishes,

& Sarah Elizabeth Turner

CONTENTS

Foreword

Lance M. Sacknoff

Before I moved to the Midwest, my conceptions of Midwestern culture revolved around Midwesterners' reputation for polite manners and agricultural prowess. Even though I knew cities like Chicago, Detroit, and St. Louis contained massive populations of socially sophisticated urbanites and acted as centers of economic trade and art, the term "Midwest" always summoned to mind the image of rural farming families eking out an existence on wide tracts of corn-swaying land. Obviously, my preconceived notions of the Midwest and its inhabitants grossly underestimated the sublimity of raw Midwestern natural landscape and the creativity, complexity, and resourcefulness of Midwesterners. I quickly learned that the American Midwest earned the moniker "America's Heartland" because the Midwest landscape and culture acted as our nation's central muscle for pumping everything from corn and livestock to social ideology and art across the country. Though I understand that all stereotypes of a region crack under the pressure of investigation, the sheer amount of diverse vibrancy I encountered baffled me. I had read more than a few pieces of literature about the Midwest, yet none of the perspectives in those books captured the vitality, intricacy, and mystery of my new home. The Midwestern identity demands further characterization and recognition.

My particular interest in regional literature, especially Midwestern regional literature, developed from my studies in the literary application of ecosemiotics. Essentially, this field of study attempts to diminish communication conflicts between humanity and the natural environment community so that human culture may appreciate the innate importance of the natural world. In other words, my field of study critically analyzes the way authors portray humans living with and in the environment. From Henry David Thoreau's *Walden* to Edward Abbey's *Desert Solitaire*, American literature possesses numerous works that celebrate the origins of all the landscapes we call home. And every literary work—whether it's a lyric essay, an epic poem, or a short story—requires a landscape to give meaning to its narrative. Human culture and all its products—language, tools, mythology, art, etc.—evolve from the landscape that culture inhabits. I argue that illuminating the relationship between an author, character, or general narrative and a given region's landscape is an intrinsic function of regional literature. And, by publishing stories, essays, and poems about Midwest culture and the relationship with the Midwestern environment, we restore the voice of the region and the people that inhabit it. My purpose for *Prairie Gold: An Anthology of the American Heartland*, then, derives from a desire to broadcast a kaleidoscope of new thoughts on the way Midwesterners think about their environment, their cultural identity, and themselves.

Though my particular motivation for crafting this anthology comes from my personal relationship with the natural environment, the literature contained in *Prairie Gold* is not simply a collection of environmental writing. Indeed, many of our authors wrote essays, poems, and stories that occur on farms, in suburbs, and even in a Chinese restaurant. Xavier, Stefanie, and I wanted writing that focused on exploring a perspective or relationship with the Midwest as a place. Whether an author wrote a free form poem about Chicago's urban history or composed an autobiographical essay on the imbricated history of an agrarian family and their farm's geology, their stories offer a precious personal insight into a culturally, philosophically, and environmentally diverse region. Similarly, some of our authors have lived in the Midwest all their lives while others moved away or just arrived. Regardless of the author's origins or their art form, they all felt motivated to produce literature about the Midwest, and writing about relationships with a landscape means writing about oneself.

Like our authors, we editors all possess varied experiences and perspectives on the Midwest: Stefanie has lived in the Midwest her entire life, Xavier has been a resident for many years, and I am somewhat newly arrived. All of us, however, consider the American Midwest our home, and we think of ourselves as Midwesterners. While we engaged in healthy debates over everything from submission guidelines to pieces ready for acceptance, we all agreed that this anthology should contain the highest quality new and unpublished work. We wanted entirely new work because, like any cultural identity, things change: people move, have new experiences, and rediscover lost interests. For example, the term "prairie gold" was originally coined as a moniker for Hard White Spring Wheat. But for us, the term invokes the intellectual and artistic wealth springing from the region much like the corn fields checkered across Iowa. Also, while I highly respect formerly published work on the Midwest, I believe that other, less published authors have just as many beautiful insights into Midwestern living. In order to acknowledge the complexity of Midwesterners' relationship with their homes and avoid stereotyping, we must always endeavor to provide room and voice for fresh perspectives on the Midwestern landscape and identity.

Each story in *Prairie Gold* extends beyond a perspective on a landscape; these stories tell us how Midwesterners define themselves. Regional literature depends on authors displaying an intimate aspect of their own character. Without this crucial personal facet, the story, poem, or essay becomes little more than a case study, a superficial summary of "local flavor," or a stereotype. A farmer in Ogden, Iowa, lives and breaths in fairly close proximity—a mere five and a half hours by car—to a social urbanite in Chicago, Illinois. And even though the urbanite and rural farmer live in relatively close proximity and understand the cultural and social mores of the larger Midwest, both characters embark on wildly different personal journeys. A hypothetical chronicle of the farmer's and urbanite's separate journeys might yield wildly dissimilar accounts. Both tales, however, would underscore how each individual grappled with their identity within the context of their most sacred place: their home. This anthology compiles the various identities developed in a region that many people value as their most intimate space. And each story, essay, and poem—regardless of the opinions and values expressed—deserves consideration and appreciated as a valid, moving, insightful, and fresh expression of Midwestern identity.

Prairie Gold represents our effort to highlight growing talent and varied mindsets in Midwestern regional literature, and as a result, we split this anthology into three roughly equal sections: fiction, nonfiction, and poetry. Each section begins with an introduction from an established Midwestern author describing the various ways they glean inspiration from Midwestern culture and landscape. The Midwest is famous for growing and nurturing the things that sustain us, and and we hope our readers feel similarly nourished by this collection.

Fiction Introduction:
Daydream

Dean Bakopoulos

Years ago, when I still lived in Wisconsin, a poet friend of mine and I were talking at a picnic at another poet's farm. It was a keen late summer day, a gathering of writers young and old; it was almost too beautiful to bear that rolling countryside without a notebook and pen in hand. You could feel it: everyone there was bursting with the high hopes and rested muses of late summer, awash in the mercifully softer breezes of late August, and eager to get to work. This poet, he was, like me at that time, a brand new father.

"The thing I miss," he said, "is the time to daydream. When you have kids, you don't have the time to daydream."

I nodded and agreed, but dismissed this notion as a poet's problem. Of course, poets, who had much lower word count goals, could stare out windows and into reflecting ponds all day long and call it work. But I was a novelist, one book out and another under contract, and I was hammering out 4,000 words a day with obsessive zeal, doing this between a full-time day job, diaper changes, an old fixer-upper of a house, and sleepless nights with a gassy baby. Daydreaming, I thought, didn't matter. Deadlines did.

It's no surprise to me now that the novel I was writing then, at the pace of 4,000 words a day, was a failure, something I have since put in the proverbial desk drawer and something that will probably never have readers. Brick by brick, it wasn't all that bad. But it lacked something. It was predictable and staid. It was boring—even though it had explosions and blizzards at its core. Something about it felt flat.

Since that failed manuscript, my wife, an artist, and I have had another child, and we've moved around Iowa a bit—from Ames to Grinnell to, finally, an old 1860s farmhouse in the tiny village of East Amana, population fifty-five. Almost all of those days in Iowa have been spent with our two kids—they are homeschooled and so we are rarely at home without children. We don't sit quietly at our desks and think all day.

For reasons too complicated to go into here, when I arrived in Iowa, in Ames in the fall of 2009, I arrived depressed. I had finished a new second novel—this one was eventually published—and I had a good job and some good friends in town. But I was worn out and couldn't write. By that I mean, I was still writing many words a day, but almost all of it in wrong directions, ill-conceived and flat, things that were piling up the word count, but feeling as flat as the country-side around us.

Around that time, I gave a reading in Madison, Wisconsin, my old hometown, and had coffee with my graduate school advisor. She, a writer of considerable fame and success, listened to me rattle off a litany of all the things I was working on: mystery novels, YA novels, a literary love story, a screenplay, a TV pilot, a collection of novellas, and essays. I made sure to mention, probably several times, that I also was writing thousands of words a day, seven days a week.

She smiled and said, "Maybe, do you think, that you're writing too much?"

I laughed and said, "That's impossible."

That winter in Ames was brutal. It seemed every day brought har-rowing winds off the prairie, and snowfalls that could be measured in feet and not inches. Back in Wisconsin, my best friend died of cancer. I missed my novel deadline and my publisher in New York filed for bankruptcy. That winter, several thousand words a day felt as flat and brittle as ever. I felt as if maybe my advisor was right: maybe I was writing too much.

I was also gaining weight and having back problems that winter and so I made a decision that instead of writing all of those words every morning, I would walk to and from campus each day, about two and a half miles each way.

I began that January, zipping myself up into Carhart coveralls to walk through campus. Only my eyes were exposed to the wind most days, and I cut through Brookside Park, picking it up at 13th street, and taking it's wooded path over to 6th, a seven-block intentional detour. I'd walk home at dusk—dusk coming before supper in those months—and, despite the cold, take the long way home again.

This was four years ago, at a time in my life when I was wondering if all the hours I spent writing were, perhaps, useless.

Let's fast-forward to a happier me. That second novel was finished, got published. A third got finished and sold this summer. But I no longer write thousands of words a day. I spend a lot more time walking, daydreaming—ambling through the countryside outside my door, working in the yard, stacking firewood, wandering along the creek with my kids. Some nights, I drive around in my truck and look at the fireflies, a million glimmering embers over knee-high corn. Winters, I make fires in the snow, look at the scattered stars and the silver snowy moon and do nothing but think. I have become comfortable with stillness in a way the younger me never was. Younger me worked himself to the point of illness—exhaustion, depression, bad back, migraines, shingles, panic attacks.

Here in Iowa, I have finally allowed daydreaming to be a part of my writing process. I think this is because one doesn't have to make time to daydream, to hole up in a room and think. Here, the brilliance of the quiet, the open spaces, the staggeringly rich skies, is living that becomes a sort of daydream. Cooking dinner, I stare out the window at the flaming streaks of the coming sunset. Playing with my kids in the yard, I smell the sweetness of lilacs in spring or pears in autumn. I see the burst of goldfinch against the endless green. Walking in the morning for exercise, I am not on a treadmill, but off in the pinking light of early morning, a light that seems to fill my veins with warmth. Driving to campus, a hilly, easy amble along Highway Six, the clouds are entertainment enough. I leave the podcasts on silent. When stuck behind a tractor at harvest time, I relish the extra time to think.

Living in Iowa's landscape, both ecological and cultural, feels like a long, sweet continuous daydream to me. (This is something worth fighting for—by the way, when big money and Giant Ag try to rob this sweetness from the public trust). When I first arrived here, I did nothing but work: write, teach, and take care of my family; I exhausted myself. Now, having taught myself to notice the unique rhythms and subtleties of this place, I always feel ready to write. My brain daydreams itself to fullness nearly every day. Sometimes you get two thousand words a day, sometimes two sentences, but the writing never feels forced.

It occurred to me recently that this feeling—of calm, of pensiveness, of joy—is at the core of why I may never leave Iowa, at least not for long. My brain, my heart, my muse, seems to have, quite unexpectedly, become dependent on the pace and scope of life here. The din of a million cicadas and the endless swishing of golden corn in early fall—these things matter to me in a way I can't quite explain. All I know is that I miss them when I am away, traveling, and when I come home, I often do nothing but stare at the world exploding around me and think long, long thoughts.

After that, maybe some words on the page. Or maybe, instead, a walk through the prairie.

Dean Bakopoulos
East Amana, Iowa
September 12, 2013

Dean Bakopoulos is writer-in-residence at Grinnell College. He was born and raised in metro Detroit, the setting of his first novel, *Please Don't Come Back from the Moon* (Harcourt), a *New York Times* Notable Book. His second novel, *My American Unhappiness*, was published in June 2011 by Houghton Mifflin Harcourt and named one of the year's best books by *The Chicago Tribune*. A new novel, set in Iowa, *Summerlong*, is forthcoming in Winter 2015 from Ecco (HarperCollins).

The winner of fellowships from the Guggenheim Foundation and the National Endowment for the Arts, Dean has taught at the University of Wisconsin-Madison, Iowa State University, and the MFA Program for Writers at Warren Wilson College. He is also an occasional critic and essayist for *New York Times Book Review*.

The Great River Road

Molly Rideout

Momma could have taken me anywhere since she'd saved the money, but she'd made it plain and clear that I'd be getting Moline, Illinois, with its big and brown dirty-river banks. She had never gone farther from Casston than the Dells in all her life, but there we were, cruising seventy like it was eighty down that Mississippi River jig-jag. Wisconsin melted away in the heat lines on the highway behind.

"No one goes to Moline unless they got something like family there," white-haired Jan, Momma's boss at the speaker-cone factory, said when Momma, trailing me by the hand, went in to ask for Friday off.

"I guess we got something like family, then," Momma replied.

We were going down to meet her maker.

This maker, she was forty-five now, a woman with Mississippi mud streaks in her amber-ale hair. Hadn't even been sixteen when she'd done the making. Didn't really know what that meant, but I did know that I had two blood grandmas, and neither of them were Grandma Flora who took care of me when school was out and who had raised Momma up proper like her own from a little basket-baby. This one was the real thing.

"Don't you go calling me grandma," the maker-woman told me when we finally met. Curls bounced around her shoulders. "I'm no-body's grandma. Keep it simple and sweet, Pineapple Cheeks. Call me Val."

Not-grandma Val looked nothing like Momma, but in the same way Momma and I looked nothing alike. It's all on the inside, Momma said. It's all in bones and muscles and hearts. We had the same teeth, Dr. Morrison, the dentist in Casston, told us. But Momma's were straight and mine grew in every which way, kept falling out with bigger ones pushing in. Val, though, her teeth were messy like mine, and when she smiled big, she smiled crisscross, like she did when she saw us coming from down the street.

"Hello Maggie!" Val called to me with a wave when we were still twenty feet away. "Hello Moe," she added when we were face-to-face. She stuck out her hand for Momma to shake.

"It's good to finally meet you, Val."

"Looks like you grew up as beautiful and bright as a warm, fall day."

Val invited us for a walk along the riverbank under the railroad-bridge and I-74. Momma clutched my hand, and I couldn't feel my fingers she held her tears in so hard. The banks of the Mississippi were all boardwalk and flowerbeds. Gentle-fication, Momma called it, but the river seemed more rough than gentle down here. Not sand rough, but river rats rough, garbage-floating-everywhere-and-no-one-cleaning-it-up rough. At the wharf down from TGI Fridays, Momma let go of my hand and said, "You be careful now, don't go stepping in goose goo or jumping off piers." I ran out onto the rocking dock, yelled, "Turbulence!" and stomped back and forth until even the planks got super woozy. Then, in one soggy wooden corner that had only one little putt-putt motorboat tied to it, I counted in the water two Pepsi cans, a tennis ball, a wiffle ball, half a styrofoam cup, bits of white that might have been the rest of the cup, a plastic fork, an empty water bottle, and a whole lot of green funk and duckweed that together smelled like our fridge on weeks when Momma got real sad. That was how a rough river looked.

Val was telling Momma a story about Dubuque when I jumped to a stop next to them, and Momma said hush, be quiet now. Momma had been born in Dubuque before Grandma Flora and Grandpa Gene had signed the baby adoption papers and driven her and her cute baby nose the forty-five minutes up the Great River Road to Casston. Now some weekends when our house there seemed small enough to walk across in two steps and Momma's chest felt sixteen-tons heavy, we'd escape back to her birthplace. "That city's better than happy pills any day," Momma said, but my Aunt Holly told her it was just another town with the Mississippi running through.

"I left Dubuque as soon as I could," Val told Momma. "Just had to. Moved out to Wyoming. Needed some air, and that sky seemed to have it."

"At the top of the bluffs you can see almost the whole sky," I pointed out to her. I slipped a hand into Momma's and looked up at this not-grandma Val and her corduroy overalls, her dream-catcher earrings, and her crisscross mouth.

She looked at me and nodded. "But not all of it," she said and then asked if we wanted any lunch.

A block off the river, Moline looked a whole lot like Casston, only with bigger streets and more of them. It had the same rundown don't-you-talk-to-me-about-this-economy look, the same Mississippi-life feel of things flowing to somewhere else. It was August-hot in Moline, and even the cars were sweating the sparkles out of their paint-jobs.

"There's just no good way to get there," Momma had told me when she'd planned the trip, maps of three states spread across the kitchen table, counter and floor. But really there was no good way to get anywhere from Casston. That was the problem: It was the type of place to get stuck in, river on one side, bluffs on the other. A driftless region, Momma called it with a weird smile I didn't like to see. "No one drifts in and no one drifts out." Momma toggled between the maps with my art supplies ruler, measuring a corner of this one, then a county highway on that one. She made the squiggly lines straight, promised me it would be an easy ride. But then, day of departure, car parked in the driveway, she gave me a plastic Ziploc to hold just in case. The puke bag. I saw she had one of her own that she stuck in her purse, folded up tight and hidden in the corner. I tucked mine into the waistband of my shorts.

For the promised lunch, Miss Val took us into Lager Haus, a German pub, one of two open bars back to back on a street that drove away from the river. It had big wooden booths, a flat-screen above the bar that flashed soccer news, and accordion music accompanied by silly voices. Every dish came with potato salad, and they had brats, just like The Drinking Well in Casston, but not the good beer that Momma liked, so she just ordered something from Chicago that was on tap. The owner, Carl, with his flat cap and water balloon belly smiled a hungry new-customer smile and filled the glass.

When we'd crossed over the Mississippi into Iowa at the Dubuque bridge, Momma had announced over the Subaru's air-conditioner rattling, "I'm gonna need a drink before all this is through." I was waving goodbye to Wisconsin, hoping it wouldn't miss me too much while we were gone. "It's good having your momma around, isn't it?" she asked. On the steering wheel her knuckles were stretched thin and long like pennies on the railroad tracks. An hour later she was singing with the radio, birthday-Christmas excited, but when we crossed the Mississippi River for the last time the corners of her mouth didn't drift up so high, and she was tearing the bits of skin off of her lip like she did when she heard mice in the cupboards but didn't want to look. She pulled over at her first chance, a concrete crossroads of clover-leafs with nowhere to get out, fumbled in the secret corners of her purse and threw up in her Ziploc. The oatmeal from breakfast hadn't digested at all. It floated there in one big putty-clump amid the foamy watered-down milkshake of stomach juices. She made me hold the closed bag until we found a place to dump it and we drove the rest of the way with the windows down and the AC off.

It was warm when I poked it.

Everyone at the Lager Haus knew Val like they were best-of-friends family. The girl behind the bar with the most wonderful pom-pom pigtails I'd ever seen gave Momma and me menus and Val a bent-over, one-armed hug.

"What're you doing here on your day off?" the girl demanded, all grins and gum, her hip snapped to the side like a rubber-band doll.

"Getting free food from you," Val replied, arm still around the standing girl's waist like Momma hugged me sometimes. Momma watched them with tight cheeks.

"Can I have chocolate milk, Momma?" I asked.

"No, Maggie. Let's both get waters. You don't charge here for waters, do you?" Momma called after the waitress as she slid back to the bar.

"Hush, now," Val said. She brushed Momma's arm, strange and awkward. "We'll split the cost."

Momma wasn't listening. "How do waters sound, Maggie?"

"Whatever," I mumbled, kicking my feet back and forth under the table. When Momma tried to give me a thank-you hug like Val had given the waitress I ducked away and pretended I was too busy to notice the unhappy in her eyes.

Back in Casston, Aunt Holly hadn't been happy either when she'd heard what Momma and me were doing. "You never cared about finding this woman before her letter," she told her adopted sister whenever she came to visit our itsy bitsy spider house all the way out where Highway 133, the Great River Road, started heading south out of town.

"It wasn't an option before," Momma replied as she picked the laminate away from the kitchen table little by little in that way that lets you avoid looking at other people's eyes. The letter lay on the table, post-marked a week ago from Moline, Illinois, inking over an eight-month-old Christmas postage stamp. "But here she is. I'm just curious."

"And I'm curious what this house would look like if you managed to get your ass up for work every day." Aunt Holly stuck out her foot and slid it around like a washcloth. Two or three needle-long black streaks emerged from under her sole. Bug juice.

"I've got a daughter to take care of," Momma snapped. "She's not gonna sit alone in this house."

"You're the one who sits alone," Aunt Holly pointed out. "Maggie goes to school now. She doesn't need a babysitter."

"I need to go. She'll have answers."

"To what?"

Momma swirled her hand about vaguely. The sweep of her fingers hit first the crusted-dry dishes and the TV remote in the fruit bowl, then my macaroni art project with most of the macaroni fallen off. They rested finally against her shoulder.

"To this," she sighed.

"She's not going to fix you." Aunt Holly had her voice to the grindstone, worn down. "It took her thirty years to even contact you. I wish you'd pull yourself together."

Momma gave a short laugh. "Pull what together? I've been in this magician's box so long, I don't even know how many parts I've been cut into."

When Aunt Holly left, Momma sat quiet, tore some of the skin off her lips in little moist bites. From the letter creased open on the table, she dialed a number, long distance, and waited for the echo in the phone lines. When she asked if, Hello, was this Val Hartley? her voice wobbled like the training wheels had just been removed. But then she indian-walked into her bedroom, stretched the spring-cord as far as the receiver would go and came out just two minutes later to say it was time for dinner now, no questions. We ate raviolis and baked beans from the can, and we made it taste good.

Before we'd left Casston, Momma had told me everything she'd known about Val, which wasn't anything more than a name and a city and the sound of her voice, but I filled in the details. She lived in a house as big as the grocery store, owned eight long-haired dachshunds, and baked even better macaroni and cheese than Grandpa

Gene. She gave bikes for birthdays and a brand new blue coat for Christmas. She liked horses, especially black ones with a little white on their noses, and she didn't work at a bar where every dish came with potato salad.

Our food arrived. Momma'd ordered small and simple: bowl of cereal, skim milk. Her empty stomach couldn't take meat, she said. I was allowed to get a burger, well done, since my plastic Ziploc was still empty and tucked into the elastic of my shorts. I watched my not-grandma brush invisible somethings off her shirt and then blow on her soup. I wondered how she liked her burgers.

"Hey, doll," Val called after the waitress. "I'll have a chocolate milk too." She winked at me as it was brought, made sure Carl was looking at the soccer scores, and switched our drinks. "On the house," she whispered with her crisscross smile. I crisscross grinned back. Momma picked at her lower lip with her teeth and watched a man out the window fill the garbage compactor across the street. She stuck a fork into the middle of her cereal bowl. I slurped away at the milk like drought-dry soybeans. The glass even had a straw.

Val took a big balloon breath. "What was it like growing up in Casston?" she asked. "Did you get a good family?"

"Yeah. Good family."

Momma had to dab her lip with a napkin because it had started to bleed, so I helped her out. "Grandpa Gene makes sure I take out the kitchen garbage and put it in the big trash can. He says it builds fiber."

Val nodded. "Good town?"

"Terrible."

"Why didn't you move to a bigger city?"

"I needed the free child care."

They looked at me.

"And Maggie's father?" Val asked, glancing at the jewelry on Momma's fingers. "Are you living together?"

"My daddy didn't know how to make commitments to anyone but himself and a fool's dream in Chicago," I quoted, chest puffed out strong.

I glanced at Momma, who gave the smallest smile, then said, "She never knew him."

"It's okay," I said with a shrug, playing cool. "He didn't love me."

"I don't know, Pineapple Cheeks, love can stretch almost any distance."

"I'll bet." Momma said.

Val gave her a long look while stirring her thick and gritty potato-looking soup. "I was going to call you Eleanor," she said at last. "But Maureen's nice."

I looked at Momma too, but she wasn't looking anywhere. "I like Maureen," I said. "Eleanor's an old people name." I slipped my hand into hers and felt only nails, but she gave a little squeeze. I kept eating my fries with my other hand.

"What was my dad's name?" Momma asked at last. Already I was getting sick of all the questions. "Is he still in Dubuque?"

Val shrugged. "Not the type to send Christmas cards. His name was Michael Saunders. One of my brother's friends."

"You have a brother?"

Val shook her head, a not-anymore shake. "Vietnam got him one through the kidney and one through the lung."

"I had an uncle," Momma said faintly.

"You've got a lot of things."

"What do you want?" Momma asked, and I started to say dessert because I thought she was talking to me. But then she added, "Why did you wait so long?"

Val wouldn't look at Momma, but she thought long and hard. "I don't think I know," she said. "Things. Excuses. They all tapped me in different places. Ran the ol' body dry."

"You're forty-five. Don't act like it's seventy."

"Do you get sad like Momma does?" I asked, because the sad-sickness tapped Momma too, ran her into the floorboards, into bathrooms, rooms with locks. Blood can help blood, the doctors said. When I got the chicken pox, they asked Momma if she'd ever had them too. Maybe she needed blood-help.

Val was looking at Momma with tree-branch eyes that could only scratch the windows. She opened her mouth a few times, then finally decided:

"Ten digits can be the hardest numbers to dial when all you can do is imagine the face of the not-so-baby-girl on the other end of the line."

"I'll bet," Momma said again.

"I wanted to see what my girl looked like grown up and happy."

"Well, here I am," Momma lifted her hands, "Grown up."

"Here you are."

That's when Momma decided to finally start eating. The bits of cereal fell apart as she scooped her spoon through them. They'd become a milky paste, and a little bit slopped onto her shorts when she took her first bite. I didn't think about the morning oatmeal at all.

Val asked, "Why don't you move down here?"

"Excuse me?"

"Rent is too high to live alone. Moline's a good enough city."

"I'm not uprooting my daughter," Momma said.

"But you could come live with us," I suggested instead, ground beef bubbling out from behind my teeth and leaking back onto the plate. "We've got a house with nine windows and seven doors if you count the pantry and Momma's closet."

"No," Momma said.

"The house needs the company."

"That would be fun, wouldn't it?" Val replied with one of those winks that made my heart go tapping against my ribcage.

"Great," I cried. "Let's go right now." I bounced up and down on the booth's bench. "But," I warned, "We've got bluffs same as Dubuque. You won't see the whole sky."

"Turns out Miss Maggie Pineapple Cheeks," Val told me, touching her nose and looking straight at me so she didn't have to look at Momma, "The whole sky is no match for some good solid rock."

She winked again like a fairy godmother in corduroy overalls, like I was the biggest princess along the entire Mississippi from Lake Itasca down to New Orleans and I had just won the blood-relative lottery. I giggled and we just stared at each other. Maybe-grandma Val wouldn't look anywhere else.

"Our house only has two bedrooms," I said, "Momma's and mine, so you'll have to sleep with me because Momma says she needs her space. We can fit a sleeping bag between the bed and the closet. The maroon sleeping bag, not the black one, because the black one is too big, unless we fold it in half. Maybe the black sleeping bag can be a mattress with the maroon bag on top."

And if I strung a sheet from the closet to my bed, we could make a fort, the best bedtime palace for the best Mississippi princess and her fairy godmother.

Momma, though, just sat next to me looking like she'd discovered that some of those raisins in her cereal weren't really raisins. I thought I might need to offer her my plastic Ziploc bag. She had that sort of look, like the whole world had just turned into winding road maps without a straight edge in sight.

"This isn't about Maggie," she said. "I'm not Maggie. I'm not you. I can care for my own child." She picked up my empty glass. "We don't need you getting us chocolate milk."

"Then why'd you come down?"

"Because you asked me to."

"I mean really."

Momma's face stretched like a worn out scrunchie that had been in my hair for too long. She picked up the saltshaker and put it back down, then the pepper, then the creamer bowl.

"I wanted answers," she said.

"So ask the questions."

"Not those kind of answers."

"What other kind is there?" Val asked with a smile, but when Momma didn't smile back, she said, "Well, have you found them?"

Momma shook her head. "Still in the magician's box."

"What?" Val's finger's slid back and forth along the table. "I could help with childcare," she offered.

Something in Momma broke clean off, left a sharp cutting edge. "Maggie's in school," she snapped. "She doesn't need a babysitter." She grabbed my hand, said I should finish my burger if I still wanted any of it because we were going now, thank you, Val, for paying for lunch.

"I wanted dessert," I pointed out. We'd only been in Moline for an hour, and the Subaru had smelled like stale car upholstery the whole two and a half hours down from Casston.

Momma stuck her hand out to my corduroyed definitely-not-grandma Val, and it looked like her arms had gone all stiff at the joints. Val stared at the fingers with their spread-eagle offering.

"I'm glad to see you're back on the Mississippi River," Momma said, black-tie formal. "It's closer than Wyoming."

"Didn't have a choice." Val said and finally took the offered hand like she was shaking an apology out and hanging it to dry. "I thought I was going mad out there. The river's got a pull, like a heart line, and it doesn't let you go. You'll do things for this water that you'd never do for another living thing."

Momma gathered up her purse with a clenched jaw and asked me if I needed to use the bathroom. She didn't bother leaving any money to help with the bill.

"You'll see, Moe." The muscles in Val's cheeks tightened a little, but she couldn't quite bring up a smile.

The air in the Subaru was burning and too thick to move when we clambered inside. Even when we rolled down the windows everything seemed to stay within the car, but Momma pushed through, started up the engine. I waved goodbye for her, and Val waved back with her dream-catcher earrings and her windy winding hair. It was a slow wave. Back on the interstate, Momma took a turn south rather than north onto a narrower state highway with a white and green sign that read The Great River Road, same as the ones we had along 133 up in Casston. The Mississippi came and went from view, a blue-brown with green lining, and Momma drove a little faster than she would with other folks around. My ears started to hurt from the wind in the windows, but she did nothing to roll them up.

"Momma," I said, but she didn't let me finish.

"Road trips are as American as apple pie," she said sticking her arm out the window to feel the currents. Her knuckles were stretched thin and nervous again, squished pennies.

"I hate apple pie."

Momma looked at me, looked up the road, then in the mirror behind, made sure we were the only ones on that snakeskin highway other than the roadkill deer coming up on our right with its head this way, legs that. She leaned way over, one-handed wheel driving, and kissed the top of my head, squeezed my shoulder. "Cherry pie, then," she said quietly in my ear with a smile of nice straight teeth. The car slowly veered onto the rumble strip and we rode those vibrations a while until Momma straightened up.

"I have to pee," I said loudly, because I wanted her to pull over, to stop smiling like that.

"You just peed at the restaurant," she yelled through the window-wind blustering in. "We're going to go a little farther."

"Like really bad," I shouted back, but we didn't stop until we needed gas somewhere south in that bump of Illinois. I dragged my feet through the candy aisle of the convenience store, said I was still hungry, but Momma pulled me through, got me outside. She buckled me all up and checked the seatbelt.

"I'm not three," I said and tried to push her hands away.

"I love you, baby," she replied.

From there we turned east and left the Great River Road.

Growing Corn
Michelle Donahue

There's something in the cornfields. After her first day at her school, Maya stares out the window of their home and does nothing but look at corn. After an hour, she becomes an expert corn-watcher. She knows exactly how the tassels move in the wind, how the stalks sway and curve like slumped spines. Her first day at her new school was a disaster.

In the far right corner of the expansive field, the Iowa corn moves, stalks splitting like the Red Sea parting for Moses. She learned all about Moses and the Red Sea today.

It went like this.

On the elementary school playground, a girl walked up to Maya.

"You're new, right? Want to play?" The girl had long pigtails pulled low on her neck. "I'm Emily."

"I'm Maya," she said, elated; she had been so scared she'd be forced to spend lunch alone, in a bathroom stall, like the new kids did in all the movies.

Emily said, "We're playing Red Moses." She pulled Maya toward the soccer field. The field had lush grass, damp from humidity. A group of boys and girls swarmed, cotton shirts sticking to the napes of their necks. Emily pulled Maya onto one of two teams, each merging into a single line and clasping hands.

"Hold tight," was all Emily said.

"Red Moses, Red Moses, send Justin on over!" Some guy on Maya's team shouted.

Justin broke from his team and ran. He leaped between two girls in an attempt to split open their clasped hands. The force of it sent all of Maya's team moving. She was pulled to the side and almost fell, but miraculously, the girls stayed strong. Their hands were still clasped, the human chain unbroken. Justin joined their team.

"See, the goal is to break through the other team's defense. You have to part the people, like Moses and the Red Sea." Emily said.

Maya said, "It's Red Rover."

"But it's funnier as Red Moses because it's like Moses parting the Red Sea, you know?"

Maya didn't. She tried to shift her confused-face to her oh-yes-I-understand face that she often used when Mom talked about her bioengineering work. But she didn't make the change fast enough.

"You don't know Moses? From the Bible?" Emily laughed not cruelly, but as if Maya were some entity so improbable that all Emily could do was laugh. Others laughed too. Maya imagined a sea of laughter sprouting from the congregation of sweaty maybe-not friends. She imagined being Moses and splitting the sea of laughter and walking between it, untouched.

"Aren't you Christian?"

Maya always envisioned herself more as a Buddhist. Her best friend in California, Kat was Chinese and Maya went with her family to temple all the time. Also her aunt in Oregon was Buddhist, so Maya knew more about Buddhism than any other religion. She found the gold shiny Buddhas so friendly. The dying Jesus-on-a-cross in every church felt menacing and gory.

She stood in the soccer field. In a movie, the bell would ring and spare the heroic, slightly awkward but likable, main character from the embarrassment of staring, open-mouthed without anything to say. But the moment stretched, wedged itself into her cranium into the part of her brain that would never forget. In the field, she thought, *life is suffering.*

Maya continues to watch the stalks move in the cornfield. They sway more violently now. She stares at the tall corn, and it bends as if something were walking between the stalks.

Something big.

She watches the corn part until dinner creeps upon her. That night it's only her and Dad, eating at the wood table, scratched now, from the move.

"Mom's stuck at work tonight. Just you and me, kiddo."

He made her favorite meal, corn tacos with pabloños and queso fresco. But the avocado is hard and mealy and nothing like the home-grown avocados from their tree back in California.

The corn billows outside their window.

"I bet Mom's making mutant corn right now," Dad says. She thinks he intends this to be comforting. But the word *mutant* makes Maya think of Frankenstein's monster, Dad's favorite book. Two years ago, when she started second grade, he read it to her at night. She loved it, but the monster's loneliness always frightened her.

"Dad, I think there's something in the cornfields."

"There's something in the cornfields," she tells Emily, the next day at school.

"Yeah, corn." Emily gives her the look, the you-don't-know-Moses look: the raised eyebrow, lips smooshed to one side and slightly open. The look that says *you're weird.* Dad told Maya that she'd be cool in Iowa, because she was from California. She knows how to surf and grew up blocks away from movie stars.

"Do you know Brad Pitt? I've seen him on the street by my old house."

Again, that look. If only Maya had seen Moses walking down the street. *Just be yourself* Dad would say. Only here, she doesn't yet know who she is. Maya pulls at the neck of her dark blue Hollister shirt and tries to think of a new approach to make and keep friends.

Suffering is caused by craving and aversion. Her aunt told her this when she wanted a horse and threw a tantrum when she didn't get one for Christmas. *You will suffer if you don't get something you want. That's the Second Noble Truth of Buddhism.* Maya was only five at the time, but she hadn't thrown a tantrum since.

Perhaps she needed to blend in. Stop talking about movie stars, beaches, and chorizo, and instead learn more about football, the Hawk Eyes and Cyclones, and eat cheese curds and tater tots. She did really like cheese curds.

Buddhism teaches: *we will suffer if we expect others to conform to our expectations or if we want others to like us.*

At home, she asks Dad to explain the rules of football.

Friday after school, Dad comes to pick her up. Usually, she takes the bus, an experience that always makes her dizzy from navigating social conventions and school hierarchy. Cool kids in the back. Nerds in the front. Those coasting between the extremes take the middle. Each section grafted young to old. Fifth graders, the real kings of the school, always in the back.

Or it went something like that. In California, her school district didn't have busses. Driving culture permeated so permanently that there was no need. So, when Dad shows up at school, Maya is both relieved and panicked because this isn't the Iowan way.

"I've got a surprise for you, kiddo."

As she climbs into the front seat, she wishes their car wasn't quite so fancy. A red, Ferrari F430. Mom makes good money; Dad likes shiny cars. She begrudges him and his ridiculous car for a moment, until he says, "We're going horseback riding."

There's a horse stable on the other side of the corn field by their house. Maya falls in love immediately. Iowa suddenly feels brighter, more magical. Miss Delilah, a woman with lush freckles spattering her face, owns the stable.

Maya climbs onto a black colt with a coat of shiny ink, and wraps her fingers through his mane. "Hello Beauty," she says and he kicks back his head as if to say *hello*. She fell in love with horses when Dad had read her *Black Beauty*. Maya rides Beauty around the stable's dirt area and then Delilah shows her an area of prairie she can explore.

"You're a natural," Miss Delilah says.

Maya likes the power she feels atop a horse. The height provides a new view of the world; the plants become small, the sky grows bluer, closer, as if she can touch the clouds. The prairie remnant is small and surrounded by corn, but the prairie plants are strange to Maya and because of this strangeness, they are wonderful. The wild turkey foot looks like split wheat and the big bluestem reminds her of fragile cattails. Even the corn shines friendly-green, the sun-yellow kernels poking through spider web wisps of cornsilk.

And then, far away in the field, she sees something. The corn bending, making way for a big object. She thinks she sees slender gray ears. She thinks she sees a tender tendril of smoke. She and Beauty tense; he must smell it too. She's going to run for Miss Delilah to warn her about the smoke, but then it disappears.

It must have been shafts of sunlight catching dust or pesticide particles. Maya knows how many pesticides protect these fields.

In the car, on the short drive back home, Maya is about to bring up the mystery ears and smoke she saw in the cornfield when Dad says, "Guess what?"

"There's been a vampire attack in Wisconsin, and they're on their way here?"

"No," he laughs. "Miss Delilah said she's looking for someone to help her with her horses. She was hoping you might want to."

Maya wants to hug him him, hard. She forgets all about the smoky ears in the cornfield.

After school, she gets off the bus near the stable. Today was another disastrous day. Emily ignored her all through recess, so Maya was forced to spend the full forty minutes alone on the swings. As Maya walks along the dirt path to the stable, her white tennis shoes grow coated with fine dust. She walks along the edge of the cornfield. The corn feels humid; it's a wet, sweet heat. But underneath that earthy aroma is a hint of acid.

She touches a corn stalk and sandwiches a leaf between her fingertips. She feels the acid absorb through her skin and tunnel deep into bone. A trail of red seeps onto her hand, from nail to knuckle, a thin line weaving like a vein. Her hand begins to burn, the flesh sagging, the skin elegant drops, curved like Dali's melting clocks. She closes her eyes. Drops speck the dry soil and sizzle.

She opens her eyes and her hand is still intact, still holding the single leaf.

"Take that, chemicals!" She pumps her fist.

Buddhism says, *everything formed is always changing. The world is defined by what disintegrates.*

The cornstalks whisper around her. Her hand has not melted. Emily could still possibly like her. Maya will not disintegrate.

When she arrives to the stable, Miss Delilah wears a furrowed frown.

"Another horse is missing," she says.

"Another?"

"Third one this month."

They spend the afternoon upgrading the locks on the stables. Luckily, Beauty isn't missing. He is the only thing Maya loves here.

Before Maya goes to bed, she puts her palm to the window and watches the stalks stirring. There is more than just wind out there. An eardrum-piercing animal sound splits the air.

The next morning is Saturday, so even Mom is home. Dad cooks fluffy pancakes, and they have real syrup from Canada.

"There was a robbery at the Kum & Go last night," Mom says, mostly to Dad. "The one close to the stable. A whole window was broken and they took the strangest things. The news said cheese puffs, gummy worms, alcohol, and packs of cigarettes."

Dad says nothing, only looks thoughtful, his cheeks puffed with pancakes.

Maya says, "There's something strange in the cornfields."

"Don't be ridiculous," Mom says.

"What shall we do about it?" Dad says.

Equipped with floppy hats, long sleeves, long pants, face masks, and stomachs filled with pancakes, she and Dad set out to explore the cornfield.

Mom thinks they are going to the horse stables.

"Dressed like this, we'll be fine," Dad says. Maya can't help but think about her imagined hand melting and dripping to the ground. But she decides she won't disintegrate yet.

The corn towers far over her head, taller than Dad. They march through the corn and bushwhack like jungle explorers. Dad holds her hand, the one that melted now feels strong and solid.

"Let's hope the farmer doesn't find us," Dad says as he breaks a corn stalk.

But Maya hears something. Hoofs. She breaks their handhold and ventures to her left, ducking between the taller stalks. As she parts the sticky stalks she thinks, *I am new age Moses. This is my sea to part.* The corn thins until she comes to an area where all the corn lies pummeled, flattened, ears half nibbled and left to rot on the ground. She can't see Dad, though he can't be far. She stands in the breezeless air.

A gray horse pokes his head into the clearing. He locks eyes with Maya. His eyes fall to slits, but Maya can still see how bloodshot and bleary they are. Small welts cover his face, and there is a protrusion at the crown of his forehead. The cornstalks obscure it until he walks a few steps forward. There, on his head, is a bone-white horn.

Dad has trouble believing there are unicorns in the cornfield.

"Unicorns don't exist, Maya."

But what if. What if like Frankenstein's monster they had been made. Biogeneticists like Mom could create all sorts of strange organisms. Maya doesn't think unicorns are less impossible than tomatoes with fish genes or plants producing their own pesticides.

Picture this: a scientist, perhaps a woman like Mom, who grew up with horses, who grew up with fantasy novels. Her hands itched to recreate that magic of childhood, that wonder she found between dusty pages. A unicorn. Isolate some of the rhino's horn genes, splice them with a horse. If Frankenstein could make a creature from corpse parts, then Maya is sure this is possible too.

But of course, Frankenstein isn't real.

But what if, like Frankenstein's monster, this creature is lonely?

Maya names him Maurice. She can't let him be nameless like the monster.

That night, she shrouds herself in protective clothes and ventures alone into the cornfield. Buddhism teaches: *it is important to develop wisdom and understanding*. She needs to understand this creature. She already knows his loneliness.

"Maurice," she calls, softly. Her flashlight beam illuminates only a small sphere of the world before her, the inverse of walking through a tunnel. The corn goes *swish-wish* around her. The silk glistens like fishing line. She imagines how lovely it would be to see another unicorn. She too reads fantasy novels. She too yearns for unicorns. She feels their presence seep into her. Her skin burns.

She can't find her way back to the clearing, so instead she only stands and waits, listens.

When the sun begins to rise, defeat creeps over her, and she turns toward home. But on the way back, for one second, weak sun filters through the corn in thick shafts, and she sees a gray horse tail flick and sway before her. She runs to follow, but it's already gone.

Monday, at the stable, horses paw at the dirt and wait to be fed. Miss Delilah sits on a wood stool and peels carrots into a steel bucket. The peeled carrots will become stew, and the horses get the peels as treats. Maya brushes Beauty.

"Do you believe in magic?" Maya asks.

Miss Delilah pauses and runs a hand through her coppery hair. "I used to," she picks up a new carrot and runs the peeler down its skin. "Sometimes I think all this science stuff, like those bioengineered corn plants out in the field and all that new pesticide, is a sort of magic." Long, dirty peels of carrot fall into the bucket. "Magic gone wrong though. It's not good for anyone."

A drop of sweat slides down Maya's face. "My mom says all that stuff gives us more food. Makes it cheaper."

Miss Delilah stands, tucking her peeler into the front pocket of her overalls.

"That might be true."

Miss Delilah has strong shoulders and a dainty waist.

"That doesn't mean it's good."

"Did you see the Cyclone game last night?" Maya asks Emily the next day at school.

"It was awesome." Emily jumps in delight, her pigtails bouncing.

Maya's hair is also pigtailed, her straw-colored locks braided messily. She never did pigtails in California, but she's beginning to get the hang of it. Although Dad tries, he's never been good at doing her hair.

Once Maya started talking about football, Emily warmed to her again. Emily's brother is on the Cyclone team so she is a "BIG Clonehead." Maya hadn't really watched the game; she finds football boring. Insufferable, even. But she googled it, read enough to fake it and lie.

Buddhism says, *you're supposed to lead a moral life.*

"Do you believe in magic?" Maya asks.

But Emily is already running toward the soccer field to play Red Moses. Maya runs after her, desperate to keep up, to make it to the field in time so that it appears that she is with Emily.

Maya can only venture into the cornfield on the nights Mom and Dad go to bed early. Mom isn't so hard; she always goes out like a light. But Dad lingers, stays up late reading.

Tonight, she gets lucky. She puts on her long sleeves and pants, her face mask, and creeps back to the corn. This time she finds the clearing quickly. She lurks around its edges, waiting for Maurice, her beloved unicorn, to appear.

She forgot her watch, so time doesn't exist out here. The dark of the night stays static; black is black is black. The corn is drier now. When the stalks move it sounds like old bones rasping. In the darkness that sound envelops her; there is an ocean of it and she can't part it.

And then. Hooves. She points her flashlight into the clearing, and there, finally, is a horse head, white, to match the white horn. *Maureen*, Maya decides. Relief and disappointment flood through her; Maurice is not lonely, he has company. Frankenstein's monster has a bride.

She had wanted to be Maurice's company.

Another unicorn pokes his head through. This one is mottled brown. He looks like a Moses to Maya. Moses is followed by Maurice, who looks a little worse for the wear. His coat had thinned, and his ears droop. Maurice carries a plastic grocery bag in his mouth. He dumps it in the middle of a clearing, and cheese puffs and packs of cigarettes spill out. Maurice nudges the bag further, and a large glass bottle of clear liquid rolls out. Maurice stamps on a cigarette pack, flattening the carton, but successfully freeing the cigarettes. He dips his head low and grabs the tip of one with his teeth, so that the cigarette rests between his horsy lips.

Maureen rubs her front hoof against a packet of matches. She does this so slowly and methodically that it's obvious she's done this before. After a few seconds, a match catches and lights the small pack. A patch of dry, trampled corn catches fire. Maurice lowers his head and lights his cigarette with it. The cigarette, the color of his horn, the color of the smoke as it rises in the weak beam of Maya's flashlight. Moses eats the cheese puffs. He takes greedy bites from the bag, a blissful expression rising to his face.

Maya stands, stunned. Maureen takes the Vodka bottle and crushes the top with her teeth, glass spattered, the shards reflecting in Maya's flashlight beam. Blood trickles from the side of Maureen's white face, but she drinks as if she doesn't notice. She holds the bottle with her teeth and tips her head back. Maurice takes a long drag from his cigarette.

Then, she sees Beauty. Lurking at the edge of the clearing, just like her. He looks different. His coat has lost its sheen, his face more angular. Already a bump has formed on his forehead. *Not Beauty*, she thinks. These are not good unicorns.

Maurice walks to Beauty and blows smoke in his face. Maurice looks rough; his body spasms at frequent intervals as if his nerve cells are trying to fight something off. Beauty chomps on a cornstalk, shuttling the leaves and ears of corn into his mouth. His eyes bulge. Maurice nods, as if in encouragement. *Keep eating.*

Don't go into the cornfield, Mom had said. *It'll hurt you.*

Maureen prances around the clearing, the Vodka bottle discarded on the edge by Maurice. She neighs, throws her head back. The small fire still burns the trampled corn, but the unicorns aren't worried. The ground of the clearing is mostly dirt now, so the fire won't burn for long.

Maya wishes she had a camera, although what she would do with such a picture, she doesn't know. Show it to Emily perhaps and say, "See there was something in the cornfield. And isn't this more interesting than stupid football?" Maya would laugh, "Look, it's Moses and he's eating cheese puffs."

Maya laughs, her stomach twisting in a knot.

Maya imagines this is how Doctor Frankenstein felt when he realized he should have never created his monster. These smoking, drinking, cheese-puff eating unicorns are not something magical. Or else they are, but they're the bad kind of magic Miss Delilah was talking about. She wants to run, only she is afraid to leave, in case they chase her.

In Buddhism, *you must be mindful and aware of your thoughts and actions.*

It was the cornfield. The horses ate the bionengineered corn with a side of pesticide, and it changed them. She can see it in the redness of their eyes, in their skin sagging from their bones. It's made them monsters.

She feels bad for them. This is her fault too.

Maurice takes a step and knocks over the half finished alcohol bottle. He crunches the glass beneath his hooves. Then he looks at her, directly at Maya and her weak flashlight beam. His spasms overtake his body, and his cigarette falls. He shakes with a violence that frightens the other unicorns. Maurice opens his mouth, and a rough neigh clamors from him. White foam forms at his lips. Beauty runs.

Maya runs.

The next day is a Saturday, the autumn light dusky and soft. Maya is afraid to return to the cornfields, but she feels it's her duty now. She needs to know what happened to Maurice. Even if no one believes her, this is what is right. She must carry this knowledge.

Buddhism is meant to be a way of life. A way to live morally and thoughtfully.

She takes a deep breath and sneaks from the house. She knows the way through the cornfield now. She walks straight west into that setting sun. The crisp corn stalks shutter as she moves past. Corn silk catches in her pigtailed hair.

Her feet carry her to the clearing. The corn stalks stamped down, bent at wrong angles. The corn is dead; there is only dirt, broken glass, cigarette stubs. Directly across from her she sees Maurice, his body on that dry pesticide-dirt.

"Maurice?" she asks.

Nothing but the long leaves from the corn whispering in the wind. She walks to his body, and she realizes that's all it is now. A body. In the dead corn, a sad unicorn, broken glass beneath him, a bright blue candy wrapper. Maurice went through so many changes. All because of these chemicals on the corn. These chemicals Maya touched, the chemicals that have not yet disintegrated her hand.

She turns, walks back toward home. *I will not disintegrate.* Her pigtails feel tight and heavy. She rips at them, untangles her hair, lets it roam free. She tries not to think of Beauty, her lovely Beauty and how the chemicals will work through him, spin him dry, just like Maurice. Beauty frothing at the mouth, violently shivering his way to death.

The world is defined by what disintegrates.

She splits this sea of corn, pretends to be Moses. Tries to part this sad burnt yellow sea. She tries to be brave and strong. But she cannot be what she is not.

Somewhere, she hears a horse cry.

Carlie's Ride

Rachel Lopez

The metal cage that curved over the two of them would surely keep them safe, wouldn't it? Two grinning, dark-skinned carnies no older than the couple locked the corroded metal bar over their chests and latched the door before liftoff, but now the bar swayed uselessly against the rhythm of the dented Ferris wheel car. They hung high above the asphalt that paved the midway. The August air, saturated with black grease, popcorn, and melted sugar, made Carlie hold her breath.

Carlie. Look here, baby girl. Look over here.

Gunner wanted her to look out at the skyline. Des Moines was for him a Gotham, a jutting mass of concrete and glass and glistening possibility beyond and above them. To Carlie, it looked like a Lego city, something a child could knock down with an enthusiastic little fist. Her eyes drifted to Gunner's strong body, at ease beside her, the way the fake leg—*the prosthetic*—resembled an actual bone inside the actual lower part of an actual leg. Their friend—they called him Tattoo Goonie—had painted for Gunner one long, bright, yellow and orange lightning bolt down each side of it like a logo on a running shoe.

You can see all the way to downtown.

He said this every time. The Ferris wheel car barely stirred above the pop and ping of strobe lights below. Carlie tried to soften her eyes over the mass of people who migrated from spinning teacups to funnel cake stands to ticket kiosks. Sweet corn cobs and paper cups dropped liked turds around the solid mass of bodies that folded in on itself again and again. All wanting to fly, to spin around. To win garishly colored stuffed animals for dull-eyed girlfriends.

Those aren't real skyscrapers, Gunner.

A hiss. Was the hiss in her voice or some pyrotechnic burnout from the ancient stadium? No sound distinguished itself from any other sound. She twirled her frizzling hair over and under her fingers and thumb, smoothing, smoothing. She was afraid of heights, but Gunner had teased and heckled her into climbing up into this goddamned thing anyway. She figured they were high enough that if the car should break from its hinges, they would crash to their deaths or lifelong quadriplegia no matter how they tried to duck or cling together inside the cage. They'd be churned up together much, much too hard when it hit the ground. She scratched at her pinky nail where the purple polish had already chipped.

Now their position, pinned up against the simmering purple evening, didn't worry her half as much as the question Gunner had just posed: If they made it out of there intact, whether she might like to marry him, seeing's how he'd be shipped out for another tour before the end of October.

"This time, you know, probably to a safer spot."

Heat prickled her pores. Gunner leaned forward and laced his thick fingers through the rust-roughened open-weave steel front of the car.

They'll probably park me at a desk somewhere. Anyhoo...

The lights flickered over his face, a blinking, hopeful moon. Carlie hated it when he said *anyhoo*.

We could start planning now, and get her done before the end of summer.

If lies mounted in measures from, say, a thimble to an ocean, Carlie figured she'd probably lied to Gunner enough to fill a swimming pool like heavy snow piled up in winter. She pictured an empty pool overflowing with snow in the middle of winter's nothing, nothingness: black trees slapping skinny bare arms against a colorless sky and muted miles of fields all around.

The massive arms of the Ferris wheel groaned and lurched and dropped them fast so that their bottoms bounced off the bench seat when the cage caught, and they jerked to a stop. Carlie was going to throw up. It was already August. He would leave sometime in October, November at the latest. Who wanted a September wedding? Of course, she could probably hide her bump for at least another month. Maybe better to do it before she got big, before the baby stormed through and wrecked her body. This made her chest hurt. She loved her body.

An image of Kirk Jepson swelled in her mind. His thick, blue-jeaned torso pushing into her open legs, her hips at the edge of the pool table at the Tip Top Tap after closing, and she told him keep going, keep going. Big hands were insistent on her black corduroy skirt, the one she'd been so proud of when she brought it home from the shopping trip to Chicago with Mom and her cousin April. No one else in town would own it. Carlie's ears started ringing when Kirk entered her and didn't stop ringing until late the next afternoon. And when the sound dulled to a hum and then to quiet, she went looking to start them ringing again. They did, in the back of Kirk's daddy's machine shop in the old uptown, sporadic rain tapping hard on the tin roof above them. She had bent forward and clung to the windowsill, her eyes locked on the cinderblock wall of the gas station next door.

Now the cage swung so slightly she wondered if it actually moved or if she imagined it, and Gunner slid his hand down her back and told her it would be alright, it would be over soon.

She really should say something, but there was too much to tell. John, and Eric, and that boy she'd sucked off in the bathroom on Court Avenue when she and April took their fake IDs to that club on the 4th of July, and she couldn't remember where it had gone from there. And that girl with the blond curly hair she made out with on a dare at the lake spot, then did more than that with her in the back seat of her car while the party died down and her friends passed out in folding chairs around the bonfire. She should say something right now. Get Gunner's crazymaking hand off her back. Carlie squeezed her eyes shut and tried to think of something, imagine the conversation.

Carlie.

Gunner's hand was on the crown of her hair now, stiff and metallic as the leg, and she jerked her shoulder. His hand fell to the hard vinyl between them, then crawled back to his own knee.

Carlie, did you hear what I asked you?

She tried to picture something other than the leg. And September, the sweating boys, the coming boys, her own sighs and the goddamned Ferris wheel.

Carlie, I mean it. I really want to.

She scanned the midway, and then fastened her eyes onto one spot in the distance: the gleaming gold leaf of the capitol dome, far from the midway's collapsing walls of noise and light. She'd learned the spotting trick in ballet. It maintained balance while pirouetting.

She lost the spot when a toddler below them threw himself on the asphalt before his parents, who argued, the woman nearly over-turning the empty stroller with her flailing hands. The man shook his head and walked away, turning back only once to yell that she was a fucking bitch. The toddler squirmed around on his back and began kicking at the woman's shins with his little sneakered feet, and the woman jumped back, clawed at the hair on her face, and rummaged for something in her purse, which she rested on the stroller's awning. Now the stroller did topple backward onto the asphalt, sippy cups and a stuffed animal of some sort, and blankets and a book spilling onto the ground. The child wailed and the woman stood still.

And then the Ferris wheel was moving, slow and smooth, all the way to a gentle stop. This repeated: slow and smooth, stop. Slow and smooth, stop. In this way they swung toward the two carnies, string-bean men who stood as if for a receiving line, grinning like fools and chatting with the riders they released, one by one, from their cages.

The Original Redskin

Jason Lee Brown

Jack Ebbers hadn't lost a lick of school spirit in forty years. If anything, he'd gained admiration for his hometown of Waning, the bellybutton of Illinois, population 4,000, a town small enough to walk across in twenty minutes, where things changed at a turtle's pace, if at all. For Jack, Waning was summer baseball tournaments and Fourth of July fireworks at the park, American Legion fundraisers and raffle tickets, the smell of popcorn at Friday night football games, the sending off of athletes in yellow buses, the driving through blizzards to tournament championships. And most importantly, Waning was the *Redskins*, a mascot name held since 1939.

Ebb, as most folks called him, scooped his fingertip through red war paint and smudged a dark red line across the bridge of his nose. He thought about the record number of townspeople who would pack the gymnasium for tonight's school board meeting. Lawyers from The National Native American Bar Association had sued the school district for refusing to eliminate Redskins as the school's mascot name, and in two hours, the Waning School Board would vote to keep the name or to change it. Ebb wasn't a violent man, never had been, but he found out the hard way that, on rare occasions, you had to go to war for what you believed in or lawyers would take everything you had, even your reasons for cheering.

He was smearing the red war paint down his cheeks when he noticed in the mirror how much hair he had lost: bald except for gray patches above his ears. His wrinkled forehead was stern with middle age and even when he tried to lower his eyebrows to flatten the skin, the creases remained deep and jagged above his gray bushy eyebrows. He smeared the red over his wrinkled forehead and watched it fill the creases like putty. When he backed away from the mirror, he didn't recognize his body, the red face in the middle of his living room. He'd lost forty-five pounds in the last two years, since the lawsuit began, and was still losing weight everywhere but his belly.

He wore a costume he'd made thirty years ago in his father's sporting goods store: light brown pants with tassels down the legs and a matching shirt with tassels and red-and-white beadwork across the chest. His father's store furnished the sporting equipment for all the school teams. The Sports Booster Club counted for more than half of the store's business, and, at that time, Ebb and his father could barely keep up with the orders. Ebb worked on his costume's war bonnet at night. It had turkey feathers that sprawled out like a white-and-black peacock. He'd dyed the feathers black to imitate eagle feathers then attached them to the leather crowned with felt. The outside had red-and-white triangles beaded across the forehead. A strip of white rabbit fur hung from the temples. He wanted the war bonnet to be perfect and knew no one would ever remember what his clothing looked like as long as he had a spectacular headdress.

The grandfather clock chimed five times. He grabbed the television remote and turned up the local news, knowing the school board meeting would be the top story. Normally, he'd already be at the high school, shaking hands, saying hi to folks entering the brick building, but tonight he wanted to make an unforgettable entrance. On the screen, reporter Kimberly Chase, a dumpy lady who had graduated from Waning High School, interviewed Dickey Moffet. Ebb considered Dickey the real deal, the staunchest proponent for keeping the mascot's name. Dickey was a lifetime resident and a former basketball star, an all-around good guy. His hair was bright red, but not as red as the splotches across his pocked cheeks. He was the president of the

Mascot/Identity Committee (MIC) and Ebb was vice president. Together they'd co-founded the MIC, gathered information, and invited nearly 7,000 alumni to attend the school board meeting.

"Kimberly, there's no doubt about it," Dickey said. "Students and townspeople voted more than ten to one to retain the mascot's name, but there's not much more we can do now but pray."

"Thank you, Dickey," Kimberly Chase said. Ebb thought of her as he used to think of himself: naïve but dedicated. Her smile stretched deep into her cheeks, and she wore a green turtleneck that made the fat on her chin bubble out like a frog when she spoke. Her eyebrows bounced with every pronunciation."

In related news, two Waning students have officially been charged with criminal threat and disorderly conduct for allegedly sending threatening emails to all seven school board members."

Since the lawsuit, a cloud of red had balled itself in his head, and when he thought about lawyers or school boards or living without the town's mascots, the cloud metastasized, swirled like a whistle of wind through tree branches. To avoid the stress, he stared at his spirit award, the gold-plated plaque that hung on his living room wall. He loved showing off the plaque and telling everyone about how he won it his senior year. His forehead used to tingle when he donned the war bonnet during athletic events in which he thought about nothing but school spirit, his only true escape. The high school band would play "The Redskin War Song," with its booming drums echoing through the gymnasium, and fans would cheer in anticipation, and when Ebb burst through a square wall of paper painted with the Redskins logo—a red-faced cartoon head wearing a war bonnet—he'd skip across the court chopping his tomahawk in the air, and the townspeople would erupt so loudly he could barely hear the band. Lately, these memories weren't as crisp and easy to invoke as they once were.

Redskins Forever stickers were plastered on the bumper of his pickup. He drove through Waning's business district, the square: a two-story courthouse surrounded by two-story flat-front buildings with large windows. He was wearing his costume, except for the war bonnet—he didn't want to add to his blind spots. His tomahawk sat on the seat next to him. The tomahawk was fifteen inches long with a leather handle and a shiny triangular gray rock with blunt edges. With one hand on the steering wheel and one rubbing the smooth rock, he thought about the meticulous effort he'd put into making the tomahawk his junior year, when he became the official mascot, the original Redskin.

He drove counterclockwise around the courthouse square that was usually packed with high-school kids hanging out on the sidewalks and cruising vehicles around the one-way street, waving arms out windows, but tonight the square was a ghost town: no screaming, no honking horns, no loud music, no engines revving, no squealing tires. He clicked on the radio, and the speakers popped like a cap gun and startled him. On the local 101 K-RED radio station, Dickey Moffet was debating a lawyer from the National Congress of American Indians. Dickey was in mid-sentence:

"…this town has used our mascot's name proudly, without criticism, for more than sixty years. Where have these critics been? Nothing was wrong until two years ago. Now, everything has to change. No questions asked. Well, I had questions and the MIC had questions, so we asked, and the results were clear…"

Ebb had heard every argument for keeping and eliminating the mascot's name. The MIC compiled pages of statistics and history and interviewed hundreds of townspeople and even went out of town and talked to people from school districts that had already changed Redskins to Titans or Cardinals or Timberwolves. He even attended a lecture the school board had paid for about identity, where a panel of professors discussed several questions: *Can you step twice into the same constantly changing river? Would Theseus' ship be the same if the rotten planks were replaced one by one until no originals were left? What if a scavenger ship picked up the planks and built another boat with the exact same pieces. Whose ship is Theseus'?* He waited for the rival town of Pana to change its name from Panthers to Stuffed Toys as soon as the damn lawyers for animal rights spoke up.

Ebb turned down the radio, and Dickey's voice faded into the hum of the engine. The businesses' windows on the square had been whitewashed. The MIC had designated that day as Mascot Whitewash Day. The Waning High School held a pep rally and parade, and afterward, athletes and students whitewashed slogans the MIC had created for weekly flyers and e-mail literature. The one that caught on the most was Save Our Skins! And if the athletes and students didn't have room for those three words, they scrawled SOS.

These three words or letters were whitewashed on windows of vehicles, restaurants, law offices, the fire station, and anywhere else the white could later be wiped away from. Ebb figured if they lost the vote the entire town would eventually be wiped away, just like his father's sporting goods store. Sophomore year, Ebb was at the store pressing *Fifteen-in-a-Row-Club* logos on T-shirts for the basketball team—the Sports Booster Club bought shirts for varsity players who'd made fifteen or more free throws in a row during games— when he'd heard two men arguing, over what he didn't know. He avoided thinking about that day because the less he thought about it the less he remembered. There were images, though, he could never forget. A tall man and a burly one. One man swung, and the crack of skin on skin didn't sound the way Ebb imagined, didn't even sound real. The men grappled, their grunts the only noise inside the store. When they broke loose, Ebb could never forget the flashing glare on the knife, the horrific screams that could come out of a man. Then blood, lots of blood, soaked into their clothes, puddled on the floor, flecked across the uniforms, baseball bats, and shoes. Ebb hadn't been able to stopped seeing red since.

The lawsuit that followed drained all the store's savings, and the Sports Booster Club cancelled all contracts because of the controversy. After two years of litigation, the payout was more than the little-to-no insurance Ebb's father had. His father never acted bitter, but his mother resented lawyers as much as Ebb. They moved to a smaller house, and his father took a second-shift job at the dog food factory. His mother worked part-time at Pamida so she could still afford nice things for Ebb. After graduation, Ebb joined his father at the factory, where everyone, on game days, rubbed his head for good luck. His parents died five years later. Father, heart attack, Mother, stroke. Ebb was the last Ebbers in Waning—no wife, no kids—and all he had left were townspeople.

He turned off the town square and passed the Waning Motel, and for the first time since he could remember, the neon no-vacancy sign glowed white like a supernova about to fade away. Townspeople had decorated houses red and black with banners and ribbons and streamers and flags the MIC had passed out, and the closer he drove to the school the thicker the red and black. Vehicles lined bumper-to-bumper on each side of the street for two blocks, and at the head of the line, the Waning High School sat on a small hill. The sun was setting behind Ebb, but ahead, the dark blue sky above the gymnasium seemed to glow brighter than the freckled stars. He strapped the war bonnet around his head as tight as he could. He tried to look at his face paint in the rearview mirror but could only see his shadow.

Outside the gymnasium, he peeked through the glass doors to the hallway where at least thirty people were standing and talking in front of trophy cases. He knew no one would notice him drawing near. They would, however, notice his entrance. He squeezed the tomahawk's handle and breathed deep three times, a ritual he'd done before every halftime show, and before he knew it, he'd burst through the tinted doors and skipped down the hall belting out a war cry and pumping his tomahawk in the air. His skip was more like a limp nowadays, and after one trip down the hall and back, he had to lean over to catch his breath. The people clapped and cheered, "Save our skins! Save our skins!"

A junior-high girl with black pigtails bounced a *Save Our Skins!* sign over her head. She had a pink shirt with *I ♥ Redskins* on the front, and other townspeople wore white shirts with a red *SOS* arched across the chest. The chant picked up, and soon people gathered at both ends of the hallway to join in. Ebb was still the original and damn proud of it. Several mascots had followed, and for decades, the school board had kicked in money for the costume, but last year, the board eliminated the mascot position, blaming it on budget constraints, despite the fact that townspeople were willing to raise whatever money needed. The chant collapsed into applause.

When Ebb straightened his posture and turned around, Dickey Moffet, wearing his blue police uniform, hugged him like he hadn't seen him in years. He'd patrolled the high school for the past ten years of his semi-retirement, the only law enforcement the district ever needed. The legend held that Dickey singlehandedly stopped a riot in the gymnasium once by unloading his pistol into the air while running across mid-court. It was true that he stopped a riot, but he didn't shoot bullets. They were blanks from the track-and-field gun. Since then, the school hadn't had one incident under his watch.

Dickey escorted Ebb down the hall of red lockers. They said nothing, the plan of attack already in place. Ebb could hear a large crowd singing "The Redskin War Song," and on pure instinct he jogged into the mouth of the gymnasium and skipped down an aisle of chairs, chopping his tomahawk in the air. The crowd sang:

> "…Fight on, fight on 'til you have won,
> Sons of Wan-ing-High. Rah! Rah! Rah!
> Hail to the Redskins!
> Hail Vic-tor-y!
> Braves on the Warpath!
> Fight for old Waning!"

The makeup made his face sweat, which seemed to feed the thoughts of swirling red clouds. He breathed deep several times to catch his breath. The gymnasium was packed with people standing along the walls and sitting on gray foldout chairs and the wooden bleachers that rose up to the large windows. Metal crossbeams angled across the ceiling like a spider web that kept the roof from collapsing. Everyone in the gym wore red, white, or black, or a combination of the three.

A man with a large camera on his shoulder filmed Ebb, and another cameraman focused on four children wearing black face paint and waving Styrofoam *Number One* fingers with the Redskins logo on the palms. A different cameraman filmed the high school students who had taken over the bleacher behind the home team's bench, all sporting bright red shirts with the words *Redskin Rowdies* written on the front. The fourth row of students had powwow drums they banged with mallets to start cheers or keep them going.

The crowd consisted of an all-star lineup of ex-athletes and alumni cramped shoulder-to-shoulder, and Ebb could taste the spirit of Waning in the stuffy gymnasium that smelled like a locker room. For the past forty years, he had seen every home game and watched students mature through high school and move on to college and never come back, but they were back tonight and were adults now, adults Ebb recognized but didn't know anymore. There was the lanky, buzz-cut Tommy Funnel, who took first place in four events at the state track meet, and the five-one Kerry Isle, who was the first Lady Redskin to score 1,000 points in her career, and Joey Flood, a huge nimble-footed man who broke into the rival team's school and stole all the band equipment and tossed it in the Waning Creek. There were too many people to name, but all of them played, coached, or cheered for the Redskins.

Dickey saved Ebb a seat in the front row. The lawyer who represented the Native Americans sat a few seats down. He wasn't even Native American. He was a middle-aged white man in a blue suit. He did nothing but nod and smile at people. If there was one thing Ebb hated more than a lawyer's smile, it was… well, there was nothing he hated more than a lawyer's smile.

The save-our-skins chant broke out again, and soon everyone in the gymnasium chanted and clapped along with the powwow drums.

Ebb knew how many Redskin wins and losses the Redskins had taken place on this court and couldn't fathom the number of memories that were born there, and more importantly, how many had been or would be forgotten because of the change. His war bonnet spread out so far behind him people had to lean around it to see the seven school board members walking across the stage. The wood stage had darkened with age and the constant trampling of feet during the halftime shows, the junior and senior plays, and the Redskin Singers, a performing group of forty boys and girls who wore elaborate costumes and flamboyantly danced and crooned.

The school board members sat on cushioned chairs behind a cafeteria table and little brown plaques with their names on them. Ebb was disgusted that six out of the seven hadn't even grown up in Waning, just moved into town within the last couple years. They had no idea what the mascot meant to lifetime locals or about its history, and for those reasons, he never made eye contact and acted like the three chairs on both sides of the president, Dusty Bales, were empty.

Dusty Bales was the worst of them all, the only member born and raised in Waning, and his part in all this sickened Ebb. Others were forced to go along, just another cog in the lawyer's wheel, but Dusty helped push it forward.

The car salesman once was Waning's best defensive back and had offers from every Big 10 School but picked the University of Illinois because of the traditions of Chief Illiniwek. Ebb supported Dusty all the way through college. He had liked traveling to Memorial Stadium to watch Dusty play, but he loved the halftime show when Chief Illiniwek war danced across the green carpet. On the long drive home, Ebb could think about nothing else but donning Chief Illiniwek's regalia and performing in front of huge crowds.

Townspeople fidgeted in their seats as if the bleachers and chairs were giving them slight electrical shocks. Dusty's white shirt and black tie accentuated the gray streaks in his crew cut. He tapped the microphone in front of him with his index finger, and the speakers on the wall thumped like a heavy heartbeat. He called roll then began the question-and-answer forum. There were only two items on the agenda: the question-and-answer forum and the vote.

"If anyone would like to speak," Dusty said, "we allotted time for quick questions or statements." His voice was deep, and he whistled when he sounded out the letter S.

Townspeople applauded when Ebb stood up in full regalia and stepped into the aisle, where he grabbed the microphone from its stand. The microphone was cold like a dead person's hand but seemed to vibrate when he squeezed it.

"I've prayed this day would never come, prayed harder than I've ever prayed," he said. "And it's not right. The MIC statistics prove this is not what the townspeople want—"

"The school board members have reviewed all the MIC reports," Dusty said.

"With all due respect," Ebb said, though he didn't believe he owed him any more respect, "This information needs to be on the record. And quite frankly, after all the money I've raised for the Quarterback Club, the Sports Booster Club, and this school district, I deserve to have my say. I have done nothing but support this town."

"No one is doubting your support, Mr. Ebbers," Dusty said.

Tommy Funnel stood and pointed his Styrofoam finger and said, "Let him speak, Dusty!"

"We love you, Ebb," shouted a woman.

The townspeople applauded.

Ebb held up his open palm next to his war bonnet to quiet them. The air was thick with static and pricked his neck and arms when he moved. His war bonnet felt like it was falling off his head, but when he reached up, the headband was in place.

"By definition, our mascot fits every criteria," he said. "Mascot: An animal, a person, or thing adopted by a group as its represented symbol and is supposed to bring good luck."

"*Webster's* also defines Redskins as: Slang, often disparaging and offensive," Dusty said. "And we've already had these debates, and let me remind you, it was The State Board of Education that recommended we drop the name. So if there is no *new* information, we need to move on to the vote."

The Redskin Rowdies heard a pause and banged the drums, and the townspeople cheered, "Save our skins! Save our skins!" The students had already voted on a new mascot name, though more than half of them refused to participate. They had many names to choose from, including The Reds, Redbirds, Red Chargers, Red Knights, Red Pride, Red Wings, Red Stars, Redstones, and Red Dogs. The most votes went to the Redhawks, a red-tailed hawk that was supposed to be common in the Midwest, though Ebb had never seen one.

"Please, please," Dusty said, quieting the crowd. "The raw truth is that the school district is having financial difficulties and any more lawyers' fees to battle this type of lawsuit, which could last for several more years, would drive the school into financial ruin. Then not only would there be no more Redskins, there'd be no more school. This is about survival."

"This is about identity," Ebb said. "Now, I know I'm not smart enough to prove or disprove if I can step twice into the same constantly changing river, like those professors you hired, but I know that the Waning Creek that runs behind this school is the same one Joey Flood tossed band equipment into fifteen years ago, and it always will be. And I don't know anything about Theseus' ship, but I know if you build a ship out of rotten wood, then it's just a rotten ship that no one wants to be a part of. So, I say, if Theseus is standing on a ship, then it's his ship. And as long as these townspeople are in this gymnasium, then the mascot's name should be Redskins. Without the Redskins, there's not only going to be no school, there'll be no Waning."

"All this may be true," Dusty said. "But nothing is going to stop this vote."

"If you change the name, it changes everything!" Ebb said. His voice echoed.

The weight of everyone's stare, an entire town's worth of hope, bore down on him. His war bonnet slipped off, and the cloud of red exploded with every desperate thought on how to stop the vote. The red swirled around him, growing in size and sound with each rotation. He climbed on stage and marched toward the school board members, the tomahawk cocked over his head. Dickey Moffet stepped aside as planned, and Ebb swung, and a slight glint reflected off the rock before it cracked the school board president across the forehead, splitting the skin. Red was all Ebb could see and the only memory he had left.

Tracks

Sheila Thorne

He was always in a hurry, always after the fastest way of doing things: the way he walked—leaning forward like a skater, or the deprecation in his voice when he saw his daughter chopping vegetables into tiny pieces for him, a cassoulet, a dinner in his honor, "But that takes a long time." What was he rushing towards? Even as a child he hurtled himself forward. Scrapes on his nose, bumps on his forehead, scabs on his knees.

His childhood home—it still stands—was a grand brick house on Lake Michigan, grass lawn sloping to bluff's edge as large and open as a playing field or a park. In his mother's garden red hollyhocks and blue delphiniums reached above his tilted head. Bees buzzed on the surface of the rolling vastness, and tiny ants ran along hidden paths at the base of the blades. All that surrounded him was his domain: the lake on the east, the North Shore village of Winnetka, the plowed prairie at the western edge. Donald. The youngest of six, he was the first to be born in the suburbs, beyond the smoke and crowds of Chicago.

Winnetka had been platted on the old Green Bay Trail in 1854 by the president of the Chicago and Milwaukee Railroad in anticipation of his line coming through. "Winnetka" was supposed to mean "beautiful land" in a local Native American language. Actually that was a lie; it was a word made up by the wife of one of the first developers. Long ago the Northwoods forest had extended along this strip of lake shore. In his lifetime, Donny would see the development of automobiles, airplanes, space rockets, the Internet. And the Bomb.

His earliest memory was the lake, its bright blueness sparking in the distance through the trees, or on overcast days its greeny-greyness; the warmth of grainy sand and smooth stones, the rhythmic thrum of lapping water, the cold that shot through him, making his back arch, and the swirl of water like laughter when his sister Lou dipped him. Lou would grow up to be a modern dancer and adventurer. She danced on an Indonesian beach, the family story went, and gave birth to her first child on a mule train trip through the mountains of Turkey. She married a Socialist, and Donny would never speak to her again.

He was bequeathed by nature a fundamental lightheartedness and buoyancy. His grandfather having made money in the Chicago lumber business as a merchant of Michigan white pine, his father used the capital to set up a tool manufacturing company, and Donny grew up enjoying a high standard of living. He dimly realized he was fortunate, and this gave him a degree of humility.

In 1910, when he was three years old, Winnetka's population was 3,168. That same year, a two-story red brick public library was built in the village to the memory of Henry Demarest Lloyd, the socialist muckraking journalist who exposed abuses of industrial monopolies. Donny's father said at the dinner table, "Henry Demarest Lloyd can go jump in the lake as far as I'm concerned, and his memory can follow him," but the children ignored him and checked out books anyway. Except for Donny, never much of a reader.

He was physically active. In summer he swam three or four times a day and played catch on the beach with his brother, Fergie, who was killed at thirty-six crashing his airplane while tipping the wings hello to his mother; he climbed up the bluff path to the house for a sandwich in the sun porch, leaving puddles on the floor (no matter, the maid would clean it up); then back to the water again. Cargo ships still chugged along the horizon on their way to and from Chicago.

He was outdoors as much in the winter as in the summer. The bluff path was a perfect place to sled with curves to maneuver and trees to avoid. He fitted a sled with a Merkel Wheel and Motor attachment to cruise around town in the snow. The family took trips out to the Des Plaines River to skate on its black ice, sometimes for miles.

He had freedom to roam. Apparently no one had the time or felt the necessity to keep too close an eye on him: his nursemaid outgrown, his mother occupied with clubs, charity work, and parties, his older sisters and brother with their own friends and social events. With his best friend, Alexander Winston, whose younger sister he would someday marry, he would bicycle through the dappled shade and green smells of Winnetka, past lawns and gardens and out as far as the Skokie Marsh on the west edge of town. "Chewab Skokie," meaning "big wet prairie," was the Potawatomi name for this low area of tall grasses and flowers, waterfowl, wading birds, songbirds, muskrats, minks, turtles, and fish which lay between two broad glacial moraines and was created after the last Ice Age by the rush of melting waters and buried chunks of ice forming kettle depressions. For two boys who did not at all mind getting wet and muddy, it was a paradise of exploration. He caught a mossy turtle here and took it home for a pet, but, out of its natural habitat, it soon died.

In 1933, the marsh would be converted into a series of seven lagoons by the Civilian Conservation Corps and become a recreational park. Donald, then twenty-six, would consider this yet another mark of the great progress of his century. In that same year he would attend Chicago's Century of Progress International Exposition whose motto was "Science Finds, Industry Applies, Man Conforms," and find most exciting the Nash exhibit of an endless chain of cars, bathed in colored lights, moving up and down in a tower of glass, and the brilliantly illuminated General Motors Building with an actual, working model of a complete assembly line, from raw parts to completed car.

During the spring melt, the marshes sometimes turned into a placid, shimmering lake extending between the two moraines, and the roads became impassible. Donny and Alex decided to build a raft. They scoured the land for winter-downed branches and small trees, pirated old planks of wood from discarded crates and such in the alleyways of town, and in a week's time managed to assemble a stack of building material which they fastened together with nails, twine and wire. They even made two makeshift seats. When the big day came to test the raft, it held their weight, and though water oozed through the cracks and wet their feet, they were able to pole out into the lake as far as they wished. The quiet waters reflected the blue sky and milky clouds.

Across the ocean, tanks were being used for the first time on the Western Front. Poison gas had been deployed the year before. In Chicago, the mayor, as well as the many citizens of German and Eastern European ancestry, opposed U.S. intervention, but Donny's father was for it: tools would be needed to fix the machines of war. Donny heard some of this at the dinner table, but it barely seeped into his consciousness: he was only nine years old.

Until the slowly draining water became too shallow, the two boys, goose-bumped with excitement, raced out every day after school to launch their "ship." Actually, there was much less to see on the lake than in the kettles and pockets of the marsh, but the adventure of navigation, the ranging over such open, wide distance, made their hearts leap and augured bright possibilities lying in the future of their apparently charmed lives. That the familiar, known marsh could turn into this chimerical lake stretched the imagination free of limits. Floating along on the mystifying water smelling faintly of mud, they talked about engines, cars, airplanes, and remote places: Siberia, the Poles, the jungles of Africa. Someday theirs would be called "the greatest generation," although Donny would be disqualified from fighting overseas, having flat feet.

When summer came and they had whole days of freedom, they ventured farther. Down Willow Road beyond the marsh lay farms and dairies and finally, a railroad track: the Milwaukee Road, owned by the Chicago, Milwaukee, and St. Paul Railroad Company. On the near side of the tracks grew a giant bur oak—the remnant of the groves of oak and hickory that had once dotted the prairie like islands in a sea, drawing the first European settlers—and next to it squatted a small general store of weathered gray wood. In the campestral land beyond the tracks the road stretched to the vanishing point in the west, while the tracks headed north. The CM&St.P owned 1,410 grain elevators and coal mining properties in Illinois and Iowa, but of course the boys did not know this.

They dropped their bikes in the grass below the oak and rested in its shade. It had taken a good two hours to ride this far. An old woman popped her head out the door of the general store to look at them, then disappeared back inside. All around lay vastness in abundance on which to marvel. In his innocence Donny wanted to someday, somehow, leave his mark upon the expanse. Like throwing a stone in a quiet pool to see the rings of disturbance. Like breaking off the branch of a tree to knock against the plants along a path, as little boys do. Such disastrous innocence. Someday he would build here shopping centers, housing developments, stadiums, freeways, though these things he could not even picture yet.

Once, these grasslands supported mastodons, mammoths, bison, elk, and their predators, men and saber-toothed tigers.

Soon a freight came growling on its way north. Flat cars loaded with tractors and rods of steel, box cars labeled Armour and Co., National Biscuit Co., Consolidated Steel and Wire Co., and rust-orange cars bearing the tilted red rectangular sign of the Milwaukee Road. Forty minutes long.

The boys went into the general store to ask the old lady if they could drink some water from her pump out front. She was sitting on a stool behind the counter, looking out the dusty window. The flesh on her face was lined with a million roads, crinkled with a thousand spokes. She had been pretty once, maybe even beautiful, but neither of them would have recognized that to be so.

She smiled and nodded, "Just don't go making a puddle now, laddies."

Outside, they giggled as Donny pulled the lever of the pump.

In the following days they came again to walk the tracks and time the freights that passed by: thirty minutes long, an hour, forty-five minutes. In one place there was a bridge, and they put their ears to the rail, and then their hands, to detect the vibration that announced an approaching train. Sometimes there were passenger trains, and they made funny faces at the staring heads in the windows. The freights moved slowly through the crossing, as they were heavily loaded and either had just left the Chicago yards or were pulling into them, and three miles to the north they intersected the Chicago and Northwestern tracks and sometimes had to wait. Alongside the tracks the grass grew long and was threaded with flowers in abundance: yellow dock, blue lead plant, milkweed, pink loosestrife, purple blazing star, Chicago wild onion. They chewed on strands of Timothy grass as they walked along the ties or balanced on the steel rails. Smells of cinder and tar mixed with flowery perfumes. Bugs made ticking noises. They didn't know it, but this was a strip of original prairie, protected from development by the tracks that nestled in it. To them, the tracks seemed to naturally belong. The trains that crawled along them seemed like an inevitable force, like storms rippling across the surface of the land.

They wondered where they were going. They had no idea the tracks reached all the way to Seattle, crossing five major mountain ranges—the Saddles, the Belts, the Rockies, the Bitter Roots, and the Cascades—connecting Chicago with the grain fields of the Dakotas, the iron range of Minnesota, the copper range of Montana, and the lumber of the Pacific Northwest. At that time, Donny still felt himself at one with everything around him: sun, sky, lake, prairie, tracks, his friend, Alex. He bled into the world and could hardly distinguish himself as separate.

Like the road and the tracks, long summer days of freedom stretched before him. Some days he stayed at the lake, and some days he played with boys other than Alex, but the track crossing was where he went most often that summer, and only with Alex; it was their secret, their special place.

One day, while sitting under the bur oak watching a particularly long train that seemed to be straining against its load, Donny said, "You know what? That train's so slow I bet we could jump onto one of the cars and then jump off again."

Alex looked at the train groaning along, then turned and nodded. Wordlessly, they both stood at the same time, approached the train and ran along beside it. It was so slow they could outrun it. Up close, its grumbling sounded like thunder. Donny felt the heat of the wheels' grinding friction. He was the first to grab, still running, onto the rungs of a hopper's ladder, climb, and swing easily onto the platform. Alex followed. They hung on and rode a couple hundred feet.

"Okay, off now!" Alex shouted. He loosened one hand, twisted to face outwards, and leaped. Then Donny followed, dropping to the ground and rolling. It was easy.

Exhilarated, they walked back to the tree where they laid in the grass and waited for the next train, smelling the moldy odor of earth and watching tiny bugs scurry around. They asked the old lady for water again, and she nodded without saying anything; she was used to them now. Then another train announced itself before the crossing with its whistle. It was a long one, and they jumped on and off again, riding a bit further this time.

The old lady came out of the general store and glared, hands at her hips. "Boys, you dassn't do that," she yelled.

Of course they ignored her. Over the following weeks they became well-practiced in judging the speed of a train and mounting the cars. Always the northbound trains, to the hinterlands. They learned to vault up onto open boxcars as well as swing onto the cars with ladders. Then jumping, waiting a little longer, and longer…letting themselves believe until the last minute they were really going to head out into the unknown and relishing the sense of free-fall, of plunging. They called the old lady "Mrs. Dassent."

In Chicago at the time, Mexican and Romanian track workers were replacing the Irish and Italians. By 1928 there would be twenty-eight camps of mostly Mexican track workers in Cook and DuPage Counties, living in boxcars in poor to wretched conditions. They had families, raised gardens, and held religious services. Donny and Alex knew none of this, nor would it have mattered to them.

Towards summer's end, they lingered to watch the horizon catch on fire, a smoldering of orange embers that grew to flames of scarlet and violet. A spectacle portending grandness, somewhere, in the distant west, in the future.

But in the present, Donny missed dinner.

"Where have you been?" his mother demanded crossly.

"Just bicycling around with Alex." It was one of the rare times he lied, or rather, hid the complete truth, for generally he didn't have to, such was his endowment of freedom and indulgence. At the end of his life he would say that he was proud of having been always honest, never having cheated, in so far as he was aware. And people would agree: he was a good man.

"Well, your dinner's been waiting for you over an hour."

The cook re-heated it, and no more was said.

One hot day, with temperature in the nineties, Donny and Alex stayed in the lake as long as possible. Their skin turned prunish. In the mid-afternoon the wind finally changed to come off the lake, cooling the air a bit. By then they were both thoroughly water-logged, and decided to jump on their bikes and go out to the tracks till sunset. They arrived at the crossing just as a northbound freight was pulling by.

Throwing down his bike, Donny impulsively raced toward the train. "Come on!" he shouted to Alex.

But it happened too fast for Alex. He was not impulsive like Donny, not quick enough or ready to leap forward at Donny's command. In the seconds he needed to consider, Donny was already vaulting himself into an open boxcar. Once up, he turned and saw Alex still standing by his bike with a puzzled look on his face. "Alex!" he shouted over the squealing wheels, the banging, clanging cars.

"Darn it!" he exclaimed. (He never swore, even then.) Throughout his life he had a quick temper, and on reuniting with Alex he would take out his frustration on him and almost lose him as a friend, in which case he might not have married his sister, and his life might have been different. Now, finding himself alone, he wondered whether to jump immediately or not. Without his best friend, the adventure lost some of its appeal. But before he could make up his mind, a voice, thin and breathy, distilled from the darkness behind him.

"Lost your buddy, huh?"

Donny spun around and looked into the shadows. He could barely make out the shape sprawled in the corner. The voice had not been unkind.

"Where you catching out to?" the man asked.

"Nowhere, sir. We just come here to jump on and off again."

"Oh, so you live around here?"

"Yes sir. I live in Winnetka."

"Winnetka." The man's voice calibrated subtly to a new tone, not quite as friendly, that made Donny unsure of himself.

"Yes sir."

"What does your father do?" the man asked gruffly.

"He owns a tool company, Munro Tools," Donny said proudly, thinking that now, understanding who he was, the man would be friendly and respectful.

"Munro Tools." The man snorted. "Is your Daddy Mr. Munro himself?"

"Yes sir."

The man spat.

"Yeah. I know who you are."

His voice had turned another full notch to cold and angry. "I know all about the likes of you."

Donny shrank, resenting the tone, and afraid. He couldn't really make out the man's features, just the broad dark shape of him, the pale moon of a face, and all the stories he'd ever heard about kidnappers and thieves flooded his imagination. He wanted to jump now, away from him. Glancing out the open doors, he saw that he was farther from the crossing than he'd ever gone. But still he waited, isolated in silence within the din of grinding metal, held by the voice. What was it that this man knew?

"I read your Daddy's name in the paper. He's one of them union busters, a fat cat pays his workers thirty cents an hour, works 'em twelve hours a day, throws 'em on the street for trying to organize a halfway decent life for theirselves. I read about that strike in the paper. He brought in scabs from the South. I bet you don't live on no thirty cents an hour in Winnetka, do you?"

"No sir, I guess not."

Donny did not recognize anything of the man's description in his father. His father always said that Munro Tools was helping build the country. That was its motto: "Tools to Build the West." He was always polite to people and warmly affectionate to all his children. He played with them, joked with them, and took the family on picnics in the car, the Locomotor. He treated Mary, the cook, and the butler and the maids with respect. Why, they were practically part of the family. Donny had heard something about some employees who hadn't been good workers, but apparently there were others eager to take their jobs in such an outstanding company, eager to help build the West.

"My father's not fat though. Maybe you're thinking of someone else."

The man guffawed, "Oh, you poor kid. You don't know nothing, do you. Do you even know what a scab is?"

"It's what heals over a cut."

The man laughed loudly and slapped his thighs in glee while Donny grew hot, shamed in the pit of his stomach. Recently he'd been shamed when his mother introduced him at a party as "the baby of the family," but that was nothing, nothing like the shame he felt now.

The train speeded up, having safely passed the intersection with the Chicago and Northwestern tracks.

The man's voice grew suddenly gentle, "You better jump, boy, ere you end up in the Dakotas working the wheat harvest with me. Once your feet hit the ground, curl up into a ball and roll. But you probably know that."

Donny looked down at the ground sliding by, the tufts of grass coming up through harsh gravel.

"It looks worse 'n' it is. Just look ahead and make sure there's nothing coming up in the way."

His voice sounded almost fatherly now, and in being so, it felt to Donny like a knee pressed to his chest, forcing acknowledgment, forcing him to consider everything he'd said, though he didn't want to. He wanted to deny him.

The man did not tell him that once he'd worked in Armour's cattle killing room, dropping the hammer on one cow after another in relentless succession. Ladies in fine clothes came to watch the killing. When the Cattle Butchers Union lost the strike of 1904, he lost his job, and had since grown old doing seasonal work, riding the rails. He'd joined the Wobblies. The previous November he'd been among the 30,000 attending Joe Hill's funeral ceremony in Chicago. Donny had never heard of the Wobblies, nor Joe Hill, nor the Meat Trust, nor the 1904 stockyards strike, even though the Armours were acquaintances of his parents and had been among those to whom he was introduced as "the baby." He only knew the man was outside the familiar social world that nurtured him so generously, and was therefore discomfiting. He also knew the man was right: he had to jump.

Still he hesitated, not because he was afraid of getting hurt—he never was and never would be afraid of physical danger. Rather, he felt weighted with something he'd never experienced before, that he did not recognize: the shock of aloneness. Insistent and encumbering, unwonted ballast that stalled his usual confidence to act—so against his grain: it made him not hate the man, for it was not his nature to hate, but to distrust him.

"You can do it, boy," the man said.

In angry acquiescence Donny jumped, newly awkward, the man's whispers (that's the way he'd remember the voice) still ringing in his ear. Jumped away from the stranger, away from what he would never understand.

Something Other Than Garbage
Jim O'Loughlin

"So, do I have a case?"

The lawyer was just a kid, about the age of Sam's oldest, but he was the union's attorney, and Sam had no reason to doubt him. And if Sam had doubted him, he would have had to pay out of pocket for someone else to represent him at the hearing.

"Well, you've definitely gotten screwed here," the kid lawyer said, yanking on his tie. Sam got the sense he wasn't used to wearing one. "But I'm not sure that there's a lot in the contract to help you, and with those letters in your permanent file, they can build a pretty strong case."

Sam's fingers tightened around the arms of his chair. Those damn letters. Ten years ago, back when he was drinking too much before he met Audrey. He'd be paying for that the rest of his life.

"So, you're saying there's nothing I can do?"

"No, I didn't say that. There's just nothing in the contract that's going to help you. But this is a really unique situation, and I've got an idea." The kid lawyer smiled and shifted in his chair. "There's a chance we could get them to drop the whole thing, but you'll have to be willing to piss a lot of people off."

Sam smiled back. "That's never been a problem for me."

He'd put in twenty-five years at the Public Works, and now he looked to lose his job because of dead trees. Could it be any more stupid? He never should have volunteered to deal with the trees. But the alternative was working on a crew under Everly over by the dam. After a day being supervised by that asshole, he'd be sure to get written up. At least if he was by himself, he didn't have to put up with bullshit. He didn't mind spending the day alone, tooling along the bike path by the river in a converted golf cart. Sam wondered sometimes if he should have become a farmer.

It had been a heavy winter, and in the spring the river crested over flood stage, taking out a lot of trees close to the water line. Sam's job was to move any of the fallen trees that blocked the path or looked like they might fall into the river. He could lift most of the logs by himself, and he took a chainsaw to the bigger downers. But it was always so sad to see the trees splintered along the trunk, half submerged in the current. He even hated to see the newer pines go down, though those were usually ripped out by the roots and went floating down to the dam where they became a more visible hazard. It was such a waste. It took decades to grow trees and just one flood to bring them down. The flooding seemed to be a little worse every year, and Sam couldn't decide whether to blame global warming, new home building in flood plains, or just a run of bad winters.

There was something depressing about it all, and that must have had something to do with how things started. He could remember the first tree now, one of the cedars. There were more of them along the banks, and when they fell they usually splintered rather than getting ripped out by the roots. One time when he took the chainsaw and cut away the top of the tree, the splintered section attached to the trunk spread out evenly like a fan or a fountain. It looked to him like a sculpture, not that he knew a damn thing about sculptures. But he trimmed off some of the uneven rough edges and shaved the bark from the stump. When he was done, it looked to him as if a tree were exploding out of the ground, and that didn't seem so bad.

He didn't change every tree he saw, but the rest of the spring he looked at the downers differently. They weren't just so much wood to be moved anymore, but something he might work with, even if he never had a lot of time for any one of them. When he had to take down a tree, he'd consider where would be the best place for it to land. Sometimes he'd try to topple a few of them together like a giant game of pick-up sticks. When he had to take a chainsaw to a big tree, he considered different ways to divide up the sections. His favorite remained the splintered trees. There was just so much you could do with them. When you cut away the tops of those, the remaining wood always seemed to hang at some impossible angle.

At home, he adapted some of his own saws so he could make some finer carvings, and he bought a heavy-duty wood boring drill that he started carrying to work. He spent a lot of the spring thinking about the trees he had changed. He even brought Audrey to check out his work one weekend, making it sound like a canoeing trip only to spend most of the afternoon tromping through the woods and looking at his trees. Audrey didn't seem sure what to make of it, but that was fair. Sam didn't know what to make of it either. Audrey's favorite was an oak that had gotten ripped out by the roots. Sam had been able to cut away the stump from the root system and then chop up the stump into a series of three-foot pedestals. He had come back on his own time one Sunday and hooked up a rope pulley to his pickup so he could hoist the roots onto the pedestals. It took him most of an afternoon, but he got the roots up on the pedestals, and now it looked like some kind of alien spacecraft taking off. That had been the hardest of the pieces to do, and Sam was pleased that Audrey liked it the most.

On the ride home, Audrey had lots of questions.

"So, where'd you get the idea to do all of that?" Audrey asked.

"I, uh, I don't know."

"You never told me you did stuff like that."

"I never did before. I can't really explain what started it."

"Are you going to keep doing this when the river is cleared?"

"I don't know. I haven't really thought about it."

Audrey paused, and he could feel her staring at him as if trying to see something she'd missed before.

"Do you know what you're going to do before you see a tree?"

Now that was a question he could answer.

"Never. I don't decide what to do until I see the tree. It's like each tree's only got a few things that can be done to it without… without messing it up. I don't know if that makes sense."

"I don't know either, but I guess I'd rather have you doing this than going out drinking."

"I'm with you there. You know, I still dream about cigarettes, but I don't miss the drinking anymore."

When Sam's work along the river was done, things got busy again. The heavy winter had taken a toll on the city's roads, and he got put on a pothole patrol. It was a whole lot less interesting than working with the trees, but after all that time alone he didn't mind a little company. He didn't stop thinking about the trees, though. He had an idea about how to modify a circular saw blade to make grooved cuts, but he would need to find someone who could do metalwork for him. Jerry, his little brother, ran a tool and die business, and he might have been able to do it, though Sam never liked to ask Jerry for favors. It's not that Jerry lorded his college diploma over Sam, but Sam couldn't help but resent him a bit. If Sam had had some kind of clue as to what to do after high school, he could have been as successful as Jerry was. But he bounced from job to job for a long time after graduation, got married to Laura when they were too young, had kids before they were ready. And, of course, the drinking. If only he had it all to do over again. But, in some ways, he was doing it all over again with Audrey. She was on her second marriage, too, and they were both now grandparents. Grandparents. That made him feel really old. Almost as old as his back made him feel after a day of shoveling asphalt. He wasn't sure how many years he could keep doing this. Driving a plow was one thing, but asphalt was young man's work, so he felt relieved when he got a call to report back to the garage early one day.

That was a stupid thing to feel because the Super didn't call Sam to the Super's office to give him an Employee of the Month bump sticker. Still, Sam had kept his nose pretty clean lately and hoped it was just some paperwork bullshit he hadn't filled out correctly. But he knew he was in trouble when he saw sheets of paper with pictures of his trees fanned out on the Super's desk. The Super didn't say anything at first. He just let Sam stare at the pages. Sam knew it was just some power game to get him rattled. Funny as it seemed, Sam felt annoyed that the pictures were such low quality. They must have been taken on a camera phone then downloaded and printed on some crappy inkjet color printer.

"I've been getting some calls now that the fishermen and hikers are out on the trails again," the Super said.

Sam didn't say anything. This guy wasn't the worst boss he'd had, but he was a boss.

"Mostly fans of your work, except for one guy who got all in a huff and called the mayor asking why we're wasting taxpayer dollars on art projects you can't see unless you're in a canoe. You may have forgotten that the mayor's up for re-election this year, but the mayor hasn't forgotten."

The Super grabbed another piece of paper off of his printer and handed it to Sam.

"Here's your termination notice, and I'm going to have to place you on leave until the hearing. I'm sorry, Sam, but this one's out of my hands."

Sam took the piece of paper, shoved it into his pocket, and walked out. When he got into his pickup, he took it out and read it. It was all legalese mumbo jumbo, but he got the gist of it. He called the union headquarters and made an appointment with the lawyer and then took a deep breath before realizing he had to tell Audrey. A drink would have felt good right then.

Sam wasn't too sure about the kid lawyer's plan, but he didn't have a better one. And anything was better than having to look again at

Audrey's scared eyes when he had told her he wasn't sure what getting fired meant for his pension. So, early on Saturday morning, at a time when he'd rather have been sleeping, he agreed to meet a reporter from the local paper and bring his canoe. They met down at the public boat launch. Sam had missed her at first, thinking she was just some high school kid with her dark hair pulled back in a ponytail. She looked about the age of his daughter, though she had to be older. This must have been her first job out of college. She introduced herself as Diana, got out her notebook and started taking notes right away.

The life jacket Sam had brought for the reporter could have fit two of her, but she didn't seem to mind. They had plenty of time to talk, paddling up river. Turned out Sam was right, this was her first job out of college. In fact, Sam's lawyer was a friend of hers. She wasn't originally from this area, but she liked her job even if the town seemed a little quiet to her sometimes.

"Hell, I've lived here all my life," Sam said, "and it seems a little quiet to me."

It was a nice day, and the river was calm, so paddling upstream was pretty easy. When they got to the first of Sam's trees, Diana stopped talking about herself and started peppering him with questions. She had a lot of questions, and he found himself struggling to come up with the right words for what he had done. He tried to be really clear that he wasn't wasting taxpayer money on these projects, that he had come back on his own time for the difficult ones. But the reporter didn't seem to care about that. She asked him when he had become an environmental artist, and he had to honestly say that he didn't even know what that was. But he tried his best to explain what he had done. He talked a lot about how sad it was to see the downed trees and to think of how many years they had grown just to be knocked down when the water rose. She wanted to know about the tools he used, and he was more comfortable talking about that. He could give details about chainsaws and drills.

She took a bunch of pictures during the trip, and she did ask a lot of questions about his termination letter. He had to be honest that he had some problems in the past, mostly insubordination, and his file was pretty full of permanent letters. But it was still just the election year crap that had blown all this up so big. She kept scribbling down a lot of notes, but he couldn't tell what she was thinking. In the end, after he brought Diana back to shore, he wasn't sure he had done himself much good.

The Sunday before his hearing, the article came out. It was pretty good. Diana was a decent writer. She had been able to put into words what he hadn't. The trees were going to be cleared no matter what. What Sam did made them something other than garbage. That's what he would have said himself if he had thought of it. She also went after the Mayor for intervening in a civil service matter and noted that this wasn't the first incident where he had got involved in personnel matters. And then she talked about how much the city had spent on the big statue over by the library, the one with the giant chicken sitting on the ball of string.

Her photographs weren't too bad either. She'd done a really nice job on one shot of a tree that had fallen with its roots pointed up in the air. Sam had drilled out big chunks of the trunk but left the roots where they were. She had lain down on the ground to get the shot, shooting straight into the root system and, though Sam hadn't noticed this at the time, straight into the sun. Normally that would have been the wrong way to take a picture, but with the roots in front of the sunshine it gave the whole picture an otherworldly quality. Yeah, that was a really nice shot.

When Audrey came down that morning, Sam poured her a cup of coffee.

"That article I told you about is in the paper today."

"Oh, yeah." Audrey yawned. It took her awhile to get started in the morning. "Where is it?"

"Right there, on the top of the front page."

Things happened pretty quickly after that. Sam's phone rang off the hook with calls from friends that had seen the article. Even Jerry, his brother, called to talk about it. Audrey bought up a bunch of copies and mailed them to his kids, and that started another round of phone calls. Later that week the mayor released a statement denying that he'd tried to get Sam fired. Sam's Super claimed there had been a "communication error," and he cancelled the termination hearing and removed the letter from Sam's file. The kid lawyer was practically giggling he was so happy about the way things turned out. And, once it became clear that Sam wasn't going to lose his job, Audrey lightened up and had him take some of the grandkids out to see the trees. The local arts center persuaded Sam to conduct a canoe tour of his work, and, though he was nervous about it, he had enjoyed giving the tour more than he thought he would.

Then one morning he got a call from the reporter, Diana. At first he thought someone had died. She was crying and could barely get the words out. She said she was so sorry, that she felt responsible for it. Eventually, she explained that the trees, his trees, had all been destroyed. Someone had vandalized them all with axes. Sam tried to get her to stop crying. He said it was okay, that she wasn't to blame. Really, what could a bunch of kids with axes do that nature wasn't going to do in a few years anyway? Diana calmed down and became a reporter again. She said she was covering the story. The police had some leads, and she wanted a quote from him. Sam said she should check the alibis of the mayor and the "taxpayers' dollars" guy. That made her laugh.

To Sam, the funny thing was that he really wasn't that upset. What he told Diana was true. In a few years, the vandalized trees would be sawdust anyways. Besides he was finished with those trees. He was thinking about next spring. There was more to be done, and he had some ideas.

Trapeze

Barbara Harroun

The last Halloween we were married, Greg took me to a party he heard about from a friend of a friend. Greg drove the country roads like he knew where he was going. We didn't talk. The Indiana farm was an hour from town, and on the ride out I thought about apple bobbing, hayrack rides, bonfires and ghost stories; activities where Greg and I might feel like touching, holding hands or at least sitting next to each other. He finally turned down a dirt lane, which led eventually to a field. Two men in fluorescent orange vests directed traffic with flashlights. Greg paid six dollars to park. I asked what was going on and Greg just said *wait, wait and see.* He said, *you'll love this.*

We followed a trail of people to a field lit like a landing strip. Small circles of strangers passed joints and bottles. There must have been close to three hundred people milling about, some in masks and costumes, though most wore jeans, heavy coats and sneakers. I dressed up for the occasion, a chocolate dress that cinched at the waist, thick tights, push up bra, make up and sleek, flat ironed hair. I wore new boots. One look around, and I saw how absurd the high heels on them were. For all those people it was quiet. I heard dried cornhusks crackle when people shifted their stances. We stood alone. Greg took a fifth of Jack Daniels from his coat pocket and handed me the keys. He drank deeply without offering. I worried about finding our way home.

Greg pointed with the bottle to the center of the field. He walked toward a skeletal structure containing two tall ladders with adjoining platforms. They stood directly across from one another, about 50 feet apart. Then I saw the trapeze high above the fallow field. There was no net. Greg moved as though the sight did not shock him. He moved the way he walked out the door each morning, a gait that suggested he wanted to sink into the floor, disappear. I hated him for a moment. Hated the way his jacket hung, hated the back of his head. But I followed, quickening my step, twisting an ankle on the uneven ground.

The girl stood at the base of the ladder. Her face was profiled in the floodlights. Her nose hooked the air. Sequins had popped off the bodice of the leotard she wore in great chunks, leaving dark spaces like lost teeth. She was thin and too young to have real breasts. The tulle of her tutu was frayed and stained. It tilted to reveal a bony hip. She leaned into the ladder and tremors ran through her arms. She hung her head. Light caught a silver strand of snot trailing from her nose. She was crying. A tall man stood behind her and whispered in her ear. Her head reared up when he pushed an index finger into her ribs. A bullhorn sounded. The man grabbed her butt with both hands and pushed her up the ladder. He followed behind her and the people around me began clapping and stomping their feet. Some let loose wolf whistles. The crowd quieted when the girl reached the platform. Greg looked on evenly and drank. The man reeled the trapeze in on a pulley.

I held the car keys like a talisman. I tugged Greg's sleeve. *Let's go*, I said. *Please. Let's go.* Greg shook me off his arm. The man gripped her by the wrist and I thought the poor girl must be cold. I wondered if the tall man was her father or her pimp. If she had run away or been kidnapped. She needed rescuing. He placed her hands on the metal bar, and she braced herself. The man took half a step back. She looked down at her feet, and I saw they were bare. The man pushed her, hard, and she sailed across the field. Everyone cheered. I knew Greg was waiting for her to fall. They were all waiting for her to fall. Her legs, those legs, tried to run on air, but this wasn't a cartoon. Then I was running, across the field, to the car. No one to catch me when one heel sunk deep into the earth, and I fell hard enough to feel the air leave me. All eyes were turned upward, all voices raised.

Across Ohio

T.C. Jones

Racing across the Ohio plains the road just goes, moaning its way east, scrolling through seas of corn planted waist-high, so straight it could slice you wide open. C.C. drives his tiny pickup, two of us squeezed in front with him, blasting a My Morning Jacket bootleg he'd recorded at Bonnaroo. My legs ache terribly, so I stretch them across Anna's lap. She doesn't say anything, but I can hear the thoughts turning in her head. She pulls a bottle of Coca-Cola from her backpack and hands it to me. We pass it back and forth, taking sips. We offer C.C. some, but he shakes his head and says he doesn't like Coke.

Every now and then Anna taps a cigarette from her pack of Camel Blues and lights up. I roll the window down half way, and she apologizes as she stretches in front of me to knock off the ash. She says she is sorry a lot, and I tell her she shouldn't be sorry so much. She offers me a cigarette, and I decline; I don't need another vice. C.C. takes the light even though I've never seen him smoke before. He drives with one hand on the wheel and drags the cigarette with his other, inhaling deeply and blowing out a long stream of smoke.

I stare out the window and watch some kids playing baseball on a tiny dirt infield. The batter slashes and the baseball rifles through the twilight sky like a comet. His little legs race around the bases, kicking up dust into a red cloud. There is no sound except the wind whipping through the truck window. I think about how the baseball speeding from the pitcher's hand scared me as a child, how I always tried to be tough and stand in the batter's box without bailing out. One time I was up against the pitcher with the best fastball in the entire Pony League. Digging my cleats in, the ball sailed wildly—I didn't bail out—and crushed into my chest. Pulling myself from the dirt infield and gasping for the breath knocked from my lungs, I held back my tears. After that I couldn't hold the bat in my hand without bailing out; I couldn't face the world without fear in my eyes.

I watch tears course down Anna's cheeks. She's been crying at random lately. We can't figure it out; it's like predicting a tornado in a Midwestern thunderstorm. She tells us her old boyfriend texts her every day and calls her a slut. Then she tells us she still misses him sometimes. C.C. and I, we tell her to quit worrying about him, that he's a deadbeat, a psycho, that he's exhibiting controlling behavior. We tell her that since he is miserable, he wants her to be miserable, too. C.C. says she needs to find a new guy: not a relationship, just someone to have sex with. Anna nods and wipes her tears.

We share everything with each other: our pains, our hopes, our heartaches, the dreams we don't dare tell anyone else. We don't yet realize this is a mistake common to fast friendships. We are based on something erroneous.

Dark is pressing in tight as the sun dips low behind us, fading in pennants of orange and red and purple. Shadows stretch over everything, long and ominous. We drive on, the land flat and seemingly rolling to infinity. I wonder if love has a starting point, an ending point, or does it go on forever in both directions?

When night falls in Ohio, it is absolute. The black road devours our headlights. Lonesome farmhouses flicker from what looks like miles away. Darkness has a way of playing tricks with your head so I look over at Anna and ask for a light. She pulls two cigarettes from her purse: one for me and one for her. I inhale and can't stop coughing.

In the Milo

Matthew Fogarty

Milo fields stretch through much of central South Dakota, interspersed with corn and wheat and soy beans and other productive crops. From a distance, like, say, from a truck on the highway that runs east to west and splits the state in two, the fields merge, mesh together, blend into swathes of golden and maize shades of yellow, light brown, and dusty red. As though the truck itself is a brush, and with each mile revealed over the rolling hills, it paints long flowing strokes on the landscape blending into the tall buttes in the background and up into the clear sky. Even accounting for the near-constant sweep of the wind, the grazing cows, the racing whitetail deer leaping through the fields, and the floating and fluttering birds, the scene is more of a still life: all the things in it having been rendered onto the same earth-sized canvas. All that's out of place are the distant spots of blaze orange, of men moving among the fields.

The thing you miss in the city is this stillness. From every corner of my fourteenth floor studio apartment in Hell's Kitchen, Manhattan, I can hear the noise of the street below, the passing taxicabs splashing gray afternoon rain on the sidewalk, the street construction, the garbage trucks, the shouting. On the street, it's a hustling go go go. Quick to the subway in the morning, quick past the tourists and their toddlers, quick up the thirty stories in the crowded elevator, quick to the sign taped to the wall above my desk: *A drop of water cannot stop in a raging river. It'll get swept away.*

Maybe on an early morning Saturday in late February when there's still snow on the ground packed firm over a layer of ice, you could hop on the F train to Seventh Avenue, walk through Park Slope, Brooklyn, and out into Prospect Park, back in one of the park's many alleys, one of the paths leading off around the back of the ball fields or under a footbridge. Maybe there, still technically in the city, you would find a similar stillness. But it will not be the same. For one, it will probably smell like urine rather than sweet corn and flowers and reeds, and it will also sound different. And for another, your view will be bounded by the tall trees of the park and whatever structures you can see rising behind them.

This is all to say that it felt appropriate when the song "Pleasant Valley Sunday" came on the radio in the cab of the pickup—*my thoughts all seem to stray to places far away*—and I hummed along. Brandon, broad in the shoulders and a tall nineteen, turned from the driver's seat to look and I stopped.

"Our field's just up the road a bit, just past that long shelter belt," he said over the dull hum of the road and the music. "There'll be plenty of birds in there. You'll see 'em running out of the patch as soon as we pull up, so make sure you're ready."

Next to me on the back bench seat, Rod flicked the safety of his empty twelve gauge on and off. "Let's do this," he said. Yesterday, he seemed giddy walking into the departure lobby at La Guardia airport and announcing to the ticket agent that he was carrying a gun, although he looked disappointed when she simply said, "Okay." She opened the hard case he had inherited from his father, confirmed that the weapon was unloaded, and secured the lock on the case before dropping it on the conveyor belt behind her. The case reappeared when we reached Sioux Falls, propelled through the door of the dedicated shotgun conveyor in the baggage claim area of the airport.

The trip was Rod's idea, a memorial to his dead father with whom he hunted as a child. Rod is one of those guys who commutes from the suburbs, two hours a day on the MTA, and gets back to say good night to his daughter by eight each night. But he cultivates a Hemingway-in-the-city, hunter-gatherer persona, a man able to fend for himself, at one with the land, even if his usual land is the hollow island of modern Mannahatta. *We'll assert our dominance over nature,* he had written in his email trying to convince me to come along. *Just don't shoot me.*

I wrote back, *But I've never killed anything before. I don't even know if I could.*

Hunting is what men do. Strong men, he replied, invoking my fear that, having lived in the city among the dominating, stifling towers for so long, I had become passive and soft, an indistinguishable pattern in the fabric of the city. Though, I was more swayed by the idea of spending a week in a cozy lodge without a cell phone or email. *Plus, there'll be whiskey,* he wrote.

When we arrived at the lodge last night, Wes, Brandon's dad, let me choose a rental from his gun room, a locked den decorated with two sorrowful taxidermied deer heads and wooden paneling behind racks and racks of shotguns.

"As you can see, we've got lots of guns. You want a semi-automatic? A pump? Side-by-side? Over-under?" Wes asked. I looked to Rod.

"Why don't you take a semi-automatic," Rod said. "Holds more shells. You'll want the extra couple shots your first time out."

The truck turned off the highway onto a county road parallel to an electric fence that I'm sure would have run for miles had Brandon not caught the only break in the fencing, a thin dirt bypass turned to mud from last night's snow and rain. He stopped the truck at the entrance to the back fields of the family farm, shifted into four wheel drive, and pumped the gas pedal to plow the truck's four oversized tires through the field toward a patch of milo.

Sensing that the birds were close, the two black Labradors in the flatbed of the pickup huffed loudly and rattled their crates, all tongues and tails. "Dark and Stormy," Brandon had introduced them earlier in the morning. "My dad likes rum," he said. And as we pulled forward into the muck, three birds—Chinese Ringneck Pheasants—ran out from one of the patches into the path of the truck. The dogs barked a loud caged symphony paced by a rabid furious rhythm.

"Look at this," Brandon said to Rod, smiling. "Here's a couple right here! Roadbirds." He gunned the engine toward the birds, steering with his left hand while loading his gun with his right, angling the shells into the chamber of his Winchester pump. He pulled the massive vehicle around to the side of the birds, like a seventeenth century gunship turning to fire the cannons. The claws of the birds dug into the pliable ground, their bodies unable to gain lift, like rolling bowling balls with wings.

The truck tottered over mounds of dirt, like crossing another boat's wake, into and out of puddles of thick mud and ruts. Brandon pushed the shotgun through the open driver's side window, propping it on the door of the moving truck. Brandon's grin occupied the whole of the rearview mirror. "Don't tell my dad," he said. He pulled his knees to the bottom of the steering wheel to keep the truck steady while simultaneously pumping the gun to load the shells and flicking off the safety.

"Close your ears, men!"

A quick succession of *Blast*! Pump. *Blast*! Pump. *Blast*! and all three birds lay dead on the ground, one of them having been shredded into bite-size pieces by each of the dozen pellets released from the second shell. At such close range, the pellets don't have time to spread into their usual patter. Wes explained last night over glasses of whiskey:

"They'll be sticking real tight. If you get a bird up real close, let him get a few feet away before firing. Otherwise, meat'll be full of pellets and you'll be covered in feathers and bird blood. That happens, you might get shot," he said.

Outside the truck, Brandon grabbed the two intact birds by their necks, twisted to complete the kill, and tossed the bodies in the bed of the pickup. He looked down at the third bird. "Coyotes' gonna eat well tonight, I guess."

The truck's cab smelled thick with gunpowder. Rod laughed, turned to me, and said, "When we get back, we ought to go pigeon hunting out of a taxicab on Fifth Avenue."

Milo is a tall, thin, sorghum grain crop harvested primarily for feed. It rises straight from the dirt toward the sun, progressing from golden yellow at the base to a dustier yellow in its plant torso to the head of the stem sprouting dark red-orange seeds. When the wind gets blowing, it kicks up pollen from the milo seeds, fertilizing the ground below. As a result, the milo on Wes' farm had grown in long, thick, messy swatches rather than in neat, tightly-planted rows, and the undergrowth grabbed at my stiff, steel-toed boots as I walked through the field, making the walk more of a push-swipe-step, push-swipe-step than a straight hike.

Usually, at home, it would take four or five miles on the treadmill at the Fourteenth Street gym, in line with sweaty faceless business-men and businesswomen in tank tops and jogging shorts running in place toward the window and the street five stories below, to exhaust my legs, but we hadn't made it halfway through the milo field before I could feel them begin to ache. I focused on my breath, and each clodding plod of the push-swipe-step, trying to stay upright with the gun in my hands.

With the rush of the wind past my ears closing off all sound but a rumbling muffle, I almost forgot our mission. Dark and Stormy had been tracing z-shaped patterns across the field about ten yards ahead of us since we entered the field about a quarter of a mile back, the dogs gleeful, mouths open, tongues out, black ears flapping. Stormy bounded across my row apparently tracking for a scent. Directly in front of me, he bounced to a stop and shot his long black tail up toward the sky like an antenna. He stuck his nose into the dirt and began to walk a slow diagonal toward the middle of the field, his nose still pressed to the ground.

"He's gettin' birdy. Get your guns ready," shouted Brandon, guiding the dogs through the field between us. "There's birds in there, Stormy."

And an instant later we heard them: a flap of feathers against the milo, a ripple in the sea of red-orange stalks. A beak poked out of the top of the milo at the center of the field, wings flapping furiously, pushing for the ascent.

"Rooster!" shouted Brandon.

I pulled the gun up to the pit of my shoulder, as Rod had shown me, and pressed my cheek against the chamber of the gun. I closed my left eye, and drew my right eye down the sight rail running the length of the twenty-eight inch barrel to the muzzle.

As the bird lifted off the milo, three more jumped up into the sky in front of it. I pointed the gun toward the center of the flock, and pulled the trigger. A *blast*! sent concentric rings of sound expanding through the air. Except that my gun hadn't fired. The sound had come from Rod's gun. My trigger hadn't worked. I had forgotten to release the safety. I flicked the button below the trigger guard, but as I did, another *blast*! *blast*! *blast*! sounded from Rod's gun to my left. I looked up and saw puffs of feathers floating on the breeze back down into the milo.

"Nice shooting! Dark, Stormy, there's dead birds in there!" shouted Brandon. And the dogs leapt through the milo to retrieve the birds.

"Were those yours or mine?" Rod shouted to me across the field.

"Didn't get a shot off," I said.

Brandon said, "Looks like we might have a runner. That was a good shot though. He's not gonna get far. Dogs'll get him. You can relax a minute."

I checked the safety of my gun and set it to the ground, securing the butt in a tangle of growth and dirt and the barrel against my leg pointed up toward my stomach. I wiped a line of sweat from my forehead with the soft cloth in my cap. The temperature had dropped in the night as a front came in from the west off the Rockies and laid down a half inch of late October rain and snow. Much of the snow melted when the sun rose, though the distant hilltops were still covered in white and the wind was still bitter. Even so, my red flannel shirt was moist. And the cold plains air was somehow snaking its way under the bottom of my jacket and chilling the flannel, so that with each heavy stepping clod of the uncomfortable boot and the resulting readjustment of the outfit, I was stung by the cold, wet shirt against the waves of heat that radiated from within my body.

Stormy appeared out of the brush at Brandon's feet with the dead bird in his mouth. "Good boy, Stormy," said Brandon. He took the bird from the dog's mouth, wrung the neck, and shoved the bloody carcass into the pouch in the back of his hunting jacket.

Rod shouted, "Loaded!" I shouldered my weapon, and we began again the trudge through the field, the dogs tracing low paths through the milo in front of us.

"Stormy, hunt close," shouted Brandon, as he triggered the electric collar wrapped around the dog's neck. The resulting yelp came from about twenty yards ahead as the dog returned to the line of hunters.

Brandon turned his head toward me. "Don't want the dogs to get too far ahead of us. They might flush the birds out of range." Last night, Rod explained how the cone-shaped pattern of pellets ejected from the shell grows longer, elongates and expands like the universe, as they fly further from the gun. Eventually, the patter gets too big, the pellets too diffuse and slow. If Stormy kicked up a bird too far away, the bird would be out of range, lost to live another day among the empty shotgun shells pocking the dirt and brush in the milo field.

We continued our slow-motion hike through the thick field, my ears muffed and whistling, all sound drowned out by the wind, like blowing across the tops of Coke bottles. And I slipped into a walking dream. I pictured myself on a European battlefield, on the beach in boots on D-Day, men falling all around me. I pictured myself in the jungle with Charlie lurking, or in the streets of Fallujah. I thought about the birds jumping up out of the milo, and instead of them flipping their tails and shooting out into the sky away from us in fear, I saw them turning back toward us, dive-bombing, going for the eyes or the knee caps, flying targets with razor sharp beaks and claws. I saw one of the dead birds emerging alive from out of the back of Brandon's coat with an uzi, like an almost-defeated villain at the end of a movie. I saw a line of birds marching together with muskets and bayonets, ready to recreate the Battle of the Wilderness, waiting for us to wade deeper into their terrain, where they'd have the advantage.

"Men," the General pheasant, regal in metal helmet and feathered plume, would have said, "This is our land, this is our turf, this is our home. This is where our children were born, where our families live and play, where we live everyday under the blessings of liberty. We will not let it be taken from us. We will not let them defeat us. We know this land. This is our land. We shall rise. And we shall fight for the glory of the Pheasant God and our birdly kingdom. Who will stand with me?" And they all would reach back into their sheaths with those pointy claws and raise their swords to the sky and chant, "Hurrah!"

A rustling in the brush behind me startled me out of the daydream, and a rooster pheasant leaped past my feet, running out ahead of me in the messy row. Dark came running after him, nearly barreling me over to get to the bird. As Dark lunged at its tail feathers, the bird flapped its wings twice, and then, on the third flap, began to take flight up out of the brush past the seeds of the milo and into the air in front of me.

"Roosters!" shouted Brandon. "Shoot!"

I swung my shotgun up to my shoulder, and clicked the safety out of position. At the edge of my vision, I could see a half dozen other birds taking flight. A squadron of pheasants began to circle overhead, almost crashing into one another in their mad flights for safety. I could hear Rod's gun exploding and could see the squadron thinning out, falling from the sky.

But I focused on the bird in front of me. Dark's black muzzle was trained on the bird as well, and he jumped from beneath the bird, aiming for its tail feathers but coming short.

I pointed the end of the sight rail at the bird, moved it a few inches to the left to lead the bird into the patter, and pulled the trigger. *Blast!* The rings of sound outpaced the patter, and the bird ringing off into the hills and the buttes in the far distance, like circular brush strokes in an oil painting. The bird stopped in midair, grabbed, connected by a trail of pellets and powder reaching from my outstretched arm. The bird seemed to pause for a moment, and then tumbled to the ground with a collapsing thud.

Tracking the bird's descent, I was filled with a strange sense of satisfaction, of victory. Out of instinct, I pumped my fist. My first bird.

And then there was silence.

Then, a shrieking yelp rose from out of the milo and fell dead on the wind.

"Dark!" shouted Brandon. He pushed through the brush toward my side of the milo, his thick shoulders and legs twisting and heaving through the patch toward the fallen dog.

The air sucked out of my lungs and the bottom of my stomach dropped through my feet into the cold ground. I would rather have shot myself than a dog, especially a sweet smiling dog like the lab we had when I was a kid. She would chase rabbits through the neighborhood, her leash trailing behind her still attached at the collar. And, summers at the lake, she would search the lakebed for the stone I had just tossed, swim back to shore, and drop it at my feet, tail wagging, for me to throw again. She grew frail in her later years, her knees having succumbed to arthritis, and climbed to the couch one last time, laid down in my arms, and stopped breathing. Her funeral consisted of a cruel car ride she couldn't enjoy and an unceremonious heave into the incinerator. And there in the field, with Brandon's dog, dark, weak, and in pain, the strength drained from my knees and I fell to the ground too.

Rod rushed toward Brandon and Dark, who continued yelping, one yelp after another. I felt sicker with each cry. Through the milo, I could see Rod hunched over the dog. And I could see the top of Brandon's head, his cap off, his hair slicked back with sweat.

Rod looked back at me. "Dude. You didn't shoot the dog," he said.

"What?"

"You didn't shoot the damn dog."

"I didn't shoot the dog?" My voice was still short of air.

"He just broke his leg. Relax, dude."

"God damn gopher hole," said Brandon. "Leg's all twisted to hell. You'd've probably caught it yourself if you'd've kept walking."

"I didn't shoot the dog," I said to myself.

Brandon pulled his cell phone from his jacket pocket and called Wes to bring the flatbed around to the middle of the milo patch. "I got to stay here with Dark. You guys want to grab Stormy and go pick up your birds?"

"Sure," said Rod. "I need to find mine. Your bird's just about twenty yards up the row here," he said to me. "You okay just grabbing it yourself or you want me to get it for you?"

"No," I said, still refilling my lungs. "I can get it."

"Sure?" he asked.

"Yeah," I said. "It's no problem."

I walked a line past Brandon and Dark to a clearing in the underbrush where the bird sat like a wooden decoy, in a sort of pheasant fetal position, its wings pressed to its sides, its head and neck tucked into its shoulders, its angle of descent traceable through a tunnel of bent and broken stalks of milo leading to the ground where it made only a slight indent in the softened dirt. The wind had stopped.

"Should'a ducked, buddy," I said quietly as I approached. Standing over the bird, I could feel the escaping heat both from the bird's warm blood and from the molten shotgun pellets in his chest. The cold air converted the heat to steam, rising up through the milo, floating a path back to the sky and into the atmosphere where it dissipated or disappeared. I thought that maybe it was the bird's soul leaving his body, rising up to the heavens, to the gods, as in that old Native American lore, wafting teepee smoke as the earthly being escaping into the afterlife.

But the bird was still alive, heaving, his heart pumping fast but slowing, his head rocking back and forth slightly like the head of a nervous child, his eyes flickering, searching, his last breaths audible. I squatted and put my hand to the tail feathers, lined with bright shades of blue and red and green.

"I didn't realize they're so beautiful," I said.

The bird looked up at me—the same look I saw in our lab in her final moments, and that I'm sure Rod saw in his Dad. Color vacated his eyes. He mustered a confined ruffle of feathers. A flourish. The last throes.

And then—

Dead rooster. Bright against the brown dirt. Colorful stalks of milo sprouting up from the ground. Me, covered in orange and hunched motionless and silent.

The Weaving

Leni Yost

Sarah had felt the chill for many months, so when Nicholas came to her one night after dinner, as the snows outside were beginning to deepen and drift against the fence posts, she was not surprised. And she was prepared.

"Will you stay with me until the baby is born?" she asked him, her hands resting in the pockets of her smock.

"I'll stay until spring," he said, and he looked past her into fall. So it was settled. Nicholas went back to his ledgers, and Sarah took up her shuttle and continued at her loom. She was weaving a tapestry in a corner near the bay window where she could watch the sun set through the bare oaks and red maples. Sitting squarely in front of the loom, she passed the wooden shuttle left to right and right to left, building inch by inch the textures and the colors that wove her stories in pictures. With yarn wound around her fingers in a butterfly, she added details to her chapters, lifting the warp threads strung over her loom and passing through the weft to make the patterns unfold a history. She favored the colors of the earth: the greens and browns of the fields, the yellows and blues of the wild flowers, the reds that burned the sky when Indian summer came.

Past the oaks and maples outside her window was a meadow, once farmed, now fallow. Wild things had taken root there—Queen Anne's lace, tiny sugary violets, pink and white clover, dandelions as tall as a child. When Sarah was a girl, she had played in such a place, listening to music on a small transistor radio. She would make a bonnet of the lace and a garland of the clover and hold dandelion blossoms under her sister's chin to see if she liked butter.

"You do! You do!" Sarah would sing, skipping backwards around Karen. "Your chin is all yellow. That means you like butter."

They would lie for hours in their meadow, plucking out tiny buds of clover and sucking nectar from the tips like hungry bees. When it was dark, they would catch lightning bugs and put them in a jar to light their way home, mosquitoes sizzling around their ears.

It had been five years since Sarah had seen Karen. Nicholas had taken his wife far from her home, and it was not convenient to go back. Her mother and father were old and no longer traveled, and Karen was busy in the city. Sarah had made a new life with Nicholas. He built her a house where she could see the sunset, but it was too far to see home.

"Is there someone else?" she remembered to ask him later, careful not to look at his eyes.

He peered over the top of his book. "No, of course not. No one else. I care about you." He hesitated, his eyes glancing just a moment at her belly. "I'm restless. I don't know where my life is anymore. I want to find out before it's too late. I don't suppose you can understand that."

Sarah looked into the trees outside her window, dark with shadows now, the moon beginning to lay silver across the bare branches. Her fingers moved lightly over the threads she had woven, smoothing out rough spots, pulling the beater bar towards her to straighten the rows. She threaded burnt orange and passed it through the warp from side to side, alternating hands, holding the vertical yarns apart as if she were plucking the strings of a harp. The faces of her parents were reflected in the window panes, young and strong as they had been when she was a little girl, determined to give their children everything love could buy.

As she watched, the scene changed, the faces lost their vitality and began to wither. She saw her parents working hard in a corn field, pollinating the crops by hand, fingering the silken threads, surrounded by taut young men burnished red under the sun, their hands cracked, ragged fingernails caked with soil. She saw herself and Karen, working alongside the men, working as hard as young girls could work before their fingers were raw and covered with blood and black earth. The meadow was far away.

At dusk, the girls would fall against each other and walk to the house with barely the strength of one girl between them. Sometimes they were too tired to eat, no matter how much they were coaxed. The lights went out early in the house, and only the mutt barking at gophers and a sow rooting noisily in her pen suggested anyone lived there.

Half an arm's length of new weaving was done when Sarah stopped for the night. Threads dangled from the back of her tapestry. With tiny gold scissors shaped like a stork with a razor-sharp beak, she snipped the remnants and added them to the pile sitting next to the basket that held her cards of yarn.

"I'm going to bed," she told Nicholas without turning around. "Are you coming?"

"I'll be up in a little while. I thought, maybe, with a baby coming, you'd be more comfortable sleeping alone. I'll take the guest room from now on."

"Yes, that's good," Sarah said, smiling. "It will be more comfortable for both of us."

She gathered up the snippets of yarn from the floor and took them upstairs to her room.

By January, Sarah had finished two tapestries, which she laid, carefully covered in tissue paper, on top of the cherry wood harvest table at the end of the dining room. She had steamed them and pressed them and begun again at her loom with new colors, a new picture, and new balls of yarn. This one would have more yellow and violet with a hint of pink and white. It would show a childish wedding, the day Sarah and Karen had pretended to marry men made of cornstalks, grass hats on their heads and wedding bands made from the stems of clover. Sarah chose a narrow shuttle and threaded it with yarn the color of the wild rose.

The afternoon sun coming in through the window made shadow puppets of the oak and red maple branches on the hardwood floor. Sarah looked into the window and saw Karen as a girl nailing boards to the elm tree behind the farmhouse, climbing high to get away from a teasing Sarah and hiding herself in the thick foliage. Sarah always found her, and when she did she climbed up after. The girls would sit on the uppermost branch, scratching behind their knees at the prickly heat rash that came with the hot, humid Midwest summers and giggling into their hands when Father came calling for them at suppertime. Only when he called gruffly for the third time did they scramble down the makeshift ladder and run into the house to wash their faces and hands and sit down at the table.

Mother dished up parboiled potatoes and beef, stretched with gravy on the second day and made into hash on the third. A pot of water stood on the back burner of the stove. Scraps of leftover vegetables went into the pot. The pot simmered all day and all night until Saturday evening, when noodles or barley went into the pot to turn it into soup. Sometimes it tasted good, and Sarah and Karen sopped it up with home-baked black bread. Sometimes there was too much cabbage, not enough sweet corn and tomatoes, and the odor made them wrinkle their noses when Mother wasn't looking. But that was supper on Saturday, and any girl who didn't eat it would go to bed with an empty stomach.

On those nights, Father looked especially tired. He ate in silence, his head dropped over his food, and he avoided looking into the faces of his wife and children. He finished his soup and gave his bread to Sarah and Karen. When the table was cleared, he would walk out to the hog pen to see if the sow was fat enough yet to butcher. In three years, she hadn't produced a litter. She'd just about outlived her usefulness, Father said, but his girls begged for the sweet old sow's life, and so the family ate soup more nights than they should and left the pork on the hoof.

Sarah would lie in bed and look into the night sky through yellow dotted Swiss curtains fluttering at the screened window. She'd count as many stars as she could see and wish on the first one. Her wish was always the same. It took her far away from the farm and showered her with riches that spilled over onto Karen, Mother and Father. The dream made her tired joints ache less and her raw hands feel softer.

From her home now, Sarah could hear the roar of the diesel trucks in the distance lumbering down the highway. As a girl, she'd seen barges on the Mississippi River with smaller boats pushing four, five, six at a time south to New Orleans. They were all moving away. Nicholas had become rich in the barge business. He wasn't much in looks, his hair mousy brown and coarse, his eyes tiny and narrow and watery blue against pink like a rabbit's, but he was good at making money. Sarah knew that the first time she met him, passing him in the hall at the bank where her father had come begging for a loan. Nicholas was well dressed and smelled like good worsted wool. His shoes were shined and the heels were new. He wore an expensive watch under cuffs with a monogram. When she looked at him, he looked back at her, looked twice at the dark hair that hung thick below her shoulders.

The vice president of the bank gave Sarah's father the loan—"I have faith in you, Mr. Cross"—and introduced her to Nicholas Jones, standing impatiently in front of the next desk. Nicholas unbuttoned his double-breasted jacket and shook hands with Sarah's father, his eyes on Sarah's porcelain face. Sarah saw that his hands were clean.

They were married six weeks later in a small ceremony with few guests. Nicholas had appointments down river that took him away the day after. Sarah made their home while he was gone, lushly appointed and nearly hidden among the thick stand of trees and wild strawberries miles from her father's farm. Karen had visited just once before Nicholas returned; he didn't like having guests. Sarah pointed out the meadow and asked Karen to hunt for four-leaf clover.

"There should be hundreds," she said, looking across acres of grassland. "We could find a bushel of luck."

"Another time, Sarah," Karen said, and the same weariness of girlhood was in her eyes. "I've found a job. I need to be behind the counter Monday morning."

Sarah thought of Karen while she worked at her weaving. Under her fingers, a tree house was taking shape, hidden by branches thick with leaves and stuffed with acorns. Karen was perched in the tree, silky brown hair pinched into two pigtails at the sides of her face.

"It looks nice."

Nicholas stood at Sarah's shoulder, watching her hands move back and forth across the tapestry.

"Thank you."

She saw his reflection in the glass, a man with hair thinning on top and graying at the sides, who stood in moribund silhouette against the verdant meadow. There had never been a time when Sarah felt comfortable with Nicholas, although they had few friends and spent most of their time alone together. When he traveled, she did not miss him. When he returned, she felt no skip of a heartbeat.

She had tried hard in the first year of their marriage to make him feel for her what she had seen in his eyes that first day in the bank—appreciation, if not love. Day by day she saw his interest in her fade, and she felt foolish trying to win him back. From the beginning, he had not wanted children. He'd made that clear. When she told him a baby was coming, she saw disappointment in his eyes.

"We're both to blame," he had said. "I don't hold you responsible. Can you—do something about it?"

"It's too late."

"You should have told me sooner."

"You were away."

"It was our busy time. I could have been contacted on the river. You could have reached me."

"Yes, I should have reached you. It's unfortunate. Now it's too late."

He looked down at her protruding belly, small and round, and it was an enormous thing that had come between them.

Sarah looked into the window and saw Nicholas's image fading as he went upstairs. She listened as he settled into bed. She knew he would slip under a blanket with charts and maps of the river and calculate new timetables for his barges, scribbling on a pad of yellow paper how he could increase tonnage and decrease fuel, hire fewer workers and secure major contracts for moving freight down to New Orleans and out to sea. In May, or perhaps sooner, Nicholas would follow his barges south for good.

Sarah pushed herself up from her chair and stretched out her arms, rubbing her wrists to ease the ache there. She took the golden scissors and snipped off the ends of yarn, rolling the scraps into a ball. She could see the meadow through the window, dimly lit by the stars and the moon. In the dark, the clover was gray, the wild flowers black and white. The glass reflected her own image as if she were in the meadow, dark hair pulled back at the neck, wisps trailing the sides of her face, her figure curved and thick. But as she skipped up the stairs, a ball of scraps in her hand, her step was light. She didn't even grasp the banister.

"I have bad news," Nicholas said early in April. "I have to be in New Orleans sooner than I thought. I'll have to leave you in a week. I'm sorry. I won't be able to stay until the baby comes."

"Yes, I thought something like that might happen," Sarah said, and her smile was not unkind. "I was prepared. I know how your business is. I'll call Karen. She can come stay with me."

He pushed a stack of paper in front of her on the table. "I've worked out the arrangement. I'll give you this much—," he drew a line under a very large figure written in neat black letters on his yellow pad. "Because there is a child, I'll also give you this much—," he indicated an even larger sum. "This will all go into an account under your name. There will be no monthly payments. We'll both be free of each other, no bother, no lawyers. Is that satisfactory?"

Sarah nodded. "Very satisfactory. It's quite generous. We'll be well taken care of. Thank you, Nicholas."

"I think it will be better this way. It's better that I'm gone when the baby comes. She doesn't need to know much about me. She'll be provided for, and that's all that counts. You'll call Karen, and she will take care of you."

"And I'll take care of her."

Nicholas put the papers into a leather case and left it on a corner of the harvest table beside the tapestries.

There. It was done.

Sarah sat down in front of the last tapestry she had woven. This was her favorite. Karen was sitting on top of a barrel painted white. Strawberries were growing on a vine that twined around the barrel. Karen's small hands were full of berries, and her mouth was stained red. Sarah had found just the right shade of blue for her eyes, and she was able to weave in the light that once shone there.

It took several hours to cast the sky around the clouds and a goldfinch lighting in a tree. When it was finished, Sarah took the tapestry from the loom and laid it with the others. She spread them out across the harvest table and saw the story of her childhood retold in the weaving. The scenes were exhilarating, and she was impatient to show Karen. Their childhood had come back to her.

The gold scissors snipped away at the yarn still dangling from the back of the picture. She balled it up in the pocket of her smock.

"I think I have it all," Nicholas said, as he put the last of his belongings in the back seat of his car and hung a suit from the hook. "I was careful to take everything so that I won't have to bother you again. Gordon will send you the other papers to sign when they're ready. Just mail them back. I've already taken care of my part."

"I appreciate that," Sarah said. She wasn't sure what else to say to her husband as he left their marriage behind with the house, the furniture and the meadow. "Good luck. You belong on the river. I belong here."

He took her hand and touched her hair, keeping a distance between himself and her round body. "I think everything is working out for the best."

She took back her hand, which had none of his imprint. "Yes, it is," she said.

Sarah stood at the bay window and watched as his car made its way down the road past the meadow. She saw her reflection in the window and began to undo the hair wound in a knot at the back of her neck, shaking it free. She unbuttoned the linen dress that covered her belly and laid it over the back of the bentwood chair. From across her stomach, tied at her waist, she removed a thick, round pillow made of muslin. As she unfastened it at the back, it fell to the floor and its contents spilled around her feet, snippets of colored yarn, once packed hard and round and womblike inside the pillow.

She picked up her dress and slipped it back on, feeling light and slender. She skipped out to the meadow, where spring was clear and sweet, and scuffed her bare toes in the grass. With a sigh that blew the stale air out of her lungs, she began to breathe in the scent of the wild flowers, and she lay down in the clover to wait for Karen.

Heartland

Stephanie A. Marcellus

W hen we pulled into our drive, our next-door neighbors were sitting in their front yard and smoking their cigarettes in the darkening twilight. At least that's where they were until we parked the car and got out. Then, the man and wife promptly, as was their habit, rose up from their crouched poses on the front steps and drug their children, even the one who was attempting to wave, into their rickety house, across from ours on Elm Street. It wasn't as if this was the first time this had happened. Rather, over the last six weeks we had lived in the crackerjack house in the middle of nowhere, in the heart of the heartland, in the smallest of small town America, this behavior had become a ritual as predictable as the evening sun filling the empty western sky each night. We would simply pull into the drive, and they would simply open their door and go in.

"There's our *dear* neighbors. Maybe I'll go ask for a cup of sugar," I commented to my husband, who was tired and not amused by my snide remarks at the end of a long day.

Since we had moved here, Cal had been working nights as a janitor at the local high school while he was commuting to a local university and finishing his degree. This janitorial work definitely wasn't his dream job. And who could blame him? Going to work just as everyone else was coming home. Beginning your work day by cleaning up someone else's toilet problem. These were things that few people would relish, but in this small town cradled on the map by nothing in particular, neither one of us could be too picky about how we paid our bills. That's why I'd been working for the last few days at the local Foodtown, stocking shelves and throwing away the overripe fruit. These jobs would have to do until we could find better, once Cal finished his teaching degree.

"What do you think they do over there in the dark?" I asked Cal once we got in the house. I was subtly pulling apart the venetian blinds and peeking across the street, trying to make sense of the shadowed windows of their house. "They never turn any lights on but that one in the basement," I continued.

"Maybe they're cooking up some meth," he said, and by his tone, I could tell he didn't want to play any guessing games tonight. He was just too tired, and he had an early morning class the next day.

"Nah, you wouldn't think that they'd be doing that—having two small kids and all and living right here two blocks from Main Street," I said as I thought about that little blond girl with her braids and sundress and with her hand posed to wave. That wave had been, to me, the one sign of heart in the heartland, an oncoming boat for a drowning man, even though it was cut short by her sour-looking mother, dragging her into the house. So much for a welcoming committee.

"You know the other day, when I was out getting the mail, that guy next door told me that one of the other neighbors said that one of us had died," Cal said.

"Really?" I remarked, feeling surprised despite the last few weeks of getting used to the politics of small town gossip. So far we'd been drug runners and other sorts of various criminals, but being reported dead was new.

"Really," Cal replied.

"Well, they could have of least sent over a casserole or stopped to see if the not dead one of us needed anything. What do you think they do over there?" I continued.

"Just forget about it," Cal said, as he started getting ready for bed.

I got ready for bed, too, but then decided that I would stay up awhile and read. I had too much on my mind, and there wasn't any use in keeping Cal up with my insomniac tossing and turning. I went out into the living room, turned on the table lamp, and checked to see if the front door was locked. What I could possibly be locking out was an unsolvable mystery, but old habits die hard. As I glanced across the street one final time, I saw the light from our neighbor's basement eerily and dimly glowing in the night like a vigil candle. Then, suddenly the light went out, and I stood there alone, peering out into the loneliness of the night.

From across the house, I could hear Cal's shallow breathing as he slipped into the rhythms of his evening slumber. The near silence was deafening, and here I was wide awake, accoutered in nothing but a ratty terrycloth robe and pink slippers. As though propelled by forces outside of myself, I found myself unlocking the door and stepping out into the darkness of the night. My movements were slow and surreptitious as I crossed Elm Street, banking on the hazy moon and the cloudy night to keep my presence a secret. I thought about the girl's half wave, but her wave became inverted, transformed into a beckoning motion, drawing me across the street. Before I knew it, I was face to face with the neighbor's mysterious window, and there was no going back.

I leaned down and felt the coolness of the windowpane as I cupped my hands against the glass and peered into the forbidden and secret recesses of our neighbor's house. As I thrillingly gazed into their basement, I wondered about what I would see. Would I see shelves stocked with meth lab chemicals? Would I see bodies of grinning dead men strung across the room? Would I see whatever it was that they kept hidden and protected—whatever it was that accounted for their terrible and unexplained hostility?

But, what I see is a drawn shade. What I see is absolutely nothing.

Yet, the longer I peer into their window, the more I can see of myself. I see a mirror image of my lone figure, my dark eyes, my uncombed hair, even my pink bedroom slippers in the foreground. The massive, open spaces of the heartland fill in the backdrop behind me, threatening and promising to envelope my small, stark figure. I feel the midnight breeze unfold against me like the pages of a vast map filled with nothing besides my red, palpitating heart and seas and seas of rolling hills and tall grass. This is the heartland. I raise my hand in a half wave and see my reflection wave back.

Nonfiction Introduction:
Not All There

Debra Marquart

A few years ago, my friend Jordan, a writer and park ranger in northern California, decided to take a month long trip to Grand Teton National Park to do some research for a book. He had worked for the park service twenty years earlier in the Tetons, so the trip was part research, part reverie, and part mournful return to the rougher mountains of his youth. He was one of those people who competed in and won biathlons—the Olympic winter sport where you ski, then shoot with a rifle, then ski some more. He liked to claim you could drop him into any unfamiliar terrain with a compass and a knife—maybe not even a knife—and expect that he'd survive as long as needed.

His whole take on the world was strange and unfamiliar to me. As a born and bred flatlander, a Midwesterner, and someone who grew up in tame farm country, not like the ranch country that existed west of the 100th meridian, I feel unsafe as soon as my car encounters the inclines of foothills. I never grew up around water, so I can't swim and am deathly afraid of water. I was never big on hiking or backpacking or camping. One time when I was around eight, I slept outside with my sisters in a makeshift tarp-tent on the far edge of our very big back farmyard, and I woke up the next morning with an earache.

As a fuzzy, red infection grew in my ear canal over the next few days and my parents hemmed and hawed about the doctor (we, none of us, ever liked going to the doctor—doctors were for when you were taken out flat on a stretcher), my parents finally took me to the doctor and discovered that a bug had crawled into my ear and died.

Probably, the night we were camping, Dr. Goodman reasoned, as he held it up between the tips of his tiny forceps for us all to see. That was it for me—no more sleeping outside. Bugs crawl in your ear and die when you go camping!

How Jordan and I ever became friends is a mystery. But, in anticipation of his Teton trip, I bought him a *Wyoming Atlas and Gazetteer* as a kind of joke because orienteering is one of his most prized skills. Before I slipped the atlas in the manila envelope to ship off to him in California, I flipped through the pages to see what could possibly make people speak in such reverential tones about Grand Teton.

When I opened the section that focused on the north-south corridor of the Rockies containing the Tetons, I was surprised to discover that practically every glaciated range, every horn, cirque, moraine, wrinkle, valley, and rubble pile that the alpine glaciers left behind in northwest Wyoming had been named, and, in fact, bore some of the grandest names in American history—Roosevelt, Jackson, Bridger.

At the time, I was working on a memoir about growing up a rebellious farmer's daughter on a North Dakota wheat farm. One of my working premises was that the place where I grew up was a no-place in the national imagination. One ethnographer dubbed the five-county area in central North Dakota where I grew up the "sauerkraut triangle" because it was so heavily populated with people from my ethnic group, known as Germans-from-Russia, and, presumably, if you drifted into this region as a hapless traveler, you might fall under the spell of sauerkraut's vinegary ethers and never find your way back to the Interstate again.

The Wyoming Gazetteer inspired me. If some of the country's most unpopulated and inaccessible peaks were so lovingly named—geological nuance after geological nuance—what might the DeLorme

Gazetteer have to say about the milder nooks and crannies of my own home ground, a lightly populated region, but certainly inhabited and well-used.

Not surprisingly, Barnes & Noble did not have a copy of the *North Dakota Gazetteer*, so I ordered it from Amazon and waited for days, anticipating its arrival, imagining all the delicious place names that people before me had coined for the topo map of my childhood.

Perhaps you already know what happened when the package came, when I ripped it from its wrapper and turned to the pages containing my hometown, my county, the township of my family land.

I found only the few names I already knew—Napoleon (town), Logan (county), Bryant (township). Highway 3, the two lane blacktop that I used to gaze at from my bedroom window and dream about escaping on, was also there.

The rest of the map was colored in with greens, brown, and tans blocking out the geographical relief of the land, the collection of concentric circle indicating small hills, black lines for roads, thin blue lines for streams. But there were few place names on the paper, nothing traced by fingers of love, mapping the curvilinear geography. The pages were full of green expanses, blank and silent about themselves.

I knew from my childhood people had lived there, worked, walked, died there. Everything imaginable and unimaginable had happened on this small piece of land, but the places must not have struck people as name-worthy—not enough to garner the attention of the DeLorme geographers anyway.

Not all there is a euphemistic phrase people in my home town used to use to describe someone who was "slow" or "developmentally disabled," as we like to say now.

In my hometown, there was a man named Rochus who walked the same route through town each day, no matter what the weather—up the main street from his mother's house where he lived, through the grain elevators, past the café, grocery store, and bar. And when he went by the Stock Grower's Bank, he would shout "big shot, big shot," at the top of his lungs. Every day. And sometimes if we kids came into his path, he'd stop and smile at us, as if he was just a very big kid in overalls himself, and he'd point his finger at us and yell, "How much, how much? Two cents? Sold!"

All this was terrifying and inexplicable, but it was explained away to us by the adults as nothing to worry about, because Rochus was not all there.

It's okay, we might say to ourselves about the unnamed state of the Midwest, *we're just not all there*. The streets you drove, the places where you slept, the willows and beech trees under which you wept and fell in love—not all there. The haunted places of my youth, like the alley of raspberry bushes on the way to my grandmother's house or the dip in the moraine east of my hometown where we used to have keg parties—just blank creases in topographical maps until someone takes the time to remember, to bring a word, then a phrase and sentence to them. To remember is to *re-member*, after all, as in reattach something like a lost limb, to bring story back to an unstoried landscape.

I'm willing to fight about this. I'm willing to argue—and come to fisticuffs in bars, drink a Budweiser even, surrounded by jars of turkey gizzards and billiard tables—that the Midwest is not a no-place. Not in the way that Gertrude Stein meant it about her own hometown, Oakland, California, when she said, "There is no there there." Despite what the world of maps, letters, and history don't have to say about the Midwest, there is *plenty* of there there.

More accurately, I think we are a "true" place, in the way that Herman Melville meant it when he wrote, "It's not down in a map. True places never are." No more *aw-shucks*-ing about the place where we live. No more digging our toes in the dirt. From now on, let's just declare the Midwest a true place full of open secrets, most of them delicious and horrifying. We have such a backlog of work to do! Whole centuries of odd facts and bizarre occurrences to record about what's really been going on here, the details of which we must now regretfully disclose to the rest of the known world.

Debra Marquart is a professor of English and the Coordinator of the MFA Program in Creative Writing and Environment at Iowa State University. She is the author of five books, including a memoir, *The Horizontal World: Growing up Wild in the Middle of Nowhere*, which received the Elle Lettres Award from *Elle Magazine*, an Editors' Choice commendation from the *New York Times*, and the 2007 PEN USA Creative Nonfiction Award. Her work has been the recipient of many prizes, including the Shelby Foote Nonfiction Prize from the Faulkner Society, the Headwaters Prize, a Pushcart Prize, and a National Endowment for the Arts Fellowship. Marquart's latest book, a poetry collection titled *Small Buried Things* is forthcoming from New Rivers Press in 2014.

Dakota Good Enough:
Loving (and Leaving) The Sunflake State

Meghan Brown

"I wish I could pick you up and put you somewhere else."

That was the first thing a kind and savvy professor said to me after I walked into her office and told her that I didn't want to be alive anymore. I was in my junior year of college at the University of North Dakota, and even after living in the town of Grand Forks for nine years, I still felt like a foreigner who would never fit in. I couldn't see the attraction of my town's favorite pastimes—hockey, drinking, shopping, hunting, church. Most of the people around me seemed to fear new experiences, and maybe because of that, they were content to live in the same county for their whole lives, perhaps never leaving the state except for the occasional vacation to Minnesota or Montana. As someone who read voraciously to feed a bottomless curiosity, who believed in animal rights but not religion, I was clearly an outsider. I wanted to travel the world, and nothing excited me more than different cultures and new ideas. My wholesale inability to relate to the people around me left me bored, alienated, and intellectually frustrated. Because people like me were so grossly outnumbered, I was convinced that I was badly made for the world around me, and if this perpetual alienation was to be my life, then I was certain that I didn't want it.

The passage of several years has since helped to heal over that fierce shrapnel wound of pain and hopelessness. I can now scarcely recall what it was like to feel so desperately afraid and alone, but I remember the afternoon I confided to my professor in crisp detail because it marked a crucial turning point for me, a change as base and fundamental as if my vision itself had been transformed. *I wish I could pick you up and put you somewhere else.* These words astonished me in their simple certainty. Medication or a new hobby would not patch over my yawning loneliness. I needed *somewhere else.*

In other words, I needed to leave North Dakota.

This was the first time someone had ever suggested that the place I lived in and its culture—and not me—was largely to blame for my overwhelming sense of intellectual imprisonment and alienation. Much of my fear and sadness miraculously dissipated when my flight from the northern plains cleared for takeoff. The last time I saw North Dakota, it was a distant horizon in my rearview mirror. I haven't looked back.

I am not alone. The nation— indeed, the globe—is sprinkled generously with refugees from North Dakota. For many, the distance they've traveled belies the magnitude and intensity of their need for novel surroundings—and of their coinciding frustration with life on the northern plains. Those who live in North Dakota seem to have one of two responses to this strange and insular place: many grow deep, tough roots and refuse to be pulled up. Yet others—people like me who were misunderstood or bullied for their quirks and curiosity—react with powerful feelings of alienation, loneliness, and boredom that seethe until they can realize their dream of leaving.

How could North Dakota, a place usually regarded as quiet and unassuming, inspire such polarized degrees of loving and loathing? Despite the state's reputation as barren and milquetoast, North Dakota is a place of colorful extremes and contradictions: One of the coldest states in the nation also happens to be home to some of its warmest people. Embarrassed by the state's reputation as retrogressive and "backwards," North Dakotans nonetheless remain deeply suspicious of outsiders and outside influence. A state that prides itself in "North Dakota nice" still struggles with xenophobia, racism, and cruelty. But a place I once considered the epitome of predictable has surprised me. Since leaving the state, I've come to realize that there are many things to appreciate about North Dakota. Maybe I was wrong to give this state my cold shoulder.

I hesitate when someone asks me where I am from. I still don't know what to say. What is that word *from* meant to impart on someone's identity? What traces do we assume a place leaves on the person who lived there? Why is *from* so important that it is often one of the first questions we ask of a new acquaintance? Is a person from the place they were born? Or is a person from the place where they've lived the longest? What if they never felt *from* that place?

The word "from" refers to one's source or origin, but it came from the Old English word *fram*, meaning a forward movement or advancement. *Fram* later evolved to mean a movement away from, so perhaps, now that I've left, I *am* from North Dakota. But I am not a native North Dakotan, and though I lived there twice as long as I have lived anyplace else, I never felt it home. Three years after I was born, my family moved from Denver, Colorado, to upstate New York so that my father could earn his master's degree. After my father finished school, we moved to a suburb of Salt Lake City, Utah. Seven years later, we left Utah for a rural house in the Black Hills of South Dakota. Surrounded by forests and grass, horses and wildlife, I felt most at home in the Black Hills. Every day, regardless of the season, was like living inside of a picture postcard. But only two years after we settled into what I thought was paradise, my father lost his job, forcing us to move again, this time to North Dakota. It was the first time I remember ever grieving for a place. I pressed my nose to the glass and watched the Black Hills recede until they were a thin blue smudge on the horizon as the car sailed east into the prairie's endless windy sea.

The first thing I noticed about North Dakota was its topography —or rather, the lack thereof. North Dakota is flat, startlingly flat. After living my whole life in hills and mountains, North Dakota's vast expanse dizzied and disoriented me, like there was nothing to prevent the austere immensity of the sky from falling down and crushing me. The eastern part of the state is so flat that sometimes there are only a few feet of difference in elevation over several miles. I've seen the curvature of the earth in its unobstructed horizon. Owing to the ease of building roads in straight lines across flat country, North Dakota was the first state in the nation to complete its Interstate Highway System. It is flat enough, so the joke goes, that you can watch your dog run away for three days. There is nothing to stop the walls of wind that blast through from east to west. As a result, North Dakota is one of a few states that lead the nation in renewable wind energy potential. The constant wind may be a promising resource to some, but I hated it. The ever-present sound of the wind made me nervous, a sort of anxious itching, as though the hairs on the back of my neck were always hackling. I imagine North Dakota natives get used to the flatness and wind in the same way that someone could get used to a constant ringing in their ears.

Forty below keeps the riffraff out goes the old North Dakota saying. After performing in Bismarck in January 2005, Joe Herndon of The Temptations remarked that North Dakota, "is where cold is made and sent to other places." When *The Daily Beast* ranked the nation's coldest metropolitan areas, three of the top five cities were located in North Dakota. In North Dakota, winter lasts from October until April, and May snowstorms are not uncommon. Twenty, thirty, forty degrees below zero isn't just cold—it's brutal, bruising, blistering, lung-shattering, teeth-cracking cold. At these temperatures, boiling water thrown into the air will instantly vaporize. Occasionally, national news reporters will invoke low temperatures in North Dakota to fill five minutes of airtime, thus allowing outsiders to peer in at our ability to withstand this place, usually casting it as a curious and charming little feat of human endurance. But those who live there know it is no joke. It is a slow interminable grind. *You know you're from North Dakota if you define summer as three months of bad sledding, if you think lingerie is a flannel nightgown with only eight buttons, if you've ever apologized to a telemarketer.* Or if a telemarketer has ever apologized to you, like the one who called my mother during a string of fierce February blizzards that put our state in the national news. When she told the telemarketer that she lived in North Dakota, he reacted with a gasped "I'm so sorry!" *Me too,* I thought.

How I loathed prying myself out of bed at still-dark-o'-clock to trudge to school, taking small and ginger steps across vast sheets of ice on the sidewalks and parking lots. It wasn't until later that I realized how the cold is good for small miracles: dazzling rainbow halos—called "sundogs"—mysteriously encircling the sun, awakening on a bitter blue-black morning to find that the foot of new snow on the sidewalk has disappeared in the night, shoveled by a neighbor. And because I learned to drive in North Dakota, I respect—but do not fear—black ice, white-out blizzards, or any other forbidding weather condition on the road. North Dakota deserves as much credit as my mother for making me a safe and savvy driver. Cold is also the medium through which one can more clearly see blessings, even a blessing as small as a warm lap cat and a new book. The cold is good for forcing strangers to be decent to one another. After all, one never knows when they'll be the one whose car skids off the highway ten miles from the nearest town.

The food in North Dakota is the simple and penitent type suitable for church functions and funeral wakes: Hotdish is the general term for a variety of casseroles whose main ingredients might include hamburger meat, cheese, tater tots, or tomato sauce. North Dakota's German and Scandinavian immigrants popularized knoephla, a German dumpling soup; lefse, a flaky dessert from Norway made from potato flour; and the notoriously rank-smelling lutefisk. Made by soaking dried fish in lye, this "traditional Norwegian food" is eaten by many elderly Americans in North Dakota and Minnesota, but few actual Norwegians. North Dakota potlucks are reliable and stolid: an assortment of hotdishes, Crock-Pots of Swedish meatballs and "Li'l Smokies," "salads" that typically incorporate lots of marshmallows and canned whipped cream, or cheese and mayonnaise, but few greens. For dessert, North Dakotans eschew Mormon Jell-O in favor of "bars," a baked confection served cold and cut into squares. The state's ethnic restaurants are mostly inauthentic and almost invariably owned by white Americans. In 2012, the long-time *Grand Forks Herald* columnist Marilyn Hagerty "went viral" after her un-ironic review of Grand Forks's new Olive Garden restaurant described the ersatz Italian chain as "impressive...the largest and most beautiful" restaurant in town. The state beverage of North Dakota is cows' milk. The state song is the fawning and serene "North Dakota Hymn." The state dance is—of course—the square dance.

Because of all this, North Dakota suffers mightily in the public imagination. The state is invariably personified as either a rural, backwards hick prone to offhanded bigotry and proselytizing, or a goofy introverted baby brother, forever trying and failing to be as fashionable as the rest of the family. Almost without exception, popular films and television shows characterize North Dakota by way of ham-fisted tropes: cold, flat, windy, repressed. North Dakota is routinely—and unimaginatively—lampooned in *The Onion* and *Saturday Night Live* as a sparsely-populated frozen wasteland.

It is little wonder that Americans have such a narrow perception of this state: they've most likely never seen it in person. North Dakota is the least-visited state in the nation, and the state's attempts to drum up tourism can be amusingly tonedeaf. North Dakota legislators have not once but twice considered dropping the "North" from the state's name because they felt it was too suggestive of a cold and bleak landscape, thereby scaring off potential visitors. My city, Grand Forks, has made its own sad attempts to become a "Destination City." Its attempts at rebranding have been remarkably superficial at times, and included pressuring an auto wrecker to erect a privacy fence to ensure that rows of rusted vehicles were not visible from a major highway leading into the city. Perplexingly, Grand Forks has resisted efforts to improve the quality of life for people that already live there. The city has been lukewarm in its support of the arts and its young people and recently voted down a measure to impose a one-cent sales tax increase to fund the replacement of its badly outdated library.

One perception of North Dakota appears flattering on its face, but the reality is much more complicated. North Dakotans are famous for their politeness and warmth. But there are exceptions to "North Dakota nice." In 2008, Cambridge University psychologist Peter Rentfrow conducted a nationwide study to determine the effects of geographic location on personalities. North Dakotans scored highest in two of the five major traits Rentfrow measured, "extraversion" and "agreeableness." Yet the state also ranked dead last in its "openness" to new experiences. In other words, the people of North Dakota are extraordinarily friendly and sociable, but they are also more xenophobic and clannish than anyone else in the nation. Rentfrow's findings underscore my own experiences. The entire time I lived in North Dakota, I never witnessed anyone utter a slur in the presence of a person belonging to a minority group. But I witnessed plenty of underhanded racism, prejudice, and hate, including bigots targeting American Indian students at my university and a synagogue in Grand Forks in multiple bouts of overnight vandalism. Vandals also targeted cars with gay pride stickers. Once, at the grocery store, I overheard one woman say to another that she couldn't bring her children to the park anymore because "too many black children" played there. On another visit to the store, a casual conversation I had with a fellow shopper segued surprisingly smoothly into a diatribe about what she hated about Muslims.

Animals, it seems, are also exempt from "North Dakota nice." Until May 2013, North Dakota was one of only two states without any felony-level punishment for the most severe animal cruelty crimes.

Big agriculture interests citing "interference from out-of-state animal rights extremists" have spooked North Dakota voters into resisting a number of animal protection measures. In 2012, North Dakota became one of the first states to protect animal industries with sweeping "ag-gag" legislation, making it illegal for whistleblowers and undercover investigators to document cruelty and abuse at factory farms and puppy mills. North Dakota has long been a refuge for a number of notoriously cruel and exploitative animal enterprises, including fur farms, battery chicken operations, and puppy mills. Long, nondescript warehouses housing hundreds or thousands of animals in darkness and secrecy are commonplace. "Coyote contests," a barbaric sort of competition in which hunters try to kill as many coyotes as possible for cash prizes, are still viewed by many North Dakotans as a wholesome day's entertainment.

The "Peace Garden" state was also famous at one time for its nuclear arsenal. You've probably seen this dubious factoid circulated on the Internet: *If North Dakota seceded from the United States, it would become the world's third-largest nuclear power overnight.* While this may or may not have ever been true, it's no secret that North Dakota once boasted an astonishing nuclear weapons cache. The remains of hundreds of defunct missile silos pock the countryside.

Former North Dakotans are drawn to one another like driftwood on the open sea. Because many of us are survivors in every sense of the word, we share a camaraderie I can't imagine existing between former residents of, say, Connecticut or Ohio. There are informal clubs for former North Dakotans all over the country. And there is a sort of unwritten code of honor that when one of us breaks free, we make a point to help others do the same. The professor with whom I confided was herself a one-time refugee from the northern plains. Seeing a younger version of herself in me, she was instrumental in encouraging me to pursue my dream of postgraduate study, writing, and research outside the state. Her fierce desire to see someone else take flight had an unexpected second coming in me. Shortly after I made my own plans to leave North Dakota, I met my partner, Nick, a native of the small town of Drayton and the first person in his immediate family to go to college. I knew right away that Nick, with his preternatural curiosity, his dark sense of humor, his introversion, and his desire for new experiences, was about as well-suited to life in North Dakota as I was. I wasn't surprised to learn that he too had big dreams of leaving, and I decided that the truest gift of love that I could offer would be to help him go wherever he wanted, even if it meant that our relationship might end.

The drive to launch one's self from this state can take the shape of an all-consuming wildfire, as it did for me and my professor, or it can more closely resemble intensely-hot coals that smolder for a lifetime, as it did for Nick. In either case, there is always an igniting spark. For my professor, it was reading about Boston when she was a young child: "By the time I was eight, I was talking about going to Boston. I read about Boston, Massachusetts, and Harvard in the World Book Encyclopedia, and it sounded like the place for me," she said. For Nick, it was his family's Packard Bell computer. The boy from small-town Drayton spent hours on that miraculous machine meeting people from across the country and the world. He grew up wanting to travel to the other side of the globe. After he graduated from college, Nick decided to go to Shanghai, China, to teach English. The terror that such a move might mean the end of our relationship clashed daily with my fierce desire to see him fly from North Dakota, which I recognized as my own desperate wish. Supporting him through the process of his departure remains both the hardest and proudest duty I've ever done. Later that year, after being accepted to a graduate program, I put everything I owned into storage and flew to Beijing to spend the summer with him.

Due to the mounting difficulties of trying to work legally in a foreign country and perhaps due to some homesickness as well—Nick decided to return to the United States at the end of the summer. We flew to Seattle and, together, rode the train back to Grand Forks. We arrived at midnight on an early August evening. After the heat and pollution we endured in China's massive cities, the cool, clean, crisp air was a shock and a delight. For several minutes after everyone else left, we stood on the station platform on the edge of town, taking deep and sustaining breaths of the sweet, pure air as though we had nearly drowned. We marveled at the deep velvet jewel box stretched open above us. It was the same North Dakota night sky that we'd both seen—and largely ignored—for decades. But on that night it changed for us. For an hour, a minute, a moment, it was our home, and it was worth anything we could trade for it.

Because I only stayed in North Dakota for as long as I did in order to finish my bachelor's degree, my time there often felt something like a prison term, time served in order to get somewhere else. It is only now, after leaving the state, that I can appreciate the many ways in which North Dakota has advantaged me. For one, my education was inexpensive and high-quality. I graduated with no student debt, in part due to my ability to work during the entire time that I was a student. North Dakota has posted the nation's lowest unemployment rates for decades. The state also performed the seemingly-impossible feat of weathering the Great Recession with low unemployment and a budget surplus. Economists chalked it up to the state's booming oil industry and the stability of North Dakota's state-owned bank. But North Dakotans' characteristic unwillingness to take risks also undoubtedly aided the state's financial security. It's true that North Dakotans are resistant to change, sometimes embarrassingly so. Yet because the state doesn't kowtow easily to fads, it is also immune from some of the more dangerous trends that have swept other parts of the nation.

That may be changing. The northern plains region has been plagued for decades by "brain drain"—the outmigration of young educated people to large cities in other states, leaving a dwindling population and all-but-abandoned towns. But with the advent of the technology needed to recover an estimated seven billion barrels of crude oil from the Bakken oil region in the western part of the state, North Dakota became the number two oil-producing state in the nation almost overnight, second only to Texas. Recession refugees from across the country have flocked to the region by the thousands in search of oil industry jobs. Now the fastest growing state in the nation, North Dakota's population is projected to grow 20 percent by 2020, and the influx has caused housing shortages in cities as far east as Grand Forks and Fargo. The use of hydraulic fracturing ("fracking") technology to recover the oil brings the looming threat of disastrous pollution and permanent, catastrophic environmental damage. Perhaps too eager to line their pockets and see their state make national headlines, North Dakota legislators have embraced the oil boom. Unlike other regions surrounding the Bakken oil shale, North Dakota has permitted horizontal drilling with little regulation and has even given the green light for oil drilling in its Theodore Roosevelt National Park. It's hard not to imagine that oil rigs may one day be as numerous as the buffalo that once roamed the prairie. The state recently proposed changing its license plate design to do away with the old bison-and-prairie image in favor of a new design featuring an oil pump and the slogan, "a well-oiled state."

Ironically, the outmigration of young people meant that the sparse and aged population remaining in western North Dakota were people who were happy with the way things were, who wanted things to stay that way. All but assured of the permanence of their lifestyle, they made their homes in the one place that seemed impervious to the highs and lows suffered by the rest of the nation, only to have their landscape rendered almost unrecognizable by the oil industry.

Witnessing this reckless takeover of my state is indescribably painful. And yes, I said "my state." The whole time I lived in North Dakota, when people asked me where I was from, I said that I was from Colorado. I clung to my Colorado birth certificate as proof that I was a stranded foreigner in a backwards land, proof that I could disown North Dakota and all that embarrassed me about it. After arriving in Iowa, I noticed myself saying "North Dakota" when people asked where I was from. It's often said that you can't choose your family, only your friends. It's also true that when you're young, you can't choose your home. In much the same way that children are forced to trust their parents to take care of them and meet their needs, young people must trust in the home they have at the time. Like children whose parents neglect them, we can feel failed when the place where we live fails to support us and help us thrive.

But I've realized that North Dakota did not fail to support me—not entirely. North Dakota holds some of her children close and sends others far and wide. For the latter, their departure is often a bitter and final farewell. But this place—this rough, strange place—stamps each of us indelibly as a "Dakotan." North Dakota has helped to make me a stronger, friendlier, and more deliberate person, while reinforcing for me the importance of welcoming people who are different and being open to new experiences.

I'm glad I lived in North Dakota. I wouldn't do it again.

Cold Feet

Sarah Elizabeth Turner

It starts with a tingle. At least, that's what I've heard. I don't really remember anything but the cold.

"Sorry, my hands are cold," I said for perhaps the thousandth time in my life upon meeting someone. I was shaking hands with a new acquaintance at an outdoor evening reading at the end of July and had long ago learned I should apologize for my frigid grip. It wasn't that cold outside, but I was in short sleeves and had been drinking from a glass with ice in it.

At a similar encounter in the middle of December, my heatless handshake caused someone to recoil, as if I'd bitten him with my below-body-temperature touch.

"Your hands are so *cold*," he said, shrinking away from my grasp in terror. Or possibly disgust. *You should feel my feet*, I thought, but I expressed sincere regret instead.

Usually, I would acknowledge the issue immediately, before the person had time to comment, but in that moment in December I forgot my manners. I haven't made the same mistake since, and often people just laugh off my comment in that awkward Midwestern let's-not-talk-about-personal-issues sort of way, not acknowledging that it's weird to have cold hands—especially in the summer—so I was surprised by the response to my preemptive apology in July.

"Are you a fellow Raynaudian?" my newest acquaintance asked.

I paused a second before saying, "Yeah, I am."

I have Raynaud's Phenomenon, a name that sounds ridiculous to me, like I'm some freak side show act, *Come see the wondrous sight known as Raynaud's Phenomenon*. My friend Krisanne refers to it as "Rainier's Disease," and I don't correct her because I prefer that somewhat self-explanatory name. Rainier's sounds like a mountain-climber's condition, something exotic that affects only those who have faced treacherous climates and battled insurmountable odds. Raynaud's (ray-*nodes*), in contrast, sounds like part of an x-ray machine.

There are two types: Primary Raynaud's or Raynaud's Disease, which, I think, is really what I have, and Secondary Raynaud's or Raynaud's Phenomenon. The disease version is an affliction in and of itself; the phenomenon comes secondary to something else, like lupus.

The basic idea is that when I'm in a cold environment, or I'm feeling stressed, the capillaries in my wrists and ankles constrict, cutting off the blood supply to my hands and feet but protecting my core from cooling. It's rare that I meet someone else who's afflicted, and even rarer for that someone to be male. According to The Raynaud's Association, Raynaud's affects approximately 28 million Americans, or about five to ten percent of the population, and women are affected nine times more often than men. One estimate has 20 percent of all women of childbearing years affected by Raynaud's. It's thought to be at least partly hereditary, although no genetic link has been identified; at least one of my aunts and two female cousins are similarly stricken.

On the scale of chronic diseases for which there is no cure, Raynaud's ranks pretty low in severity for the most part. I don't have to take medication or do special exercises, and I have full function of all of my limbs and organs. I don't have to monitor my blood or follow a special diet, and my condition rarely comes up in conversation— many of my friends wouldn't even know I have it, that's how little my disease impacts those around me. Even I don't think about Raynaud's as much as I should— don't take care of myself as *well* as I should— because it's just sort of there. Only when I have physical contact with someone else (or with a non-affected part of my body) do I remember, "Oh, yeah, I have Raynaud's."

It's not that I don't realize my hands and feet are cold, I just can't *feel* it the way other people feel when their extremities are cold: from the inside. I'm more likely to notice when my hands and feet are warm. Having cold hands can be helpful when I have a headache or a burn: instead of frozen meat there's frozen me to soothe your fevered forehead. In addition to being chilly, or perhaps as a result of that, I have lessened sensation in my fingertips and toes, which means I have to be careful, especially with my feet, so I don't injure them without realizing it—because I can't feel what I've done—or so I don't burn them in an effort to warm up.

People often think of Raynaud's as a winter disorder, but flare-ups, or what they call "attacks," can strike at any time. A cool summer evening, not wearing socks or long sleeves, handling frozen food (for *any* length of time), even holding a glass with ice in it can cause my hands to cool and turn red. Or white. I can't handle the frozen turkey on Thanksgiving, shouldn't put my own ice cubes in my drink. I shouldn't even open a bag of frozen vegetables or touch an ice pack without wearing gloves, no matter what the temperature is outside.

At least twice, I've had what I believe to be mild frostbite, but it might have been just a severe attack. Two or three toes turned stark white, and I had trouble wiggling them. Both times this happened because I wasn't dressed warmly enough for the Minnesota weather on an evening when I had to walk several blocks through wet snow because of transportation issues. Both times, I tried pounding my feet on the ground to warm them up, thought warm thoughts, braced for the worst. Both times, I ran a lukewarm bath and stood in my tub, crying, as the water ran over my feet, which stung and ached at the same time, buzzing and tingling like they'd been electrocuted. Where they were normally numb, they hurt with the same intensity as a brain freeze.

SmartWool socks are a Godsend, but only if I remember to put them on when my feet are warm. They act like an insulated cooler or thermos: whatever temperature your feet are, that's what they'll remain. With Raynaud's, my feet don't generate enough heat to keep my SmartWools warm, so I have to warm my feet before I put them in socks or they'll never warm up, even at home.

On one particularly cold day in the heart of winter, I waited longer than normal for the bus to arrive, standing in the direct path of a bitter wind and stamping my dress shoes against the snow-covered cement. My toes didn't thaw during the 45-minute bus ride, or the three-block walk from the bus to work, or even as I sat at my desk bouncing them up and down in an effort to increase circulation. Eventually, I sneaked off to the bathroom, peeled off one thin black sock at a time, and stood at the cramped sink running water over my clammy feet to warm them up, grateful for the privacy of the single-person restroom so I didn't have to explain myself or ask my boss if we could please turn up the heat for my sake. Even though no one could see me, I felt humiliated over what lengths I had to go to just to warm up at work, especially since I'm from around here and therefore should have adapted to the cold ages ago. I'm more than a little concerned that one harsh Midwestern winter I'm going to lose a toe.

I can't help but wonder if I'm partially to blame for my condition. After all, I hardly take care of myself now that I'm aware of it. I go out without warm winter wear, carry cold pop without gloves, bare my feet beyond the balmy bounds of summer. I still seek out the coldest patch of my bed and smother it each night, hoping for a respite from the heat, even in winter. I was born in Wisconsin at the end of February, and it seems my body wants the frigid weather.

My dad is a human furnace. He would happily go all year long in T-shirts, oblivious to the winter winds. He emanates heat, and I am my father's daughter, often overheating just like he does in the summer. I would much rather freeze than sweat and could never live down south in the muggy marshes of Louisiana or the arid zone of

Arizona. I can't imagine living somewhere without four defined seasons, and although I can't enjoy winter activities the way I used to, I still hold out hope that someday I'll be able to ski again without repercussions from Raynaud's.

I have never officially been diagnosed.

I first noticed the change when I was in sixth grade. The blue tinge to my skin when I'd go outside, the way my hands were cold to the touch like snow led me to believe they were formed by hoary frost, not heat and blood and bone and skin—icicles on the ends of my hands instead of fingers. My hands felt like death to the touch but internally seemed unaffected. I don't really remember the tingling sensation that's supposed to accompany early Raynaud's, but I do remember visiting several doctors, at least one of whom brought up the disease.

"Hold this between your fingers," she said, sliding a piece of paper between my pointer and middle fingers. I'm still not sure what she was looking for, but after watching me for a few seconds, she told me Raynaud's was likely. Afraid to find out if it's something worse, I've been living as if "likely" were "true" ever since.

Luckily, my current apartment has heat included with the rent. Not only that, but the heat's usually on quite high, which is good since I can't control the thermostat. I joke that I have the heat of an old person and the feet of a dead person, but, really, a coroner would have a hard time pinpointing my time of demise if all he or she went by was the temperature of my toes. By their standards, I've always been dead for several hours.

I've heard that one cure for Raynaud's—if you can call a short-term solution a cure—is to stand somewhere cold, such as outside at night in early fall or on the porch in winter, wearing shorts and a tank top and place your hands and feet in hot water. The thinking is that you can train your body into realizing that your hands and feet need heat too, not just your core. Knowing this is a treatment adds to my worry that I may have contributed to my condition: I've been a swimmer all my life, but your body loses heat more rapidly in water than it does in air, and often the pool I practiced in was kept at a very cool temperature. Not only that, but when I was little I used to wash my hands in cold water, only cold. I'd stand at the faucet in our downstairs half-bath and switch the handle to "C," waiting for lukewarm to splash ice cold before rinsing my hands in it. I worry that my cold water-washing trained my hands to react the way they do now, that my passion for swimming has been bad for my health in the long run.

My aunt Patty told me about the aforementioned treatment, but I've never tried it. She said it took two weeks to fully work and only lasted six months, and I have this problem year-round. My Raynaud's only used to be an issue from late September until late April/early May, but I find it happens when I'm tense or nervous or sitting too close to the air conditioner without long sleeves.

There is, of course, another solution: move somewhere warm.

No one knows the exact origin of the term "cold feet." It means to hesitate or have reservations that prevent an action, particularly marriage, but its usage cannot be traced to a single source, just like Raynaud's can't be traced to one cause. Some theorize that the term "cold feet" means that your feet are frozen in place, immobile, and others believe it comes from the fact that fear (like stress) causes the body to divert blood from your extremities inward. I don't know that I believe one theory over another; they're both plausible. But, in my case, indecisiveness hasn't usually presented a problem.

I will admit, however, that I hesitated before moving to Minnesota four years ago, even though I grew up in Eau Claire, Wisconsin, and to many of my friends this seemed like a return, an easy choice for me to make.

I remember sitting in my apartment in Brooklyn and second-guessing my decision, for reasons both emotional and physical. Was I ready to leave? Did I want to say goodbye to New York City, probably for good? After four years of acclimating to a slightly milder climate, could I handle the below-zero temperatures of January? If I were to leave a northern city that I loved, wouldn't it make more sense to travel somewhere south?

It's not that I wasn't cold, really cold, sometimes in New York. I endured ribbing from my East Coast friends that I should be hardier—"You're from Wisconsin, you should be used to the cold," they teased.

"We don't walk around in it," I countered.

But the lows aren't as low along the coasts, and the coldest I remember it being in New York was in the high teens. It's not unusual for the temperature to sink to ten, twenty, even thirty-below with the windchill in Wisconsin and Minnesota.

Part of me wishes I had listened to that hesitation. The four winters I've lived in St. Paul have been harsh, and not just because of the cold. The first year I dealt with a couple of break-ins and a car accident, the second year we had record snows, the third year I spent writing my thesis, and this last year I went through a painful breakup, and it snowed on-and-off throughout April and each of the first three days of May. Added to all of that, I have never felt settled.

The other big trigger for Raynaud's is stress—living in flux, making it through graduate school—even during the summer my condition has intensified. I've moved four times in the past four summers, and the last time I didn't unpack all the way; boxes and bags still sit where I left them that first day.

The irony, of course, is that now that I can move away, possibly back to that neighborhood in Brooklyn, perhaps even to the same apartment, I find myself hesitating again. There's nothing rooting me to Minnesota specifically, but leaving, even if it's better for my emotional health (New York, Chicago), or my physical health (California, Hawaii), scares me.

I've spent the past four years getting acclimated to the Twin Cities, making new friends—like Krisanne—and building contacts for my writing, a network I value. Just the thought of starting over exhausts me. Even if I went somewhere warm, the stress of learning a new place and trying to make new friends might counteract any benefits I might gain by living in a warmer climate. And moving somewhere familiar (but not warmer), like New York, might not help my health much at all.

If I'm being honest, there's more to my hesitation than just the inconvenience of moving. Many of my reasons for moving back (apart from the graduate program I've now finished) are still valid. New York (and Chicago and California and Hawaii) is expensive. My family will never move away from Wisconsin. My closest friends from forever live nearby. My sister and her husband just moved to Minneapolis, and I'm seeing there might be nieces and nephews on my horizon. The region is a great place to raise a family, and the people have values that closely align with my own.

And, although I don't love Minnesota, I love the Midwest and I love being Midwestern.

Being Midwestern, however, also contributes to my Raynaud's. Living in a colder climate is one of the main characteristics of its sufferers. But I wonder if that's just because Raynaud's would only appear in a colder climate; when you live somewhere warm you're less likely to have a reason to develop it.

I recently learned that at the apartment I like, the one with the heat befitting an old person, or a Raynaudian like me, they're raising my rent. Again. For the fourth time this year. I have until the beginning of winter to decide what I'd like to do—commit to a lease paying way more than the apartment is worth or move, which has added to my conflicted feeling about the area. What do you do if where you're from—where you live—is hazardous to your health?

Sometimes, when I'm feeling particularly annoyed with how cold my feet get or I've tried warming them for several minutes to no avail, I think mean thoughts about my Scandinavian ancestors. I mean, c'mon—you're already moving halfway around the world, the least you could do is *upgrade*. You'd think someone along the way would leave the land of 120-degree temperature variances for something milder. More temperate. But, except for a few adventurous outliers, my family is rooted in the Midwest.

And yet it's these ancestors who make me love the land of my birth. Part of being Midwestern is having a fierce attachment to family and a quiet pride in place and lineage, and I told everyone who met me in New York that I grew up in Wisconsin. I understand how hard it is to move away from what you know; the familiar landscape of the Midwest must have comforted those early settlers as they transitioned to a strange land, and perhaps the same intolerance of the heat that my father has prevented them from venturing south. Even if I silently curse my roots every year near the end of January, I value my relatives. Like my grandmother, who turned down my grandfather's marriage proposal when she was 19, because, in her words, "I had things I wanted to do." They finally married when she was 28, in 1944, when the median marriage age for women was 21. Her confidence and independent spirit are qualities that have stuck with me, particularly in my times of doubt and hesitation. Gram died my first year in New York, and I can't help but think that some small part of me wanted to be closer to her, that this desire for closeness was a contributing factor in why I moved to St. Paul, the city of her birth.

I think about Gram as I walk through the neighborhood where she spent her early childhood, not far from where I live now, or when I pass the duplex where her parents lived after Gram had grown up and borne seven children of her own. My second apartment in St. Paul was less than a block from that duplex, in a mirror duplex down the street. I loved living there and imagining what my great-grandparents must have been like. Did I inherit my sense of humor from them, my "Midwestern wit?" Did one of them suffer from Raynaud's as well?

For as long as I knew my grandmother, she read two papers: the *Eau Claire Leader-Telegram* and the *St. Paul Pioneer Press*. My mother remembers Gram taking her and her siblings shopping in the Cities, and I wonder if Gram felt as unsettled as I do—her house in Wisconsin and her home in St. Paul. I know she loved my grandfather—"I quit going out with him, but he just kept coming back," she told me, but there was a smile in her voice and a twinkle in her eye when she said it, like it didn't take too much for him to convince her to marry him. To stay. Her heart was in two places, just like mine. If only I could carry my body the same way: my core in northern states, my hands and feet somewhere warm.

Field Stones

Zachary Hawkins

In the winter, cold creeps down from the surface of the garden and touches the tops of buried stones. The rocks gather heat from the earth below; they pull the warmth upward, out of the dirt, until the water in the soil underneath them freezes ahead of the descending frost line. The ice crystals expand. The ice nudges the stones upward. In the spring the ground thaws, leaving voids beneath the rocks, and the soil moves to fill them.

I pick rocks from the garden. They are scattered about, some half buried, some sitting atop the turned soil, heavy and warm with the sun. The earth is flecked with the dead stems of winterkilled oats. When it had been dry enough to work my father hooked the disc harrow to the tractor and pulled it through the cover crop. The sixteen-inch cymbal-shaped blades cut through the oats, weighed down by fifty-pound rocks set on top of the frame. The discs turned and stirred the earth, breaking clods and smoothing ridges, reshaping the surface of the garden, leaving behind a wake of dark soil. The sandy grit scoured the steel, the field stones struck the discs and left notches in their sharp edges, and the sound of scraping rose up from the ground.

I walk a meandering course over the garden, stoop to gather stones, cradle them in the crook of my arm, elbow to fingertip, and hold them against my stomach. As my burden increases I must stop and kneel at each stone to pick it up without spilling the others. I pull them from the dust and find the colors of the sky. Gray flecked with mica. Blue streaked with orange. Rusty red. Dark purple seamed with white.

On Easter morning, the week before my grandfather died, we sat in the church sanctuary with the lights turned off. I watched stained glass burn—blue, red, and purple—in iron frames. Streams of brown and green eddied in asymmetrical panes that fit together like dry stone walls at the center of each window. Outside, the blanket of snow was turning back, revealing rotted leaves and matted grass. Behind the church, the river rose up with melt water and churned its burden of soil. Along the banks a congregation of trees offered their bare limbs to the sky.

Three days earlier, Maundy Thursday, the earth flirted with equilibrium after a season defined by darkness. Day matched night, and the world turned its full face to the sun. Sunrise defined due east, sunset marked due west: the first day of spring. And the next day, Good Friday, the balance shifted. The light lasted a moment longer than the night as the world began to bow.

A boy in an acolyte's robe walked to the front of the church, balancing a single flame atop a large Paschal candle, and the sanctuary lights lit up with the opening chords of the processional hymn. The incandescence mixed with daylight like snowmelt swirling in river water. We stood to sing. My grandfather gripped the back of the pew in front of him, set his jaw, and rocked himself to his feet. He opened a hymnal and turned over the thin pages as my grandmother looked on. They joined their voices with the others.

"See the grave its first-fruits giving, springing up from holy ground; he was dead, but now is living; he was lost, but he is found."

The sun climbed higher in the stained glass, and we traced the shape of the liturgy through prayers and hymns. Sunlight filled the windows and flooded over the faint paths worn into the red carpet. Beyond the pews, the wooden communion rail curved beneath the promontories of the pulpit and the altar. It passed near the baptismal font where a shallow bowl of water shimmered like a puddle.

When the time came we stood to gather at the rail's edge like the trees along the river, reflecting its arcuate sweep. Again, my grandfather willed his rawboned body to rise from the pew. He walked alongside my grandmother toward the front of the sanctuary, resolutely covering the ground to the rail, and placed both of his hands on the wide surface. He gave his weight to the wood, bent his legs, muscled himself to the hard floor. He settled on his knees, held out his open hands, and became still. The pastor tore a piece of bread from the loaf and held it in the light before placing it in my grandfather's palm. I watched a few crumbs of the broken body scatter across the surface of the wood.

My grandfather maintained our aging fleet of farm implements, brought them out of winter dormancy for planting in the spring. He changed the fluids and filters on the 1959 John Deere 530 tractor and greased the bearings on the disc harrow every time it was used. He oiled the floors of the livestock trailer and the flatbed trailer. I often found him bent to his labor in the workshop. He wore a long-sleeved work shirt and loose overalls. His cap sat crookedly on his head, cocked a little to the left, the same way his hats did when he was a young man. Beneath its bill his thinning face could look like a fall-plowed field left open to the weather, the furrows deepening—especially when he was setting up a joke. Then his face filled with a grin as quickly and completely as a crop of wheat greening up in the spring.

A few years before he died, my grandfather spent a winter rebuilding an old manure spreader. My father and a friend got a deal on it at a farm auction. It didn't work very well, but my grandfather thought it should be cared for anyway. This is the fashion in which he fixed it up: He took it apart, piece by piece, cleaned it, and assembled it anew. He put in a new floor of salvaged boards, the length of it one hundred and two inches and the breadth of it thirty inches. He swabbed the inside with oil, and the outside he painted with orange paint. As a finishing touch, he wrote the words "OLD IDEA" in pitch-colored letters on both sides. It was a farmer's lark, a spoof on a popular brand of farm implements, New Idea. He waited for the weather to warm in order to finish the paint job, and then he pulled the manure spreader out of the shed into the barn lot to dry. When a neighbor boy came by and saw the joke, he put his hands on his hips and guffawed like it was the funniest thing he'd ever seen.

My grandfather kept an ongoing task of sorting and organizing the miscellaneous hardware scattered about the workshop: nails, screws, bolts, nuts, washers, fasteners of every kind. He discarded all that was corroded or misshapen and combined the rest in old tin cans he'd saved, cans bearing labels for McLaughlin's Manor House Coffee and Planters Salted Cashews, ordering the oddments by kind and keeping them for later use. He gathered and preserved things that would have otherwise been destroyed; his work was a relief to us as we went about our daily toil around the farm.

There are ruins beneath us here in northern Indiana. David Dale Owen, the state's first geologist, wrote about them in 1837. He was mapping the sequence of Indiana's underlying rock formations and spent the year crisscrossing the state on horseback, traveling a thousand miles, searching for evidence of iron ore, coal, and building stone for a burgeoning state. He left his hometown in the lower Wabash Valley in the spring and followed the final miles of the Wabash River until he lost it in the Ohio. There he turned east against the bigger river's current and went along Indiana's border with Kentucky, tracing the sinuous terminus of the state, searching bank and bluff, looking for bedrock exposed along the river's edge. After he left the river and moved northward, Owen found it increasingly difficult to survey the bedrock below.

"On crossing the National Road," he wrote in his report to the General Assembly, "I found the greater part of this northern country covered by a diluvium of sand, gravel, boulders, and clay sometimes to a very great depth."

Diluvium, he called it—from the root *diluere*, to wash away. To Owen, the jumble of grit and stone shrouding the bedrock was evidence of a great inundation, of a time when water covered the earth and left in its wash so much debris. A deluge. A great flood. Owen found here a landscape remade in a baptism of cold, broken stone.

The last glacier, the Wisconsin ice sheet, was thirty thousand years upon this place—frigid and slowly swelling, a gradual cascade stretched across time. Ice prevailed, increasingly, exceedingly, miles thick in some places. The crust of the earth sank into the mantle beneath its weight. The ice covered the hills and filled the valleys. It smoothed the terrain like hands over a wrinkled bed sheet. It ground the rock to cobbles, to pebbles, and bore them away—solitary boulders, constellations of gravel, streaks of rock flour—suspended in the ice. And the glacier prevailed until thirteen thousand years ago.

Then the ice retreated from Indiana. The ice receded, dropping the pieces of the world, broken and scattered. The far-flung bones of the earth were heaped across the land and left to weather, left to endure: wind and water, freeze and thaw, winter and summer. Rock turned to grit; grit turned to soil. Now the soil gives birth to field stones.

That spring, my grandfather felt pain in his chest for days before asking my father to drive him to the hospital. Once there, his condition worsened. We sang hymns in the hospital room.

"Abide with me, fast falls the eventide."

We gathered around the bed and sang.

"The darkness deepens; Lord, with me abide."

Beneath a thin sheet, my grandfather's heart pulsed at an irregular tempo, a machine adding every third or fourth beat.

"When other helpers fail and comforts flee," we sang, "help of the helpless, oh, abide with me."

Light from the overhead fluorescents pooled in the dark glass of the hospital room windows, while outside a spring drizzle hung in the night air like an exhaled breath. Remnant scraps of dirty snow melted at the edges of the parking lot and carried grit toward the storm sewers.

"Earth's joys grow dim, its glories pass away. Change and decay in all around I see."

My father prayed from the Commendation of the Dying service.

"Almighty God, look on Glenn," he said, calling his father by his first name, "whom you made your child in baptism."

I removed a toothette swab—a small sponge on a stick—from a plastic cup of water and touched it to my grandfather's cracked lips. He mouthed the sponge, squeezing a few drops across his tongue. After he finished drinking, he tried to speak. I leaned over his bed to hear, bringing my face close to his. I smelled the stale breath in his parched mouth, the odor of his perspiration rising into the antiseptic air. The sheet swelled as his lungs expanded, remaking the landscape stretched across his chest. His voice scraped across his throat.

"What's that, Grandpa?" I asked.

He tried again, fighting to speak through the fatigue and the plastic tubes stemming from his nose. The weary muscles in his jaw tightened. He ground out the words in a gravelly voice. They sounded distant, fractured, like they were picked up by the wind and carried away. I nodded, helpless.

The stony coldness started in my grandfather's feet and moved across his legs, advancing by the hour. My grandmother stood at the end of the bed and held his feet between her hands.

"They feel like ice," she said.

We kept vigil, knowing the cold would soon reach his heart.

Not far from the hospital where my grandfather died stands a mound, much wider than it is tall, a lilt in the landscape. It marks a moment of pause, a long backward glance. The Huron-Erie Lobe of the Wisconsin glacier lulled there in its retreat, caught in equipoise between growth and decay. It was the last sheet of ice to cover the region, holding on as long as it could in a warming world, ebbing in fits punctuated by long stretches of stillness. During each weary respite, the glacier laid down its burden of sand and gravel, outlining the curve of its terminus. It left a series of these inscriptions across the Bluffton Till Plain, memorializing its passage in a language of quiet landforms called end moraines.

At the glacier's edge, frigid wind poured off the ice sheet over a landscape of mud. Chunks of ice fractured and fell into the melt. The water roiled away, scouring valleys in the drift, making rivers—the Mississinewa, the Salamonie, the Wabash.

Driving home from the hospital, I followed the memory of rushing melt water. My father sat in the passenger seat with his head bowed, and we traveled along a small stream, a tributary of the Wabash called the Little River, as it trickled through an oversized valley once thunderous with the sound of the glacier's retreat. The valley turned to the south, but we continued west across a great emptiness.

When the ice subsided, the wind blew over the face of the abandoned till. It picked up fine particles of silt and lifted them into the air, breathing life into the rock. The dust, called loess, spread across the landscape and settled atop the debris. It filled the cracks and crevices; it blotted out the features. In the early hours of morning, the farm fields, the brick houses and barns, the clumps of trees all gave way beneath the weight of the darkness. Under the stars I saw the structure of the world as it was created by the ice: shattered, exposed, endless.

I carry the field stones to the north side of the barn and spill them, relieved. They clatter over the pile and wait to be used as borders around flowerbeds, to hold open doors, to weigh things down in the wind.

When I work in the barn or the shed, I find scraps saved by my grandfather. There are varying lengths of two-by-fours, pieces of plywood, old coffee cans full of nails pulled from lumber and pounded straight. Iron fence posts, skeins of baling twine. Boxes of latches, brackets, hinges, and doorknobs. Shreds of work shirts, undershirts, dress pants, socks, towels, and wash cloths torn up for rags.

My grandfather's handwriting is everywhere. Measurements scratched into joists, blocky numbers etched with a stubby carpenter's pencil he whittled sharp with a pocketknife. Scripture verses. Proverbs. Labels on the tool cabinet's drawers: *hammers, pliers, files and rasps.* A hand-painted sign: *It is the neglect of timely repair that makes rebuilding necessary.*

I once went with my grandfather to tend his parents' graves. We took his Chevrolet, traveled south through the center of the county, and crossed over the Wabash River into the landscape of his boyhood. He grew up among the farms between the Mississinewa and Salamonie rivers. So did his parents, and they are buried there in a small country churchyard tucked among the fields. At the north edge of the cemetery a corridor of trees follows a creek, interrupting the expanse of corn and soybeans. It is one of many small streams draining toward the Wabash—tributaries reaching back into the farmland, spreading out like open fingers over the till plain.

We walked among the modest assembly of graves until we found our surname etched in rose-colored granite. We stood for a while in silence. Then my grandfather walked from the headstone to a nearby patch of open lawn.

"This is where the church stood," he said.

He paced the perimeter from memory, recalling its shape. It was the church where he'd been confirmed, the building where his mother attended services every Sunday as a girl, long since dismantled, the bricks and beams torn down and taken away. I watched as he walked over the grass. He paused, as if standing before a door. Then he stepped inside.

"These were the pews," he said, making his way where the center aisle had been, as if he were looking for a place to sit. He continued to the front of the sanctuary, speaking out loud, furnishing the chancel with his voice.

"Here was the altar," he remembered. "Here was the pulpit. Here was the baptismal font."

He held out his hands as if to touch the objects, finding each shape even in its absence. I went to join him on the lawn and we stood in the memory of the room with the breeze in our hair and the grass beneath our feet. We stood in the open space, the gravestones gathered at the edges, in a silence like the moment before the service begins.

We buried him in the cemetery just down the road from the farm. I could almost see the garden from the graveside. We gathered around an opening in the gray-brown earth. Then we left the casket at its edge and walked to our cars. The columns of headstones resembled the rows of last year's corn stover in the surrounding fields, broken stalks rising from the dirt. The ground was thawing, softening in the sun and freezing at night. Daily, farmers walked across their land and knelt in their fields. They squeezed handfuls of soil to see if it crumbled, if it was ready to be worked.

I wished I'd brought a spade, the steel oiled, the edge sharpened, to dig the grave myself. I wanted to feel the weight of each shovelful of soil in my hands.

I closed my eyes and saw the metal bite into the ground, opening it. I heard the grit scrape against the tool. Deeper and deeper, I passed horizons in the soil. The earth changed in color and texture, growing darker. Brownish gray became yellowish brown. I passed clay loam dotted with gravel. Gravel-speckled sandy loam. Loamy sand, coarse and friable. Gravelly loamy sand. Loose gravelly sand. The weathered minerals of the earth coalesced into larger pieces—clay to silt, silt to sand, stones to boulders—the broken rock that holds up the living world.

Maintenance

Catherine Lanser

Buying my first house with a friend wasn't conventional, but living in Madison, Wisconsin, isn't like living anywhere else. Here people tend to look at things a little differently. So when my friend Sheri, who knew I was having trouble finding a home in my price range, asked if I might be interested in buying a duplex together I didn't think it was too out of the ordinary. It was a way to extend our single incomes a little further. We'd still each get our own living quarters but at a lower price than we would pay for a house of our own. As a single woman I liked the idea of having a neighbor I knew.

But finding a duplex that we both actually wanted to live in had been difficult. Which is why we were so excited when we toured a small, but nice, three-bedroom duplex. Except for one thing, it seemed perfect. We could afford it, and it was nice enough that we wanted to live in it, but the location left something to be desired. We wondered if the duplex's location on the southwest side of Madison, near Allied Drive, one of the city's worst neighborhoods, would be a problem. Allied Drive was about two miles away, which in a city like Madison seemed like a world away, but the city had recently started buying and rehabilitating buildings in that area. In an effort to "clean up the neighborhood" they had forced many long-time residents to move out into other areas of the city, including our new neighborhood. Still I imagined how lovely it would be to live in an area with such diversity, in a city where I didn't necessarily see that characteristic every day. As

I drove through the neighborhood I saw African American, Caucasian, Hispanic, and Hmong people living side by side.

In the end we decided to buy, partly because we were weary of the search and partly because we felt the neighborhood had potential. We talked about the multitude of expensive homes and older couples who still lived in among the more run-down and rented places.

After living there for 10 years I didn't regret the decision even if I had seen things in the neighborhood that had made me question our choice. The area was definitely not as tame as the town of less than 10,000 I grew up in two-and-a-half hours northeast, but I figured it was just part of living in a mid-sized city. If I was disappointed about anything it was the yard work and snow removal I hadn't thought about when I bought the house.

I was thinking about that as I stood on my front lawn, surrounded by a sea of leaves, when two boys in dark hooded sweatshirts rolled by on their bikes. The first slowed down to make sure no one was in the car in the driveway before speeding away. The second pedaled more slowly and seemed to be taking in the urban scenery. When he turned his head his soft round face made me smile.

"Excuse me," he yelled out.

"Excuse me," he said again, coming to a shaky stop on the slick pavement. "I was wondering if you needed someone to rake your leaves?"

It wasn't the first time I received such an offer. It was one of the surprises of living here. Boys like this one, as well as grown men, offered to rake my lawn, shovel my snow, or mow my grass for a little cash. On snowy Saturdays kids roamed the neighborhood carrying shovels. They'd yell to each other, their voices bouncing around the cold air, about how much money they were going to get.

"How much would you like to be paid?" I asked.

"I would ask for $5 or $10," he said.

"Great. It's getting dark now, but stop back tomorrow," I said. "About 3:30?"

The next day, at exactly 3:30, I looked out my window and saw the boy riding slowly down the street. He was surveying the houses. He pulled to a stop just past my driveway at the property line. I opened the door and waved to him. He smiled and drove up the driveway.

"I forgot which one it was," he said.

"What's your name?" I asked.

"Delon."

"Do you live near here?"

He pointed a few houses up the street to a blue duplex.

"I guess we're neighbors then," I said.

I gave him the rake and went inside. About 45 minutes later the doorbell rang.

"I think I'm done," he said.

"It looks great," I said. "Come on in."

I fished a $10 bill out of my wallet. "Here you go. You did a great job."

He grinned.

"Do you think you might be interested in coming back tomorrow for those?" I said, pointing to the leaves piling up under the 20-year-old maple in the backyard.

"Oh, wow!" he said, nodding.

"Okay. I'll see you tomorrow then. About 3:30?"

I nodded.

The next day the doorbell rang promptly at 3:30. I saw Delon holding a rake as I peered through the peephole. When I opened the door I jumped, noticing an older boy standing off to the side hiding in the nook between the side of the house and the garage door. For a second, I wondered if I had been naïve the day before and if they planned to rob me.

"That's my brother Keandre," Delon said. "He's going to help me rake."

Keandre nodded and looked down. From the kitchen window I saw that they worked easily together. I kicked myself for assuming the worst. They didn't seem anything like the other kids in the neighborhood. Groups of teenagers and younger kids would congregate on the sidewalk near the open green space along Sheri's side of the house until we put up lights. After that they went somewhere else. But the street was still a busy thoroughfare for kids on their way to the gas station for a snack. They didn't pay much attention to the homeowners unless they used our lawns as trash receptacles for their snack wrappers.

When the first snow fell Delon appeared again. I stayed inside drinking coffee while he labored. As the snow continued to fall he continued to show up. On days when I worked late I found crisscrosses marking the spot where he had rested his shovel on my doorstep.

When the snow stopped falling and the grass began to grow again, it wasn't long before I saw Delon. I was driving home from work and saw him riding his bike a few blocks from my house. We waved at each other like long lost friends as I passed him on the street. By the time I pulled in the driveway he was at my house. He told me he was ready to start mowing the grass and we agreed that the next Saturday would be the day.

That Saturday I pried for details. "How old are you?"

"12."

"How old is your brother?"

"He's 14."

"Do you and your brother go to Toki?" I asked, remembering the stories I had heard about the neighborhood school. I knew a teacher who had quit teaching because the kids at Toki were too rough. Another, a substitute teacher I knew, refused to take assignments there.

"I go there, my brother goes to Cherokee."

I asked more questions, finding out again which house he lived in, but not much more.

As we got closer to summer, I saw more and more of Delon and Keandre as they rode their bikes or played in front of the blue one-story duplex where they lived. Delon set the schedule for mowing, showing up once a week or so. Sometimes I saw him in the neighborhood and told him to come on a certain day, but he'd come a day earlier.

"My mom says I should ask if can mow tonight," he'd say.

Other than that she existed, I didn't know anything about his mom. I surveyed the blue duplex as I drove home, but never saw a woman. One day as I drove past, Keandre was practicing his dribbling. As he bounced the ball between his knees it hit his shoe, rolling into the street and into the path of a truck. The driver didn't brake until he had flattened the ball. Instead of apologizing, he stopped and yelled out the window at Keandre, who ran back into the duplex, leaving his flattened ball in the street.

As the weather warmed up, the streets around our duplex brewed. I heard of fights between rival gangs and of shots fired on the side streets. I had grown accustomed to the sirens coming from the police station up the street. One night in June I heard at least six police cars speeding past my house. The next morning I read that a 17-year-old boy was shot dead five blocks from my house.

A few days later, Sheri and I met on the sidewalk in front of our duplex.

"Do you think we should sell?"

"I'm not sure," I said. "At least it's not happening right here."

"Yeah," she said.

"I'd like to stay, but if you think we should sell we can think about it," I said.

"Maybe we can see how the summer goes," she said.

"I just want to believe everything will turn out all right."

"Maybe," she said.

A few days later Delon told me he wouldn't be able to mow my lawn anymore since he and his family would be going to Chicago for the summer. Unsure of his exact departure date, I wished him well before he left. Over the next few weeks, I said goodbye numerous times, as he put the lawnmower away.

At the end of June, the doorbell rang at 7:45 p.m. I was leery to answer the door at that time of night but opened it after seeing the familiar face through the peephole.

"My mom said I should come over and ask if I can mow your lawn," he said. "We're leaving tomorrow morning, early, early."

He pulled the lawnmower around the back for the last time. "Man, this is going to be long when I come back," he said.

"I guess I'll have to mow it myself a few times while you're gone," I said. "Are you coming back?"

I had seen a "For Rent" sign on the lawn of the blue duplex.

"We'll be back in one month," he said.

"Oh, yeah?"

"Yeah, one month," he said. "I'm going to Cherokee in the fall like Keandre."

"What time are you leaving," I asked again.

"Early, early," he said. "I have to get cleaned up before I go to bed, and wear my clothes to bed tonight because we're leaving real early."

We said goodbye again, and I thought about hugging him but waved instead.

The next morning when I left the house, I saw that the green Taurus that usually sat in front of the duplex was gone. A few days later I noticed a pink wingback chair, a television, a spare tire, and a number of indistinguishable smaller items had been pulled out of the duplex and were abandoned on the curb.

I didn't see Delon again until September. He rang my doorbell just as it was getting dark. When I opened the door he was bent over and resting his hands on his knees trying to catch his breath.

"Hey, I didn't know if you were coming back."

He looked up at me and smiled.

"Where are you staying?" I asked. "I didn't see you around the duplex."

"We're living in Allied."

"Did you walk the whole way here?" I asked.

He nodded.

"What do you have there?" I asked, pointing at the papers in his hands.

"It's for school. Would you like to buy a subscription to the newspaper?"

I had recently cancelled my subscription but grabbed the papers and signed up. I watched him turn back toward Allied Drive, wishing I had the courage to offer him a ride.

Before we decided to finally sell the duplex, I would tell people I wasn't going to leave the neighborhood. "You can't save a neighborhood by leaving," I'd say.

But I couldn't save the neighborhood by staying. Or by paying neighborhood kids to mow my lawn. Or helping a boy with a school fundraiser. The neighborhood needed more maintenance than that.

That doesn't make it feel like less of a failure, though. I feel an ache in my chest where the hope used to be when I drive through my old neighborhood on the way to my new condominium. When I get there I know I won't have to do any snow shoveling or lawn mowing at all.

Letters After Achilles

Stefanie Brook Trout

I.

May 2, 2013

Dear Bees,

I feel I must apologize. I'm new to this apian life, and I regret not thinking of you first when Achilles came to Iowa. The cold air settled on my exposed back this morning, and I awoke from the chill. Snow shrouded the world outside my window, colonizing the tree branches like arctic lichen. Today, the snow didn't fall simply down. It fell east and west, north and south. It blew up, buoyed by the wind.

Yesterday they warned us this storm was coming. They, who attempt to prophesy these kinds of events. They, who termed this record-breaking storm Achilles. I wonder how deeply they who selected the name understood its history. I wonder if they knew the word's etymological origin—*akhos laos*, "the grief of the people." I wonder if the name made them think of Homer or Brad Pitt. And I wonder if there is a slain hero Hector out there whose wimpy brother Paris will summon all of Apollo's courage to save us from this storm with his arrow.

I would have been more concerned with you, dearest bees, if I had believed the forecasters, but I was in denial. Impatient. Just two days ago, I pulled the canvas bag out from under my bed, the bag with swimsuits and sandals and other articles of clothing that reveal more skin than they cover, packed with a strip of cedar to keep everything fresh. Two days ago, I donned a tank top and shorts. I bared my pale skin to the bright sun, and I sweat in the eighty-degree afternoon.

I was embarrassed about showing so much skin after having spent so long covering it up, and I have more skin now than I did the last time I wore these clothes. I have more skin than I've ever had before—more breasts, more stomach, more hips, more ass, more thigh. I have what I've always been teased for not having: meat on my bones. My boyfriend—as much as I hate the juvenile sound of the word, that's what he is—doesn't mind the extra flesh. I know I probably shouldn't mind it either, but I do. I'd had the same body for a decade, and I no longer recognize the vessel that contains me. But I was done covering it up and content to pick up more sun and more fresh warm air on account of my increased surface area.

This morning, however, my body only picked up cold, pushing against me on all sides as Achilles bore down on Ames, Iowa. Sleeping next to the window was lovely in the summer when my boyfriend—just a roommate back then—and I moved in and arranged the furniture. I would wake up to sunshine and, when I left the window open for the night, birdsong and bursts of fragrant foliage. I woke up to the signs of life. It was like a Disney movie or a transcendentalist celebration of the world's glory. But through the long winter, it has felt like sleeping in front of a walk-in freezer with the door ajar because of a faulty latch.

The air coming off the window tells me how much clothing I will need before I'm ready to face the world. This morning, the cool air told me to wear all of the clothes—or at least all of the warm ones I haven't grown out of. (It's a funny thing, "growing out of" clothes at twenty-eight years old instead of just wearing them out like usual.) The bag of bikinis and skimpy shorts that probably won't fit anyway will have to go back under the bed for now.

From the window, the snow looks soft and quiet just as all snow appears from afar. It tumbles off the branches more quickly than usual, though, falling fast like fat white tears. Once I ventured outside, I found the snow neither soft nor quiet. The temperature hovers just above freezing, so the snow does not drift as gentle flakes but rather drops as airborne slush, pockmarking the white carpet upon impact. The fat white tears cannonball into puddles on the street. They collided with my head like well-guided slush missiles. Moisture beaded on my glasses; my vision blurred.

And at that moment, I finally thought of you, dearest honeybees. It hasn't been a week since we in the recently-formed Bluff Creek Bee Club released you into your new hives at the Casey Land. If we had anticipated the arrival of Achilles, we might have waited for calmer skies. But by the time the storm was foretold, it was too late. If your colonies were already well established I wouldn't be so concerned about the weather. If you survive this storm and the summer that must eventually follow it, you will winter out-of-doors at the Casey Land. By then, hopefully, you will be strong. A superorganism adapted for life on all continents save Antarctica, your species has survived cruel weather before. But right now, your queens are fresh out of the cage. You are all just starting to get to know one another and your roles in and outside of the hive. And I worry.

I want to save you from Achilles, but leaving you alone is the only way I can help right now. I hope you huddle close in your hives the next few days, ranks closed around your respective queens, shivering to raise your body temperatures. I know you can keep warm as long as you have food. I hope you conserved your sugar water wisely, stretching the reserve until Achilles has gone and the air is safe for us to open your hives again for a top off.

Since you're probably (hopefully) tucked away in your hives, you likely haven't had a look at the world outside. It's strangely beautiful. I hadn't realized how green and vibrant the grass had become until it was silhouetted against bright white slush. As courageous and ambitious as any Trojan, the grass fights back against the spring snowstorm, radiating the energy of life and thawing the dimpled snow before it even stops falling. Put another way, it looks as if all of Ames has been TP-ed by some angsty teenagers just before a downpour, the soggy tissue torn through by raindrops to reveal glimpses of the verdant landscape beneath.

Somewhere, a bird sings. Though I can't identify the species, I think I know the words to its song.

I promise to write again soon.

Yours truly,
Stef

II.

May 3, 2013

Dear Achilles,

Your freshly fallen snow still frosts the mostly bare trees. Yellow buds shouldering bright white cloaks explode above my head. It's like walking into a cathedral but even more heavenly, calling for more reverence.

My eye rests in the negative space, where the angular branches frame the blue steel sky, making it seem more tangible, no longer abstract. Like something you could hold in your arms. Here I find the true nature of the tree—not in the bulk of its shape but in the way its form alters my vision of the world. I cross myself in a conditioned response to the holy. I wish there was some other way—one not tainted by the connotations of religion—to express my deference to this sight.

Namaste, I whisper. But that can be problematic too.

What I mean to say is, *Thank you.*

Sincerely,
Stefanie

III.

May 4, 2013

Dear Tallgrass Prairie,

The snow melts in the spring sun, dissolving into dewy grass. Good news for bees.

The bees' home at the Everett Casey Nature Center and Reserve is seventy-six acres straddling Bluff Creek. Five years ago, 1946 Iowa State Engineering alum Everett Casey gifted the land, valued at $201,000, to the Master of Fine Arts program in Creative Writing and Environment. Why he did this, I'll never know for sure. Casey cited an excellent writing class that he took at ISU for an explanation. A single class. I like to think that it was for me and others like me in the MFA program. Casey was from Detroit—not too far away from my own birthplace and childhood homes in West Michigan. I like to think that Mr. Casey knew about my type. That we would need a piece of wildness to be able to make Iowa home. I know it sounds selfish, but I like to think he reserved this place for me and others like me so that we never forget the privilege we have to live on this land.

As you know, the property should be carpeted with tall prairie grass—as should the majority of Iowa. Forty percent of the United States was once covered in you, my dear Tallgrass Prairie, but Iowa led the rest of the union with the largest percentage of its land area devoted to the native grasses. A sea of grass that can be just as disorientingly awe-inspiring as the open ocean or, something I'm more familiar with, a Great Lake. Your beauty has always been subtler than that of other landscapes. You hid much of your treasure underground, in your amazing, complex root system that held the wet, rich soils in place.

Now Iowa leads the race to the bottom—with more than 99.9% of its natural landscape gone, replaced by a system governed by drainage tiles and an excessive amount of chemicals. Thirty million acres of big and little bluestem, Indiangrass, and switchgrass—all plowed under to make room for cornfields. The hardy stalks grow taller than men. Their ears boast hundreds of kernels arranged in tidy rows like widgets on a factory line, packaged efficiently in a husk and swaddled in long blonde silk for safer shipping and handling. Eight thousand years of prairie legacy disappeared, so Americans can get fat on soft drinks and corn-fed cattle.

I prefer to get fat on honey.

I miss you.

Love,

Stef

IV.

May 8, 2013

Dear Rain,

I lay in bed before the open window. The prophets say you will come tonight, and I believe them this time. The cool air preceding your arrival curls up against me. I cannot suffer these suffocating clothes any longer.

Despite what my bras might think, I'm no longer thirty-four and no longer an A. My cups runneth over, and I acquire daily grooves in my skin from where I tried to reign in the flesh and fat with underwires and straps and clasps. The miraculous wonder padding I paid extra for is now redundant, bordering on ridiculous. My underwear, likewise, fails to fit over my new and enlarged backside. Instead, the barely there fabric bunches up in the crevices, constantly requiring re-extrication. I am hyperaware of my clothes all day these days, constantly attentive to their needs. Pull down, push up, pry out. My clothing cares nothing for my needs.

With the blinds closed and the door shut, I have no need for these scraps of fabric that hurt me in order to hide the landscape of my body from myself and the rest of the world. So I strip and cast the restraints aside. My boyfriend kisses the extra meat on my ribs, next to a small scratch of unknown origin. *You're beautiful,* he murmurs into my soft body as the night breathes its cool exhale around us. *You're beautiful. You're beautiful.*

See you soon.

Best wishes,
Stefanie

V.

May 10, 2013

Dear Casey Land,

At last, the skies are calm enough to expose the hives to the elements. Emerging apiarists pile into a van and set out to visit you. We must check on our bees—make sure the queens are still alive and the workers are building comb for brood. We must replenish the sugar water. Soon the bees will feed themselves.

We burn scraps of burlap in the smoker, pumping the bellows to fuel the fire. Standing to the side of the first hive, we puff smoke into the openings. The smoke calms the bees, so they won't attack us. We lift the outer cover, give them more smoke, and then remove the inner cover to reveal the built-up frames. Right now, the hives are short—with only the lower deep in place. The lower deep is the brood chamber, where the queen lays her eggs. Soon we will add the upper deep—the food chamber—and a few weeks after that, a queen excluder and a shallow honey super. We don't expect to harvest much honey this year, but we're optimistic that we'll each get to taste the sweet products of the humming hives. For now, however, we just hope our colonies survive. Between *Varroa* mites, the mysterious Colony Collapse Disorder, and now the bizarre weather, our bees face much adversity.

We pull out frames for inspection and find our girls have been busy despite the chill. They built extra comb between the frames, too much comb in places, and a large piece of the hexagonal wax breaks off and falls into the hive. A brave beekeeper sticks her gloveless hand into the depths of the chamber and pulls out the fallen chunk, covered on all sides with bees. There's no way to glue the brood comb back together, so we gently brush the bees off and back into the hive. We save the piece as a souvenir. Later, on the drive back to Ames, we'll notice the tiny rice-like eggs the queen has laid in each cell. Since we will be too inexperienced at this point to recognize the queen among the crowd of workers and drones, the presence of eggs serve as our proof that Her Highness is alive and performing her royal duties.

We shift some frames around, moving the heavily built-up frames toward the outside and moving the barer frames toward the middle, the heart of the hive where the queen lays her eggs—as many as two thousand per day. We refill the sugar water, close up the hive, and proceed to complete the same tasks with the second hive.

The business of our visit taken care of, we decide to enter your lovely forest to look for blooming wildflowers. Evidence of the early prairie restoration efforts is apparent—most of the invasive species we lopped off in the fall have failed to sprout back. We all wish it could have been accomplished without the aid of Roundup, but unfortunately it's our only effective weapon against the intruders. If we want you to look natural again, we will have to take some unnatural measures. That's what I'm told anyway, and though it feels wrong in my gut, I listen to those with experience because I know they hate how toxic our environment is too.

We hike down the steep hill, the trail newly widened, through invasive cedars and into the oak forest, past the agricultural field recently converted from corn rows to oats in preparation for alfalfa planting—your only source of income and now on its way toward becoming a much better source of nutrition for the bees—until we reach Bluff Creek. The fast water fills the channel more completely than we've ever seen. Our feeble rock bridges have been submerged by the snowmelt, creating exciting riffles.

No longer a stagnant, desiccated remnant, the creek rushes nobly. We straighten our spines, pull back our shoulders, and beam like proud parents. *We made this*, we think, but like proud parents, we're wrong.

As you well know, Bluff is a meandering sort of creek, and we follow its winding way downstream to the sandy point bar that demarcates the edge of the property. Though our English Department holds your deed, we stewards don't like to think of *owning* you. You aren't *our* property. You've been home to all varieties of native and invasive flora and fauna, and now that includes a pair of bee colonies, but please don't get the wrong idea. This kind of colonialism is rather different than the kind you might be apprehensive about.

On our way back to the van, we lose ourselves in your woods. We unknowingly follow what is most likely a deer path forking off our main trail. Hopping the barbed wire fence could be our first clue that we are losing track of where you end and the neighboring land begins. An arbitrary line, yes, but still legally significant.

We emerge from the woods on the edge of a freshly planted field and follow it toward the road hoping to see our hives just around the bend. We don't.

So we reenter the woods, no longer on any path at all, blazing our own trail that includes crawling under and climbing over fallen trees. We shinny down a gully, hop the muddy bottom, and scramble up the other side. We scale another barbed wire fence—a promising sign— and emerge from the woods again. This time, we see the white hives and know that we are home.

On the van ride back to Ames, we find ticks all over our bodies. Another souvenir. Thanks for that.

Respectfully,
Stefanie Brook Trout

VI.

May 21, 2013

Dear Morel,

My boyfriend and I are hiking at Ledges National Park. It's part of a healthy living habit we're trying to establish this summer so each of us can start feeling better about our bodies. He's tried to take me out running, but I haven't had the appetite for it yet. Hiking through the woods, however, is a workout I can get behind. We bring our dog, Lily. It's the kind of workout she can get behind too, running ahead of us to mark the trail.

We aren't far from the Casey Land, where the bees are now feeding themselves. Ledges is beautiful—in much better shape, a more natural condition than the Casey Land though that state is probably the product of much planning and hard work—but I can't stop myself from thinking about the bees. It's funny how beekeeping has caused us to break the only two rules of the Casey Land: take nothing and leave nothing. We left a couple of hives packed with tens of thousands of bees. For now, we've just taken the broken chunk of comb, but we're hoping to take honey home eventually. And beeswax. And propolis. Maybe even mushrooms now that we have a taste for low-impact, sustainable agriculture and we've identified several edible species growing at the Casey Land.

While hiking at Ledges, I tell my boyfriend to be on the lookout for you, in particular. When a member of our bee club went out to the hives to remove the sugar water feeders and fill that space with extra frames for brood, she found some morels on the Casey Land. My boyfriend doesn't know what you are yet, Morel, but I describe your brainy appearance, and we both keep a distracted eye out for you. There's a lot else to look at, however. I watch my footing since I'm hopelessly clumsy, even on an easy trail like this. I watch Lily, nose in the air, picking up the smells of life and death around her. At least I imagine her expert nose smells this in the forest, with the decaying leaves still littering the ground among the emergent grasses and sedges and young saplings. I watch the landscape framed by ledges and bluffs. Before moving to Iowa from Indiana, I wrongly assumed the places would be equally as flat.

And then, despite my distracted thoughts, I see you. A single morel, large and grayish white, right next to the trail. I can't believe our luck. No one could walk this path without seeing this delicacy, and yet you are still here when we happen to pass by. Waiting for us. I pick you and start telling my boyfriend stories about mushroom hunting with my dad as a young girl. This is the first time I've held a morel in twenty years, and I can't wait to savor you. We look for more, but you are it. The land has delivered this solitary gift, and we will appreciate it at that.

With gratitude,
Stefanie

P.S. Is it legal to pick wild mushrooms at a National Park?

VII.
May 22, 2013
Dear Hawk,

Last night, I quartered the morel and soaked it in a salt-water bath to cleanse away the unsavory elements. Today, I throw the quarters in my cast iron skillet with butter, beer, and salt. They expel their moisture and shrivel up. I'm thrilled.

My boyfriend has never eaten a morel. He's never eaten any mushroom picked fresh from the forest, and he's skeptical of my find. He's happy that I am happy, but he wonders if I'm going to kill us. *Are you sure this isn't poisonous?* he asks, a shriveled piece of gray matter dangling unappetizingly from his fork.

You can look it up if it will give you peace of mind, I tell him. *But I know this is a morel. There is such thing as a false morel, but they don't look anything alike in my opinion.*

Then why do they call it a false morel? he asks.

I shrug. *I don't know. I guess some people who don't know what they're doing think they do look alike.*

He doesn't look it up, and I'm impressed by his trust. We each eat our two mini-morsels of morel and praise their deliciousness and our own luck.

We walk Lily and find your body behind the garage. I say you're a hawk. My boyfriend swears you're a falcon. A hunk of meat is still suspended in your clenched talons. There's enough fur for me to think it used to be a rabbit, but that's only an educated guess because there's no body. Just raw flesh and gray fur.

I can't imagine how you ended up here, at the terminus of a dead end gravel alleyway. Boyfriend picks up a stick and moves your large body around. Your neck swivels properly. There are no signs of injury except in one small place where your wing meets your body, charred black. You probably collided with the power lines on the ascent. Foolishly hadn't looked all ways before alighting. Having concluded the necropsy, my boyfriend drops the stick with the solemnity of a coroner removing his latex gloves.

In sympathy,
Stefanie Brook Trout

VIII.
May 23, 2013
Dear Morel,

The hawk is still there. The flies are coming. I expect the wind to carry the rotten stench of carrion to me, filling my nostrils with the scent of decay. Call it selective smelling, but I can't pick up the rotten stench. The air still smells sweet. Soon enough, the hawk will just be feather and bone, and then bone, and then nothing.

I call my dad in Michigan and tell him about you. Having taught me to hunt mushrooms, he oozes pride. *I haven't found any myself yet,*

he confesses, *but Joanne—my step-mom—found a bunch yesterday too.*
He also warns me about the false morels, which he's never done before because I've never before gone mushroom hunting without him. He describes how the caps of the false morels can look similar to a true morel but aren't connected to the stem at the base.

You were a true morel. I know this. But I can't help thinking that it would have been too easy to accidentally poison us. Carried away by enthusiasm, nostalgia, and a little hubris. The tiny meal could have been our last. That would have been unfortunate.

Fond regards,
Stefanie

IX.
May 31, 2013
Dear Bees,

This morning we—my boyfriend, Lily, and I—are finally running. For me, it's the first time in seven years. Seven years ago, I ran the Detroit Marathon on a relay team to raise money for a summer camp for kids with heart problems. My leg was only six miles, a lazy day for a marathon runner, but it was longer than I'd ever run before, and I found out later that it could have killed me.

I ran for my nephew Dominick, who was too young to attend summer camp yet but had needed two heart surgeries in his first year. I knew I had a congenital heart problem too, but I hadn't known how serious it was when I had agreed to run the relay. I found out four years later, when Dr. Sheik diagnosed me with an atrial septal defect, a hole in my heart two centimeters in diameter that allowed the blood from my left and right atria to slosh back and forth at will, sullying up the whole system of veins and arteries and valves and vena cavae that work diligently to keep oxygenated and deoxygenated blood from mixing.

Dr. Sheik plugged the hole in my heart without taking a scalpel to my chest and, after a few months, cleared me for strenuous physical activity. But I was terrified to ever run again. I've gained twenty-five pounds since the surgery. I blamed it on my new birth control, my busyness with graduate school, my laziness. Now, running through Ames with my boyfriend beside me, Lily leading and wishing I could go faster, I feel my heart rate quicken and the subsequent anxiety, and I know that it was fear that kept me inert. I had a new heart, and I was afraid to stress it too hard. I didn't want to go through all of that again.

Running, I feel my heart beating, thrumming its chord of life through my body, awakening my senses. My heart might have been faulty at first, but my skeleton is built for running. All that I am rests on two long legs. As a teenager I wore hot pink skinny jeans to the zoo, and my sister, who lives in California and hasn't seen me in the past year, still calls me a flamingo. My thighs never used to touch, but they're rubbing now, which is inconvenient but really not a big deal. The fresh air fills my lungs with a forgotten power. The extra flesh is cold, but I am warm.

I will come for a visit tomorrow.

Faithfully yours,
Stef

Lucky

Paula Sergi

After weeks of snowfall and other winter weather phenomea, our city has become a different kind of place. Even the bowling leagues have cancelled due to record snow levels and wind chills in the minus 40 range. Last weekend's brief rain and sleet mixture added another layer of mystique when more snow fell over slushy streets and sidewalks. Another deep freeze followed, and so we are walking and driving on crunchy surfaces. When a car pulls up our dead end street it announces itself with a sort of screech, a small grinding of tire over chunks of gravelly ice.

We hold bragging rights in the neighborhood for having the longest icicles. They cover our second story windows like monster teeth or curtains made of ice. I feel like I'm living in Dr. Zhivago's winter palace, except ever since we bought a new furnace a few weeks ago we have heat. Of course we'll need a new roof come spring, but I'm not about to knock those monster teeth off the gutters. Some are shaped like Edward Scissorhand's hands.

I'm unpopular these days. Folks in the hardware and grocery stores keep complaining about the weather. "It's beautiful!" I exclaim. "If you don't like winter, why do you live in Wisconsin?" I'm thinking there will be a mass migration to California or Southern Illinois and we who stay behind will find more fish in the lakes come summer.

Last night I released my students early from the clutches of English composition and found myself driving towards Main Street. I knew there was nothing to eat at home, and I was hungry. Though I could detect no human activity on the streets of town, I was hoping the Chinese restaurant was open.

I found a parking place right out front and took this as a good omen. No one else ventured the ice-laden streets, and I think myself lucky.

Only four other patrons were inside, and they chose the buffet in the back room. I wanted carry-out and waited in the empty foyer. No newspapers, no posters, nothing to read. I stared out the window at winter.

Then I detected movement. Through the frosty glass I could see that some patrons had wandered out from the bar across the street. I thought it odd, because here in Wisconsin at that time we could still legally kill one another with second-hand smoke. Why would these folks venture out in the cold for a cigarette? Their frozen breath and exhaled smoke formed a double halo above their heads. They all three looked skyward, as if asking for an icicle to impale them, a swift sword of justice.

A cell phone broke my reverie. The restaurant manager had a brief conversation, then went out on the sidewalk himself to look skyward. I felt a stab of pity for him, understanding the weight of roof damage for a small business owner.

Back inside he gestured to the cooks with his hands. He formed one large ball, and then separated his hands, showing two separate balls. He shook his head in frustration when the cooks didn't understand, grabbed a paper menu and drew something I wasn't privy to. A spirited cackle of Chinese broke out. I was curious, but my order was ready, so I left.

As I pulled out of my lucky parking spot, I looked back for signs of smoke or fire at the restaurant. In my year view mirror I saw them, three Chinese chefs in white aprons, staring skyward. Then I remembered the news report from earlier in the day, looked up, and saw it for myself: the lunar eclipse, easily visible on this clear, cold night.

Try to explain it in any language, this passing of Earth between the sun and moon. Try to remember why we stay on this planet as it rotates, how our cars do not slip off into space. Try *not* to love the smokers and the Chinese chefs, together on this frozen wonder.

Small Town News

Paula Sergi

As the string of hot days in Wisconsin lengthens, even the heartiest among us suffer. Though we love our brief summer, temperatures have hovered near ninety for weeks on end, and the humidity wilts our good humor. Even the black-eyed susans droop, avoiding eye contact. Tensions rise, giving way to dramatic events.

Last week, for example, Herman and Evelyn heard an interesting incident reported over their police scanner. Herman had been out to water the tomatoes, and Evelyn was drinking her third cup of coffee, elbows resting on the oiled table cloth bearing rooster icons.

From what she could tell, a mother and son tangled in the parking lot of a local discount store. This piqued her interest, as it had been a slow news week. "Hermie, listen ta this!"

Apparently the ruckus began inside. Witnesses reported seeing the duo waiting in line at the pharmacy for the son's steroid cream. It seems the mother knew enough to refrain from referring to his situation as "prickly heat," but could not help but suggest a tepid bath with Epsom salts. Sullen behavior gave way to dirty looks.

Evie and Hermie watched for the city beat column in the newspaper for more details. By Tuesday it appeared, near the end of the publication, page 3. Other shoppers reported that the culprits may have been planning a day at the lake. Items in their shopping cart included sun screen, a Styrofoam cooler, and sandwich bags.

It's unclear who first spotted the bright display of water toys, but it seems their attraction to the fluorescent-colored water noodles was mutual. *At ninety-nine cents each, those water toys were flying off the shelf*, said Erv Schrufnagel, store manager. The son protested his mother's initial choice. "Not the pink floral," he was overheard to complain in a whiney voice. They ultimately agreed on two green and one yellow.

The malcontents then proceeded to the checkout line, where another wait ensued. It may have been accidental, no one is sure, but when their shopping cart wheels skinned the woman's shins, a minor scuffle, characterized by verbal exchange, broke out. The mother, described as middle aged, suggested her son proceed to their car. Perhaps neither anticipated the angst which befell the son when he realized the car keys were in his mother's purse. He was seen waiting in the bright oven-heat of the asphalt parking lot, hands stuffed in his pockets, kicking at loose gravel. At one point a fellow shopper witnessed a crude utterance from the direction of the car, after the young man in question leaned onto the side mirror, possibly burning the tender skin of his underarm.

When the mother appeared, Al Wehner from gardening noted that the son violently exhibited his impatience by snatching the shopping bag, which tore to bits, sending the contents across the parking lot, some spilling under the car. Their eyes met in an angry gaze, and the son crawled onto the melting asphalt to retrieve various items, braising his knees.

Witnesses say a bottle of Epsom salts and a jar of Noxema face cream rolled from under the car, causing the mother to lose her footing. Legs became entangled. When the two sweaty figures got to their feet, a melee broke out. The mother grabbed a yellow noodle and began to beat the son about his head. The son returned her aggression. Sweat flew. Insults were exchanged.

Security was notified, which triggered the call to authorities. By the time local police arrived, the scene was subdued. The melee had fortunately broken out near the hose display, and a water source was available. "Hosed 'em down, officer. Won't be no more trouble from them two," store security reported.

The weather forecast on page four reported more of the same. Security detail at the discount store has been redoubled, in the hopes of forestalling such future incidents.

Fuckaroo!

John Linstrom

Up North, rivers lie like tapped veins in the arm of a monster, crossing and recrossing over themselves, picking up in rapids and eddies, turning through walled corridors of sedimentary history, tearing over fallen trees and glacial boulders, emptying into the million calm lakes before spilling out the other side again, all racing as if away from the heart of civilization, or maybe toward the heart of Canada, that Far North that exists beyond or among the big woods. Here, in the North Woods, we are not "south of the border," not west of the Big Lake, but North, "up," over the centers of everything but the wilderness.

The drive had been long, from the heart of Iowa through the vast corn/soy plains and into the patchy woods and towns of Minnesota, settling into a midway campsite after dark and leaving before any ranger could ask a fee, continuing the drive up 61 along the north shore of Superior and then, finally, breaking off at Grand Marais and taking the old Gunflint Trail up through the ragged forest and the million lakes to its very end and the campsite that was there, the stack of university-rented canoes and the sandy bank we would set out from. It was worth it, we said. This was the escape we afforded ourselves, the way out of grading more composition papers, the weekend off from visible horizons, the break from grad school and the solace of the wooded dark.

Welcome to the MFA Program in Creative Writing and Environment at Iowa State, better characterized by our escapes from the academy than by any of the conversations we have in our moldy workshop room.

My first canoe trip would have been my tamest if David hadn't been left behind, but there he was, standing onshore with his lifejacket on, next to the last boat but with no partner.

No one knew how he ended up stranded like that, but he was *my* academic advisor, and *I* was just sitting as a duffer in my canoe, so the decision was made without much discussion. And then David had to go back to the van to get something, and then I went up too but couldn't find him, and after fifteen or twenty minutes there we were, standing on shore where he had been alone before, no canoes in sight.

"So have you done this recently?" David asked. We were just about thirty yards offshore, rocking gently, and had completed our second 180-degree twist backward. He instructed me to stop paddling as he got us facing forward again.

"This is actually my first time."

"Canoeing, ever?"

I nodded.

"Oh, wow," he said, sort of softly. "Huh, that's funny. You're so outdoorsy though! Not to mention beardy." He liked to call me beardy. "Weren't you ever in Boy Scouts? It seems like I read that in your thesis."

I contemplated this, pretty sure I hadn't mentioned it in my thesis. "I guess we didn't do as much as most troops," I said. "I ended up in the boring troop of my town. We didn't do much besides an annual camping trip at the Flywheelers Festival out in the country. We always went to help park cars for them. But canoeing's not as big a thing in southwest Michigan."

"Oh, we'd go canoeing all the time with the Scouts in Georgia," David replied.

The canoe was facing forward, so I asked him if I should start paddling again. He seemed irritated, I thought. Still, the sky was blue and the air piney, and once we figured out how to move straight we'd probably catch up with the group in no time. We'd stop at Seagull Palisades, do a writing activity, and eat lunch. (This is what terminal degree programs in "Creative Writing and Environment" do, I thought to myself.) My bread and peanut butter were in a friend's bag up ahead, but nearly everyone else's lunches and notebooks were in the big waterproof bag that Steve had left onshore and that David and I had now as a duffer between us. I smiled, thinking about how they wouldn't be able to start eating without us.

As soon as I started paddling again, the canoe veered to port. "Oh dammit," David said. His cusswords were usually tamer than that. "You know, how about if I just paddle for now until we catch up? I'm fine doing this on my own; I just can't remember how to do it with two people."

I lifted my paddle out of the water, set it across the bow, and rested my arms on it. I could hear a woodpecker working on a tree somewhere. It was pretty easy to cool off in a setting like this. This is actually great, I thought. I decided to make the most of the morning, while my academic advisor began to huff behind me, alternating sides, pushing us toward the bend up ahead.

In a meeting with Steve a week or two earlier, the five of us second- and third-year graduate students, who planned to join the first-year group up North received the directions we'd need to unite with them at the "End of the Trail" campsite. Then he told us, just in case they headed out before we got there, how to follow the rivers to get to Seagull Palisades for lunch. I had written the directions down, nodding and scribbling dutifully, in my little pocket notebook. I had not actually planned to use them.

This annual fall bonding retreat is the kind of tradition that emerges from our strange hybrid program, but I should say up front that most of us, with a few exceptions, are soft-handed writers. Not exactly mountaineers or voyageurs. We write about different things, be they wilderness, farming, or urban environments. I'm in it for Liberty Hyde Bailey. Liberty Hyde Bailey, the Father of Modern Horticulture. Liberty Hyde Bailey, the farm boy from my hometown, South Haven's Favorite Son. Liberty Hyde Bailey, the infinitely quotable jack-of-all-trades, plant-collecting, globetrotting philosopher. Liberty Hyde Bailey, the man with the weird name that no one has ever heard of and with whom I have fallen into a strange dependency. Tell me where to go, Liberty Hyde Bailey. Tell me how to be happy.

He always seemed to do and study what he wanted. "My life," he said at his ninetieth birthday party, "has been a continuous fulfillment of dreams." Bailey liked the woods, and he explored these same Boundary Waters when he was a young man in his late twenties. So, when I heard that this fall's trip would be to the Boundary Waters, I was thrilled enough about going that I took responsibility for writing down the directions. Thank goodness. When we were on shore and David asked how we'd find the rest of the group, I replied with confidence that Steve had told me where to go.

The little notebook lay open on my thigh as we drifted down the river, now somewhat in a straight line, and as we neared the bend in the river I lifted it, looked at the bend, and looked at the directions again. It wasn't actually so much a bend as a distinct Y. "Which way did Steve say to turn?" David asked.

"Well, it's not totally clear. He said to 'go straight and keep to the right,' and then we're supposed to go over 'a small rapids,' and Seagull Palisades will be the big rocks on the left. But neither of these look like 'straight' to me."

After a pause, David asked, "So which way do we turn here?"

I shrugged, looking down both forks of the Y. "He said to go straight, and keep to the right."

"Ah, the right! Okay," David replied, suddenly sounding a little too cheery.

Sometimes I think you really can intuitively tell that a decision you're making is wrong, but, because there's no evidence to support the feeling, you're likely to go through with it anyway. I'm not sure whether this comforts or depresses me.

Our newly chosen branch of the river curved around a bend and soon we could no longer see the fork behind us. This is about the time we began to hear the rapids. David asked if I could hear "that," and I responded that I could, and that the directions said we should go over "a small rapids."

"What's going over a rapids like in a canoe?" I asked David. I had heard of such things in relation to kayaks, but not really in conversations about canoes—let alone big heavy university-rented ones.

"Well, he said 'small rapids,' right? If you're going *with* the rapids, it really shouldn't be much trouble at all. You'll want to look out for big rocks and try to push away from them, but don't worry about it too much, because I'll be steering anyway."

I still had my red plastic paddle crossed over the bow of the canoe. "Alright," I said. He was still working audibly behind me, and I felt a little guilty for not being a good enough canoeist to help us reach the others more quickly. I determined to be as helpful and positive as possible, although something about the gradual narrowing of the river and the continuing absence of any other canoe in sight made me uneasy. The sound of falling water grew louder. "So, I'll just keep my paddle up unless you say something? Or maybe if I see something?"

Around the bend, from my perspective sitting at about water level, a flat line emerged over which the still river water disappeared. We seemed to be moving a little more quickly. "Just don't worry about it," David said. I rocked forward onto my heels and lifted myself up a bit to try to see over the edge of the drop, which continued to emerge as we rounded the bend. Over the edge, the entire river transformed into a maze of currents that twisted around dozens of boulders. *Damn*, I thought, *that's bigger than I expected.*

David noticed. "Wow, this will be fun," he said. I sat back down and gripped my paddle harder.

Soon we could see that the flat line spanned the whole width of the river, and that the river continued on in a rapids like that until it disappeared again around a tree-topped ledge of rock. There wouldn't be any portaging; the slopes of the river rose dramatically on both sides of us already. We could turn around now, but that would be working against the slowly strengthening current.

The canoe rocked, and I realized David had stood up to get a better look. "I guess that's the rapids, huh?" He shouted so I could hear over the water rush, and then he laughed, sort of shouting as he did. "I think we can shoot 'em!"

He steered us just to the right of a large boulder around which the river rose and fell, and as the bow edged near the drop, I could see that the water fell some five feet. I gripped my paddle across the bow and started to lean backward.

David laughed again. "Are you ready?" he cried. I looked out, the rapids expanding to fill my entire field of vision, turning over every boulder and depression so unendingly it seemed almost static, glossed like blown glass but loud as a china shop emptied onto its own parking lot.

The water on either side of us lay flat. The sky hung still and bright. The trees shivered. And slowly, the canoe's end pushed out, me in it, straight into the air, and began to tip forward.

We each yelled different things—I don't remember what—as the bow tipped earthward and the hull began rolling to starboard. As it did I lifted my right leg and stuck it out of the boat, crashing into the river and hitting slick bottom just as the canoe's stern swung out to the right behind me and splashed down the fall with David, who I turned around to see floating on his side in the river. I reached over to grab his small red cotton backpack before it got soaked, and the canoe, half full of water, righted itself.

"Fuck-a-roo!" David shouted.

I pointed at the small, dark writing things in the water of the boat, and asked David if they were leeches. There were probably a hundred floating in the boat, and then I also picked some off of my exposed calves in the river. The water was above our knees.

David denied that they were leeches.

I had never seen leeches, but they were leeches.

David thanked me when I handed him his mostly dry backpack. "My lunch is in there," he said. "Triscuits and deviled ham."

"Deviled ham?"

"Thought I'd try to share some with the vegetarians in the group." He smiled.

I looked back upriver, which was weirdly close to eye level beyond the boulder behind us. I looked at the steep slopes on either side of the river. I looked downriver, at the continual rapids that we still couldn't see the end of. And I looked at David, who was looking at the same things. "Well, there's no turning back," he said. He looked down at the canoe with the leeches. "And the good news is, that didn't really count as a dump! Everything's still in the canoe."

And for a moment I was actually glad that, of all people, I was stuck on a rapids with David Zimmerman. David's one of those guys who tends to make awkward people feel comfortable. He speaks out of turn, asks inappropriate questions about significant others, and tells self-deprecating stories about subjects like toe fungus. And he tends to see the funny, if not always the bright, side of things. As much as I'd rather not be stuck in the rapids with anyone, now that I was, David would probably prove the more entertaining companion, even if only because he might have less sense of the danger we were in.

I wondered how much danger we were in.

We stood on either end of the canoe and rotated it so that most of the water poured out, and then got back in the boat, which the rapids made difficult. We weren't in for more than a few seconds, moving forward, before the canoe swung around another boulder and tipped again, spilling both David and I into the river this time and filling up halfway again.

"Oh, fuckaroo!" David said. He didn't smile. "This is bad." We emptied the canoe again, and placing everything inside we began the slow process of walking it down the rapids, David holding the painter at the bow and I hanging onto the stern, picking our way among the algae-slick boulders and through the insistent roaring current.

This was not the river we had entered only half an hour ago. That river was glassy blue and cut by reflections of sunlight and treetops, clear so that you could lean over the gunwale and spot the mindless-looking fish floating by, and with my paddle across the bow I could enjoy the sounds of woodpeckers and the occasional breeze through the pines. This river, on the other hand, was boulders up to my neck and the white crashes around them, eddies where the current got confused swirling clear and deceptive, and an invisible underwater carpet of algae coating a million rocks, fist-sized but jagged, that David called "ankle-breakers." The current twisted around our shins and kneecaps like anacondas, strong but smooth, egging us on.

So we continued, David issuing a periodic stream of "fuckaroo's" as he slipped along, more and more regularly losing his footing and falling into the rapids, and me behind him, trying to learn from his mistakes and keep upright as much as possible but constantly feeling inadequate in my ability to support him. I became more aware of our age difference and started to worry more about his ability to physically weather these rapids than about my own ability to make it out. I wondered how long it had been since he had been on a canoe trip like this.

We grew hungry. David spoke repeatedly of how hungry he was, and of how much he looked forward to finding everybody and tearing into that box of Triscuits. "The Triscuits and the deviled ham," he'd say, sometimes affording a grin. And, of course, we told each other plenty of lame jokes to make the time pass more easily, most often returning to the old one about how at least things couldn't get worse.

"Oh my god, look," he said at one point and pointed to the bank on the right. Pine trees stood silently some forty feet up—I didn't see anything. "I know where we are," he said, still pointing. He recognized the bank; we were just below the place where the first-years had camped the night before. We had long since admitted to ourselves that we had taken a wrong turn. "That's a relief. At least now I know I can get us back." Up ahead at this point the rapids finally emptied into a wide still lake after a few more significant passages—so, once there, we could safely beach the canoe and make our way back up to the campsite, which as it turned out we had barely ever left. At the edge of the lake I could see where it emptied into another narrow stream that turned and made its new way farther into the woods.

And at about that time two blond-headed girls, aged maybe seven and ten, emerged from around the edge of the lake opening, skipping and climbing over the rocks along the bank. Their long hair wagged behind them, and I believe they wore matching white dresses. "Jesus, look at that," David said. I laughed, just long enough that I could regain focus again on the task of not slipping, but when I would look back up and see them again I couldn't help laughing all over. David did it too, and we alternated with these sort of painful, short bursts of laughter. The two girls could not hear us from where they were over the rapids' din, but they stopped to watch us briefly once before heading back, probably thinking that they looked down on two adults who were having fun and knew what they were doing.

We finally reached the last major drop before the rapids spread out and reached the lake. The tangled limbs of a fallen tree blocked the left side, and to the right sat an unreasonably large boulder. The only sensible spot to descend was through the middle in a horseshoe-shaped step between the boulder and the tree, but the current was the strongest we had felt, and the water below the horseshoe roiled as it fell from all sides. The ground beneath us also declined, or the water rose, as we neared the boulder, so that David and I were both waist-deep, and the current pulled hard on the hull of the canoe.

"Fuckaroo," David muttered, keeping a safe distance as he peered over the edge.

I think what happened next was that I wanted a look too. This was the largest drop that we'd have to step down, and I didn't feel confident that my legs were long enough to do it, let alone while hanging onto a canoe that wants to whisk away and spill the contents of several other people's bags into the rapids, all while trying not to slip on the algal stones and crack my head against them in the process. My legs were already shaking against the current, tired after about forty-five minutes of cautious strain.

That was when I led the stern of the boat around to the right of David so that I could at least judge the drop for myself. Maybe I stepped too close, maybe I became distracted by more leeches on my legs, or maybe the turning of the boat perpendicular to the rapids would have caused it either way—but I lost my grip. I staggered on the stones, and as the boat started to do a 180 right there by the drop I realized I couldn't keep up with the stern. It tugged away, and I let it go. David held onto the painter but was nearly toppled as it swung right and then, smack against the big boulder, flipped entirely upside-down, half over the fall and suctioned tight to the diagonal falling water, our bags and paddles floating in the air bubble below it, and David, teeth clenched and feet tenuously planted, leaned backward like he was playing tug-of-war with the painter.

"Not good!" he shouted. He glanced around, holding the line. He shimmied to one side of the canoe, then to the other. He looked down at the water that was too fast to see, and he took a breath. "I mean, we just have to right it."

I no longer understood why this was the case. The lake was a stone's throw away—we could see its glassy stillness and the green ring of forest around it (and I imagined there were really magnificent Seagull Palisades off to the left where we couldn't see them)—and without the boat we'd be able to make it much more easily. Once in the lake I figured we could fix everything, swim and retrieve the boat if it floated too far, whatever, but we had to get down this fall somehow first. Let the thing go, I thought—give up—the river wins the boat!

Instead, David grabbed the gunwale, worked his way around to the boulder side, and tried to lift it. Against the boulder, the water reached well up his stomach. David leaned back, wedging himself between the rock and the boat, strained against it, sighed. "Try to grab from the other side and pull toward you," he said.

I don't honestly know if I've ever felt so incompetent. I tried. I reached over the hull, tried to get some kind of grip on the gunwale, but couldn't do barely anything beyond what David in his curled wedged position was doing. I did get hold, I did pull, but I couldn't get a good footing, and ultimately it was mostly David who pried it up.

It happened with a sloppy pop. The canoe flipped back for a moment into canoe position, and we had it as if frozen in time, floating there above the rushing water at that crazy diagonal over the crest of the drop—but the current and gravity had it too, and it was stock full of water. It took off, and, as I teetered, still without good footing, I let it go.

The entire canoe plunged downward, and my academic advisor went down with it. Boat and David vanished. *He should float*, I stupidly thought. The boat came up first. I could not see David, but the painter was still underwater. Downstream, one of the plastic paddles snagged on a fallen tree, and in the middle of the stream, as if framed there, the red cloth backpack with the Triscuits. I did not panic as much as I should have. I mechanically scanned the drop—the slickness of the rocks, the depth, the height of the drop as compared to the length of my leg. I still didn't know how to get down. For several seconds, the amount of water that poured over that ledge must have been immense.

Liberty Hyde Bailey was a world-explorer into his nineties. He travelled far and wide, from deep Amazonia to inner China, to collect and catalogue plants in the name of systematic science. This is not so different from a writer who travels far and wide to write and document the world in poetry—in both cases, at some point, you probably start to wonder what the point is, whether all your findings printed on so much paper and all the life-energy you sacrifice really add up to a true career, an occupation with meaning and weight. No one asked Bailey to document the palms or the raspberries or the sedges, and he did not accrue wealth from those pursuits. And many times, on rough sea voyages or, I imagine, on long canoe trips in the Amazon, his possibly gratuitous exploits (He admitted that he reveled in the adventure, that he did it out of a personal love for and obsession with plants and cataloguing them.) certainly endangered lives, and not just his own.

Staring at the white water at the edge of the drop, I did not know what to do. If I jumped down, I guessed I would probably die. I did not know that, in another twenty minutes, I will have picked over the last thirty yards of rapids and will gather most of the things that had spilled from the canoe. I did not know that the back seat and one of the thwarts of the canoe had each cracked in two against stones on the river's bottom and that the hull had very nearly stove through in its subaquatic voyage, that I will help lead the busted-up canoe and our soggy belongings around the bend and onto the shore, noticing the unsettling number of large fish passing between my legs and then a sign that read "NO FISHING OR SWIMMING—SPAWNING AREA." I did not anticipate lying on the shore beside my academic advisor as we both rested our tired limbs beside the broken canoe, nor that we would discover that all the lunches and notebooks in Steve's "waterproof" bag would be totally soaked. I could not imagine all those soaked pages, the ink run amok, no longer notebooks of writers but slabs of soggy pulp, water-consumed language. I never would have guessed how welcome, after that exhausting hour, the salty taste of deviled ham would actually be. I did not visualize the way Steve's eyes would bulge a couple hours later when we described where we had gone, that he would laugh and tell us that no, those weren't rapids, they were falls.

Underwater, David lost sense of direction. Many pounds of water thrust him down and his head struck against a rock. He would later describe two thoughts in that instant: the first, *What will happen to John if I die?* And the second, a memory from Boy Scouts, *go limp and let the current take you.* He instantly relaxed, and after what felt like half a minute the river carried him in a surge to the surface.

So David's orange hair emerged, followed by his flush face, his sunglasses gone, T-shirt bunched up around his chest and back revealing long scratches rubbed out of his sides by rocks. He might have simply breached like that and fallen back, but a single foot caught something solid, then the other. He jerked to a stop, spluttered, and stood, teetering. He didn't make eye contact, and he didn't look for words. The empty canoe trailed lazily behind him, the painter still in his hand. He almost lost his balance, and then he sat down on a rock and looked around a little.

"Fuck," he said plainly. "The Triscuits."

A Need to Know Basis

D. Gilson

My mother likes to tell stories. She exaggerates truth, if it ever actually exists, and yet, my siblings and I never question the emotional authority of the tales she weaves. They are part, surely as she is part, of our very existence. My mother enjoys the chase of a narrative. And this is a trait I have inherited, most likely one of the very passions that led me to writing. My father, however, loves facts. Plain and simple.

My father is like *Dragnet's* Sgt. Joe Friday. In weekly episodes from 1951 until 1959, Friday, played by Jack Webb in gray suit and black tie, gave a simple introduction to the show, yes, but the two simple statements also revealed his general philosophy: "My name is Friday. I carry a badge." There is nothing wild here, nothing worth note, really. And yet, the simplicity of the syntax speaks volumes to the man behind the badge. Every week we find Friday investigating a new crime on his beat with the LAPD. Every week he questions a key witness. She is always a woman, and like my mother, perhaps, a person who enjoys the chase of narrative. She posits and interjects tangentially in her own view of the crime. Friday interrupts and asks for "just the facts, ma'm." This is not unlike the man from whom I received half my DNA. My father, Duane, for whom I am named. My father loves *Dragnet*, which strikes me now as no surprise, the show we watched every week in syndication from our living room in the Ozark Mountains of Missouri.

A few weeks ago I emailed my father, asking about his military service, particularly his time in Southeast Asia. Like many soldiers having served in any war, and perhaps especially those who served the American conflict in Vietnam, he's never spoken at length about this period. I assume it was pivotal and that even this assumption is a gross understatement and over-generalization. And what, of me, does the fact of emailing betray? Could I not have picked up my cell, dialed the only home telephone number I can ever remember my parents having? Would my father have not picked up, and in the low whistle of his central Missouri drawl, say, "Hell-low?" A question instead of a statement. Could I not have asked, when home visiting just weeks ago, the question already on my mind, without a doubt, for my father to explicate his military career? Over coffee, perhaps? On the back deck? No. I emailed my father because a question of this kind, in a category I cannot even begin to define, makes us both too uncomfortable. Or rather, it makes me uncomfortable, to be clear, to place blame, if that is what it can be called, on me and not my father, sitting on his plaid sofa in the den back in Missouri, a sleeping dog at each of his flanks, a large-print Western novel open upon his lap.

When I emailed my father to ask about Vietnam, I should not have expected elaboration, a narrative of any sort. Instead, via post a week later, I received two handwritten pages, amounting to a timeline of his journey in the United States Air Force. I decided to attempt what I already knew impossible: to chase the narrative of my father, or at least, this part of him. I decided to place my word alongside his, though I fear, there is no map to this place deep inside of him.

I enlisted in the Air Force on 10 February 1959. A group of enlistees were sent to the Kansas City Induction Center by bus, where we received our physical examinations and swearing in. We left Kansas City by train for San Antonio: basic training at Lackland Air Force Base.

At the beginning of basic training, every enlistee in the United States Air Force swears, aloud and en masse, an oath. Called "The Airman's Creed," it begins: "I am an American Airman. I am a Warrior. I have answered my Nation's call. I am an American Airman. My mission is to Fly, Fight, and Win." My father wanted to fly, to leave behind the fields of the family farm in Billings, where he watched the cropdusters fly over, dreaming of his own escape. He was short, 5'6", and thought by his own sympathetic mother, perfectly built to be a pilot. At his physical in Kansas City, however, it became apparent he could not see well. On his medical write-up, the doctor likely wrote "not eligible for flight school." Or, "young man, what have you gotten yourself into?"

Dad boarded the train in Kansas City. He rode along the great prairie that sits east of the continental divide and knew he would never fly.

But there is, here, a point of legacy. In 1959, Private First Class Duane Gilson, my father, received what the military refers to as Regulation Prescription Glasses to correct his vision. These are frames made of sturdy black plastic, known for durability and cost-effectiveness. They are called Regulation Prescription Glasses, or RPGs, or Rape Prevention Glasses, or birth control glasses, or BCGs.

One spring in college, I found my father's BCGs in the back of a filing cabinet and asked if I could have them. Perhaps, I thought, they would give me a certain air: trustworthiness earned by a life fought for and lived. I took them to the optometrist and had them filled with the prescription that corrects my vision. I have worn them ever since, and when my father looks at me in them, I am unsure if he is flattered—*my son wants to be like me!*—or if the emotion is something altogether different, inverse to joy, unsayable.

Following basic training, I was transferred across base to attend basic apprentice medical training. We had an opportunity to choose different specialties. I chose veterinary service, and was sent to Gunter Air Force

Base in Montgomery for Veterinary Apprentice Training. This was the summer of 1959.

The Air Force Medical Service, or AFMS, became an official entity on July 1, 1949, when the Air Force itself was only two years old. The division was subdivided into six major corps: the Medical Corps, Dental Corps, Nurse Corps, Medical Service Corps, Women's Medical Specialist Corps, and Veterinary Corps. The Air Force Veterinary Corps was always a somewhat vague part of the military industrial complex. During my father's tenure, from 1959 until 1979, their primary responsibilities were animal medicine, treating and rigorously training military dogs; food quality and sanitation, often seen as outside the scope of the Corps and fodder for both internal and external complaint; general public health initiatives; and animal research. The Vet Corps was small, and my father toward the top of its hierarchy. And I cherish this fact, his position, though the Corps no longer exists, disbanded in 1980 from lack of need and direction.

I have gleaned my father joined the military to escape the strict hand of his own father, a rigid man whom I only remember and, even then, only vaguely. My grandfather: spouting racial epitaphs to a busboy at Western Sizzlin, rolling his eyes at my grandmother, beloved by both me and my father, her middle son. I have gleaned my own father longed to learn and that for the seventh of fourteen children living on a farm in rural, central Missouri, college was not a possibility. The military was a way out. By the mid-'50s, the Korean War was over, and a conflict in Vietnam barely bubbled under the collective American consciousness. My father, to this day, is a quietly peaceful man; that he chose the Vet Corps is of little surprise.

But the map into this part of him becomes blurry. What is this place even? I fear the country's name: *Place-You-Will-Never-Know.*

In December 1970, I departed for assignment to Bien Hoa Air Base, Vietnam.

There is one picture of Dad that I hold dear, possibly more than any other possession. He has traveled to Bien Hoa but is now in a rural village, a haven for children made parentless at the hands of a world political system that regards the process of orphan making as a necessary part of progress. In the photo, my father holds a piglet between his knees. His back is to the camera. A group of Catholic nuns, dressed in shockingly bright white smocks, compose the remainder of the foreground; they watch my farther, and learn how to vaccinate the pig against jungle diseases. In the background, within the doorway of an ordinary building, two children, about eight years old, watch the scene between them and the camera unfold, their eyes wide, their smiles shy, yet obvious.

And though I cannot see the look on his face, I know my father is happy here. Helping, even if the circumstances are shit. Helping, the thing he continues to love today.

As I write this, I sit in a coffee shop in Pittsburgh. I moved here from Missouri two years ago to pursue a second graduate degree. My father helped me move to Pittsburgh. Early one sticky August morning, we stood in his garage, in the middle of a little town named Nixa, Missouri. We bickered as we crammed the last of what could conceivably fit into the back of my Jeep Cherokee, two people, both men now, thinking they were experts on packing one's life into a small space. I relented and let Dad reorganize the trunk. When it came to the open interstate, however, I did not relinquish control of the radio, though we listened to that which binds us: Johnny Cash, Bob Dylan, Simon & Garfunkel, and Ira Glass in past episodes of *This American Life*.

Twice I have seriously considered joining the armed forces. Once, in my junior year of high school, when I was deadset on attending the United States Naval Academy in Annapolis. Once more, in my senior year of college, when I spoke with a recruiter from the Air Force Officer Corps. "Son, we would love to have you as a writer in our information services division," he said. But our country was fighting two, seemingly unending wars under the umbrella of a larger *War on Terror*. "Bullshit," my father told me, "they need soldiers, son. Combat. Don't do this." And I didn't.

Somewhere on Interstate 70, around Dayton, Ohio, I turned to my father, "I am going to be a teacher," I said, "Do you like that?" My father, who is not apt to show emotion and who never said anything of this sort before, who hasn't since, and won't, I imagine, again, said this to me, "Yes. I am proud."

Here I am, in a coffeeshop in Pittsburgh. My father's thick black glasses bare fact upon my face. His handwritten timeline lies on the table before me. I pick it up, thumb the script, the place where his hand has brought—*himself?*—to the page. We are all reaching out, and it is, perhaps, the truest cliché. We are all trying, or should be trying, to understand one another.

At the end of 1971, I returned stateside, to Keesler Air Force Base in Biloxi, Mississipi.

This sentence isd the only explanation after his departure for Vietnam. There is nothing written in between leaving the United States and returning. In his poem "Vietnam Epic Treatment," Donald Revell goes to a similar line of questioning: "The 20th century? / It was a war / Between peasants on the one side, / Hallucinations on the other." I remember eighth grade.

I remember eighth grade and Coach West, our history teacher, assigning us a research project. Seven pages on a historical issue from the twentieth century. I chose to write about the American conflict in Vietnam and gave myself over to facts. From 1955 until 1975. Some 58,000 American soldiers killed. Some two million plus dead Vietnamese civilians. Tet Offensive, Anti-Communist Sentiment,

Kent State Protests. I am in the eighth grade and cannot understand countless complexities.

I am in the eighth grade and walk into the den, notebook in hand, to speak with my father. "So Walter Cronkite claims we didn't win the war in Vietnam, but I'm finding conflicting information. What happened?"

My father looked at me, his eyes widened. It was not anger. It was bewilderment, or some emotion, unnamable, akin to astonishment. "Son," he said, "I can't..." and his dialogue trailed off. He calmly put down the book in his hands, unfurled from his easy chair, walked to the garage, and locked himself inside.

I don't know if my father was always a quiet man, though I suspect he was. Statistically, his involvement in Vietnam likely deepened this introversion. Vietnam, the American conflict with the highest rates of post-traumatic stress disorder among its returning veterans. Vietnam, according to the United States Department of Veterans Affairs and explicitly explained in the findings of their "National Vietnam Veterans' Readjustment Study," is also the war with the highest rates of psychological problems and disorders that go unreported, and therefore untreated, amongst veterans from nearly all demographic subcategories, across class and race and any number of indicators. Most-prevalent lifetime disorder, they say: antisocial personality disorder. I will never know if my father is just a quiet man, or if he is quiet with just, and external, cause.

But I am trying to write this. I am trying to fill in the holes, to chase the narrative. I am trying to draw the map to that place deep inside of my father and to march through the newly-found path. Though I fear this place is called *You-Will-Never-Understand*, I do know this: a river leads me there, a steady stream named *You-Must-Never-Stop-Trying*.

When I am home visiting for the holidays, I wonder, why do I think of all this now? Why is it suddenly so important, so urgent? It is Christmas: my nephew Kyler, fresh back from Afghanistan, and I drink beer on the back porch. The last time I saw him, Kyler was a senior in high school. It's been over two years since, and he's filled out, become chiseled in the chest and arms. His blue eyes, rare in our family, shine bright, though they're sunk a little further back in their sockets now. I ask Kyler, "how's it going, man?"

He says, "ah, you know."

No, I don't know, Kyler. I don't know, sir. I don't know, Dad. But I need to. "Tell me," I implore. You must.

Lost and Found

Marc Nieson

In 1991, I drove from Midtown to the Midwest with a vague sense of finding someplace where I could feel more grounded in my life. Today, we might call it entering a new GPS, but back then locating oneself on the map wasn't quite so precise or swift a process. Indeed, I'd spent years bouncing between cities as exotic and far afield as Manhattan and Venice, yet each was an outpost where I again grew misdirected, lost. I decided to try out school again and applied to a graduate writing program in Iowa. The Midwest struck me as a new kind of landscape, offering fresh vistas and horizons, perspective even. And a steady pulse. The heartland.

I can still recall those burgeoning acres opening before me. Outside the car window, row after row of cropland was whizzing by, strobe-like and hypnotic, lush. As did Ohio, Indiana, Illinois. Then I abandoned the interstate altogether, meandering north into the dairy land of southwestern Wisconsin. With each passing farmstead the horizon grew more rolling and manicured, the air thick and fertile. Finally I crossed the Mississippi River at the very spot Joliet and Marquette first documented 300 years earlier. On the other side of the bridge stood a shiny green road sign reading "*IOWA: A Place to Grow.*"

Huh, I thought, maybe this is the ticket.

Bypassing any instinct toward an Iowa City apartment, I proceeded to find myself something more remote—say, a rural rental some 15 miles outside town. An old one-room schoolhouse, in fact, perched on a hillside overlooking hundreds of acres of pasture and woodland and nearby crops. Yet I took up residence in early autumn, the neighboring combines quickly sheering every cornstalk to stubble.

Snow soon followed. Faint flurries quickly gathered into multiple inches and drifts. Temperatures and wind chills I'd never before imagined, let alone endured. Winter blanketed everything, and even my skin thickened. Huddled inside my schoolhouse, I felt as bound and beleaguered by my bearings as ever. Perhaps even worse.

All the while, though, I nurtured that tiny glimpse of green road sign within—*A Place to Grow*. I'd slide my black and white fiction drafts aside to thumb through Technicolor field guides instead. I took diligent notes on any and all of the local flora, as if by memorizing their names I might somehow conjure them from below the frost line. I intoned my stubborn mantra to the schoolhouse's four walls: Sprout. Sprout. Sprout.

Finally spring arrived, her budding display deep and wide as my desire. First, the curly hairs of hepatica pushed through the last few patches of snow, and within days were followed by violets and bellworts, Dutchman's britches, anemone. Daily the woods' floor exploded into a palette of lavenders, whites, and yellows. Then came scarlet cup mushrooms, burgundy trilliums, nearly any color you could imagine. Soon I was filling my nostrils and arms alike. I gathered young dandelion leaves to spice up my salads, and sprigs of curly dock and nettle tips to steam with splashes of lemon. Then one day, I heard someone whispering about another delicacy sprouting in the woods. Some mushroom called the morel.

Some say they arrive when the bluebells first bloom. Or when young oak leaves get about the size of squirrel ears. Some say they favor northern slopes, others say western. Some swear morels hide under Mayapples, others near dead elms, and still others flanking young moss. Some wield divining rods before them like the blind, others tote lucky talismans in back pockets. As far as I could tell, every mushroom hunter had his own opinion as to how to find morels, but not a single one would divulge precisely *where*.

Tina, my landlady, was kind enough to show me what one looked like, holding out its odd honeycombed head and squat stem in her palm.

"That small, huh?" I said.

"Some," she said.

"I thought they were supposed to be flesh-colored?"

"That's another species, the yellows. This one's a grey. It's more rare and pungent. You'll only find these for a few more days. The yellows will follow and last a couple weeks, depending on the heat and rain. But that's it. Not much of a season for slackers."

"Where'd you find this one?" I blurted.

She stared at me as if I were something worse than a slacker even.

"Can't answer that, can you?"

"Nope," she said, and started walking away. "They're out there though. You just have to look for them."

I started out haphazardly glancing at the slopes and stands nearest the schoolhouse. After I spied a couple of the greys, though, it was like I got sprayed with magic fairy spores and turned into a little child again, darting about on a secret scavenger hunt. Soon I was hugging old fence lines and combing through the spreading bloodroot and Virginia creeper. I foraged as close to the ground as a chipmunk, rubbing jewelweed on my forearms to counter any poison ivy. After a while, I began to spot morels where there weren't any—those twisted forms and leaning heads surely beneath that next leaf.

Come evening, I'd spill my cache onto the stone tabletop, then arrange two buckets of water for their washing. I sliced each mushroom lengthwise and stripped tiny slugs from their bellies, squadrons of spilled ants soon commandeering the schoolhouse floor. But it didn't matter. I had my morels. Sautéed in olive oil and pepper, they dripped with a flavor as thick and enchanting as smoke.

Late one morning, I came back from mushrooming to find one of my current professors sitting outside the schoolhouse. As it turns out, James Alan McPherson was also an old friend of Tina's, and had come over for a tea with her on the schoolhouse deck. Over the course of the semester, I'd grown to admire and enjoy his presence, too. In a heartbeat, he'd shift from an almost painful shyness to an irreverent humor, telling off-color jokes or quoting the Bible to help prove a point—risky things in these lean years of political correctness in the academy—yet always remaining deeply vulnerable and giving.

I'd also responded strongly to his writings and teaching style. He didn't harp on our drafts' technique and content so much as on their context and accountability. Our assigned reading list spanned the globe and several centuries, and his dizzying seminars were jazz riffs on questions of ethics and race and communal responsibility. Or perhaps the blues might pose a truer metaphor, both for his voiced pangs and hopes. His empathies.

Beneath such tutelage, I felt something deeper taking root in me. Not just lessons in point-of-view and voice but on the intersection of place and character. On what might hold and center one beyond any given landscape or address. Call it gravity. Or one's moral compass.

"What's in the bag?" he asked as I approached.

"Lunch."

I extracted a couple of morels and set them on the deck rail. McPherson dipped his head to peer over his glasses.

"Strange looking mothers," he said.

"Yeah, they are, aren't they?"

"And they're safe to eat?"

"Better than safe, Mr. McPherson."

I showed him the rest of my stash, naming each leaf and flower of the greens I'd gathered for a salad.

"You're really into this stuff, huh?" he said.

I looked up at him, then past his shoulder at the splashes of purple thistle on the hillside. On one perched a perfect goldfinch.

"Yeah," I said. "Yeah, I guess I am."

"Well, maybe you should write about mushrooms then. About this place." His voice sounded both muted and mischievous. I gauged the slight curl to his lip, the warmth in his eyes. Another kind of heartland.

"Actually I have," I admitted. "But only in my journals."

"That's OK. Grist for the mill. Grease for the pan."

"Oh, I don't know," I said. "I'm not so sure anymore. The more I document, the less I seem to know, or at least grasp. I mean, to tell the truth, lately I'd much rather just live it than record it."

McPherson chuckled.

"Well, there's that," he said. "There's documenting and then there's interpreting. The difference between what you find, and what you make of it. What you do with it."

Mnisota

Benjamin Vogt

> "Ole is walking by Sven's house one Saturday afternoon and
> notices a sign out front that reads 'Boat For Sale.' Ole hollers
> to Sven, 'Ey der Ole, ya' don't have a boat. All ya' got is a lawn-
> mower and snowmobile.' Sven replies, 'Yep. Der boat fer sale.'"
> —Garrison Keillor, *Prairie Home Companion*

At my parent's house there is always the echo of Canada geese,
their splashing forms on Lotus Lake muted by maples and birch. Even
in early winter the geese are still on the move, as some stick around
foraging from lake to lake. In cool mornings, just before sunrise, my
foggy senses catch their stark, vibrating calls and direction to one
another—it is especially piercing then, a still deeply foreign presence
that reminds me of who and what I've adopted, where I'm from.

When my family moved from semi-arid Oklahoma to abundantly
moist Minnesota when I was ten, there were immediate physical sen-
sations that washed over me and planted themselves into my psyche.
I suppose this is the same sort of event that happens to babies; I've
heard psychologists say that our first impressions are our deepest,
lasting for the rest of our lives in the subconscious and coloring how
we perceive each subsequent encounter.

In any case, when we moved it was August. In Minnesota, this
month can veer into two distinct modes—god-awful muggy and rav-
aged by the last batch of mosquitoes, or precariously crisp and brisk

in preparation for a long fall. In 1986, it was the latter. We moved into a moldy duplex for a few months (complete with mothballs), and outside were clumps of mysteriously sharp trees—pine and spruce. The needles littered the ground, and the moist shade of those conifers was a musk I'd never experienced before, an almost unexplainable scent. It is a decomposition and a composition, a rest and a feverish action, fear and liberation, trepidation and discovery. It was cool in these shadows, the sweetness of the sharp aroma indelibly marked on me, just like the sudden overhead calls of passing birds, the same size as pterodactyls.

I'd never seen birds so large, so uniform, like an army pacing the sky. Their first calls made me rush out from the tree's shadows into the low light of early autumn and feel something charge within me. As those geese slid south, my heart was still racing to head north and catch up to my body in this strange place. My mother had grown up in Wisconsin, just next door, and explained to me what these birds were, as much as she knew—but what was sure in her voice was that she was closer to home than she'd been for a long time, and I was further.

This disembodied, disconnected sensation was wonderful. It was liberating. It would take months, even years, for me to realize how horrible that can be at the same time.

Each spring, and especially each fall, the geese came ordered in their appearance, chaotic in their calling, bridging the gap of their lives. Sometimes they'd fly so low I could hear their wings, the combined catching of their feathers like leaves in the breeze, pulling and pushing upon the air. They were just out of reach, moving at a pace I felt I could catch up to if I willed it a little bit harder.

The Canada goose has been clocked flying as fast as sixty to seventy miles per hour but rarely keeps up that speed. They are exceedingly efficient as the lead bird breaks the wind and reduces drag for those behind. Such work is exhausting, and after a while the leader will drop to the back and be replaced as each takes its turn along the lines, falling back, sliding up, keeping the pace. I always stop what I'm doing and look up when I hear geese approach, admiring the elegance of the V, that arrow of purpose and faith so ingeniously discovered and adapted to over millennia. The formation helps them expend much less energy, thus being able to cover as many as 650 miles a day with little rest. Most geese in the Midwest and Great Plains follow the Mississippi, whose banks are full of shelter and food and open landing spaces. Since the Mississippi begins in northern Minnesota, at Lake Itasca, I've come to feel that the geese begin with me as well, as if I let them go, and with the geese some part of me that never could have been nurtured in another place.

My parents took a huge risk moving north. My dad had built homes since he was a boy, along with farming wheat. After they sold the tractors and combines to pay off debt amidst the farm crisis of the early 1980s, and as the housing market subsequently cooled in Oklahoma, they ventured north. They were nearly the same age I am now. My dad arrived several months ahead to make contacts and scout the market, then to begin building his first spec house. I celebrated my tenth birthday without him and, a few weeks later, preceded the Mayflower moving van into a former prairie called Eden Prairie—a large western suburb of Minneapolis. My parents had spent all of their money on the move and financing the business. As the first house was finished we moved in until it sold, then moved into the next house until it sold.

In the summer, just after hatching, several species of adult geese molt and lose their feathers. As they and their flightless goslings bobble about on the ground evading predators, they are pretty much stuck in the same boat. By the time the goslings get their flight feathers, the parents have regrown theirs. This explains a mid summer line of geese that walked through a very busy local highway. Cars normally going sixty miles per hour stopped in each direction for a full minute as seemingly defiant parents led their families across six lanes of asphalt from one catch pond to the other—no one in our car had ever seen anything like it. This wasn't a country road, waiting for a lone and disinterested cow to move to the side. There was purpose, even dignity in this brave parade. It's hard to imagine that in the 1960s, Canada geese were nearly extinct, as they now thrive in the world of golf courses and housing subdivisions, living comfortably and amiably among our flattened landscapes

Whenever I wake up cold and unsure in the mornings, I smell the damp pine needles of those first months, and when in my hazy pre waking I hear the geese call, I am at once comforted and frozen in trepidation of the new day. Their call is a call south, hungry and driven by some hormone deep inside them that's triggered perhaps by the waning summer sun. Parents mate for life, teach their children the way south and back again. Children nest where they were born, and their lives and their purposes form complete circles, perfect in shape and efficiency of being. Even now, years later and having just woken on a chilled fall morning far from Minnesota, their chaotic calls break the air around me, ease me into my life and a new day I remember having intensely lived before. In leaving, they've brought me closer to my home.

The fourth house we settled in is where I eventually grew up, and it is in a valley. Or, more clearly, it is in a valley overlooking a valley. Glaciers carved out over 14,000 lakes in Minnesota—though this is officially the land of 10,000—leaving, at one point, a much wider and deeper Lotus Lake that once would have submerged the neighborhood. Our house is in the second level valley, overlooked by a ridge of trees to the west, and itself sitting on a rim of trees—replete with new houses growing like mushrooms—all overlooking the water. It's like a football stadium.

On some mornings in early spring, after the last sheets of ice have melted off, the whole watershed takes on a crisper, newer feel. I can't fully explain it, but the shadow of the brown water, like a large pupil, finally opens to the world, seeing out, released from the gray film of the ice. The trees and soil and the shadows of each seem to link up, reverberate with the reflection of water, sparkle in the light coming off the waves below a stronger mid day sun. Lotus is only about a mile long, angled southeast to northwest, and not even thirty feet deep at its middle. I imagine that the snowmobiles and ice houses, lost to brave souls out on the ice too early or too late, will someday emerge as an island in the middle, much like how the Hawaiian islands formed as volcanoes grew beneath the ocean's surface. The first winter here, back in 1989, my sister, dad, and I walked halfway down the ice-covered lake, holding close to the shore. When we reached what looked like an active storm drain, the ground below began to creak violently—at least to my wary ears—and we hustled back the way we came, careful to retrace our steps on the ice until we heard nothing but our own footsteps.

During the summers my dad and I would fish on Lotus along the edges of lily pads, eventually sporting the lotus flowers which gave the lake its name, but which could, in fact, have given every lake in Minnesota its name. We'd sit on the boat, he up in the bow, me dangling my legs off the back, both risking our casts as close to the lily edge as possible where largemouth bass strike when the bait first hits the water. Every other cast for me came with praise for hitting the four foot swath of bare water between the shore and lilies, followed by agonized frustration that, once again, I snagged a lily stem below water and we'd have to practically beach the boat to rescue the lure. It's a felony to pull out lilies, but I never felt guilty, unable to understand the law's inconsistency: our neighbors on the north end could chemically clear a lane of them to gain access to their shallow dock.

Lotus used to be much larger, partly because it used to be part of Christmas Lake, a few blocks north, and the massive body of Lake Minnetonka, a bit past that. Water still flows underground between all three, but Lotus gets most of its body from the hills around it, directing rain, car oil, fertilizer, and soap toward itself. At 246 acres, Lotus is well over twice its phosphorous limit, and the few marshes around it, partly due to the hilly terrain, can't filter out much so the lake suffers periodic fish kills, like the one in 1999 that saw masses of crappie wash ashore. This was a sad event for me, as I fondly remember the time when over just a few hours I reeled in thirty or more crappie on a windy, cold, cloudy day as we trawled back and forth over a large school. I probably caught the same fish twice, even three times that day, but it was the only time I felt like a true fisherman.

Lotus sits in the northern part of Chanhassen (rhymes with *ban-lass-in*), in northeastern Carver County, about thirty to forty minutes due west of Minneapolis, and on land that was formerly home to the Dakota Sioux—a group that included the Isanti and the Santee, who had once come all the way from South Carolina. The history of the region is much like the history of any region west of the original thirteen colonies. The Northwest Ordinance of 1787 cleared the way for settlers northwest of the Ohio River. At the time, the Ojibwe and Sioux split Minnesota along a northwest to southeast diagonal. The Ojibwe, having pushed the Sioux west with the help of French-made guns, were in the northeast stretching back into present day Michigan and Canada, while various Sioux tribes to the south and west fanned out through Iowa, Nebraska, the Dakotas, Wyoming, and Montana.

In 1849 the U.S. government created the Organic Act, which outlined the physical location of the Minnesota territory and simultaneously created a government, while stipulating $5,000 for a state library and $20,000 for a capital building in St. Paul. I see very little that's "organic" about this act, though. In 1850 the seven council fires of the Sioux nation, subcultures of the larger whole, had their last annual council meeting and sun dance in northern Iowa. It's unlikely that this is a coincidence.

Chanhassen was first settled by those of European descent in 1852. Did Joseph Vogel, settling near the Shakopee Station just south of present day Chan (what the locals have come to call it), and Joseph Kessler, four miles northwest of Vogel, create some sort of settlement pact? I wonder if they did, or at least, if the two families—like distant monarchs—created a combined dynasty when Vogel married Kessler's sister, Veronica. It helped, I'm sure, that both families were German immigrants and that both patriarchs shared the same first name. Perhaps they had too much in common on this virgin prairie.

A year later, in 1853, the Indian land title ended, freeing up settlers to come pouring in by the wagon-train load. It's during this time that a woman named Clarissa Cleaveland, in an act of displaced irony, chose the name of Chanhassen for the developing area—a name derived from the Dakota Sioux word for the sugar maple. Today, the Mdewakanton or Shakopee Sioux, just 20 minutes south along the Minnesota River, are buying up as much land as possible with profits from a casino, expanding the borders of their rare suburban reservation.

I wonder what the first Chanhassen town meeting was like back in 1858, at Carver County's only school house, when the first law was to allow all animals except pigs to run free from April 1 to November 1 each year. (A year later the pigs were set free.) In 1896 the village was incorporated, sporting Pauley's General Store, the requisite saloon, feed store, lumber yard, and the State Bank of Chanhassen. Did it look like those old west sets I've seen in a dozen movies? Was it a dusty rectangle carved out of lush green prairie? When the Milwaukee and St. Paul Railroad trains stopped, did the steam engine chug and whistle through the streets like Lutheran church bells on Sunday? The town was a beacon on the prairie, decried Reverand H. M. Nichols in 1855: "Two years ago, Chanhassen was nowhere. Now, there is hardly a vacant claim left in the township. The settlers are far above average of new settlements, in respectability, morality, and intelligence; and rarely can a pleasanter or more desirable community be found than that now settled in Chanhassen." Chanhassen was recently home to a Jehovah's Witness convert, Prince, his recording studio Paisley Park, and his compound replete with a windmill.

After negotiating a treaty that confined the Dakota Sioux to unfamiliar country, the U.S. government agreed in turn to provide them with annuity payments to buy staples that they, no longer with suitable access to hunting grounds and arable lands, could not produce for themselves. After crop failures, a long winter, the diversion of resources to the Civil War, and the refusal to allow payment for grain by credit, in August of 1862 five settlers in a hunting party were killed by four Dakota. Later that night Little Crow—leader of the Mdewankaton Sioux—convened a war council that reluctantly decided to attack settlements along the Minnesota River Valley to drive the settlers away. Little Crow knew they were outgunned and outnumbered.

The Sioux won a few battles in the six week Dakota War, even burning New Ulm but after only a month were routed at the Battle of Wood Lake, so Little Crow fled to Canada. It's estimated that 300-800 civilians were killed during the war, the highest number of civilian deaths until September 11, 2001. After the conflict, and by the end of December, over 1,000 Sioux were in jail. While 303 of those were found guilty of rape and murder, their courtroom appearances lasted no longer than five minutes, and were not allowed legal representation or explanation. Abraham Lincoln personally reviewed the records before deciding that 264 sentences should be commuted. Of those commuted, nearly one-third died of disease after four year prison terms in Illinois. On December 26, the other 38 Dakota were hung simultaneously in Mankato as part of the largest mass execution in U.S. history. Buried in a single grave at the edge of town, several bodies were later exhumed because there was a shortage of cadavers for anatomical study by local doctors. This was a common practice of the time, and one of the beneficiaries was William Worrall Mayo, of Mayo Clinic fame.

After the executions in 1863, most Sioux were forced west out of Minnesota when the U.S. government declared all previous treaties null and void, and offered a bounty of $25 per Sioux scalp. In July, Little Crow and his son returned from Canada and were foraging for berries near Hutchinson. Trespassing, Little Crow was mortally wounded by the local farmer. (His son escaped.) His body was carried to town and mutilated by the residents, while the farmer received the standard bounty for Little Crow's scalp, plus a $500 bonus when it was found out who he had killed. The scalp went to the Minnesota Historical Society in 1868, and the skull in 1896, both returned almost a century later to Little Crow's grandson. A small stone tablet sits at the roadside of the field where Little Crow was shot, and in 1937 Hutchinson erected a bronze statue of him overlooking the Crow River.

I don't know if I loved growing up in Chanhassen, but it was home, and my most tumultuous and important years are tied to this place. Maybe any city nearby would have done just as well. I was not born here, I simply lived here for nine years. My Oklahoma accent was cancelled out by the Minnesota accent I encountered, so now I speak "normal," whatever that may be. No one, by listening to me, can tell where I'm from, though I have a tendency to slur my "rural" and favor my "rut beer," but also occasionally say "botuh" (rising cadence on the 'o'). And in many ways, I've become less sure of where home is, my youth cut perfectly in half and spread over a continent.

But I know I am a Minnesotan. I may not wear shorts on the first thirty degree day in early February, or know many Olie and Sven jokes. I don't enjoy ice fishing or following closely behind snowplows going sixty miles per hour—but I am from this place. My first winter in Minnesota, our fourth grade class spent a long weekend near the Boundary Waters Canoe Area Wilderness along the Canadian border. This was my sudden, trial-by-ice immersion into the culture. I had my southern accent, leaned on my "y'all" when telling my teachers I'd be fine not climbing the sky-high ropes course in minus thirty degree wind chills. But at camp, I found I enjoyed snowshoeing and especially liked cross-country skiing, drinking Barq's from the vending machine, and comparing the similar indoor and outdoor temperatures on my new thermometer key chain.

But I am a Minnesotan—I can pass the tests. I know what "oofta" means although I don't use it in my vernacular. I won't touch lutefisk, but I would, actually, like to have my head carved in butter. I will eat Spam if I must. I've visited Paul Bunyan in Brainerd. I was here for the Great Halloween Blizzard when the Twins won their second World Series—I remember tickertape parades in the halls of grade school. I appreciate the biker-gang-leader-looking Ragnar the Viking, the only human mascot in professional sports (in real life Joe Juranitch, Hopkins school district assistant dean and holder of the world record for shaving a beard with an axe). I own a Helga hat. I get smug when people complain about their "terrible winters," and I go on a diatribe.

I can smell Minnesota wherever I am. I can taste it and touch it in my daydreams. The damp, musty chill of autumn rains anywhere is Minnesota. The dark winter days with wind-driven snow penetrating the sweaty scarf, stinging the face like glass shards, is Minnesota. I can almost savor the sweet penetrating itch of the state bird—not the ghostly-calling loon, but the mosquito. I love a blueberry muffin (the state muffin) in the morning. There's nothing like fresh walleye (state fish), though I've never caught one. I am a Minnesotan because I awoke here, or was awakened by the place, and those first memories are stamped so deeply on my psyche that I experience all new places with the echo of this state. But I can never really be a Minnesotan.

The name "Minnesota" comes from the name of a river in Isanti Sioux territory, Mnisota—"*mni*" for water, and "*sota*" for hazy/smoky. And yet this is how I see my life in this place, trying not to, a land covered in water filled with hazy memories and discoveries that form a distorted image of where I'm from and who I am.

Learning Shift

Will Jennings

"The moment there is an 'other', all movement becomes gesture."—Robert Karp

Trempeleau County, Wisconsin 1971. County D out of Ettrick runs north through the Co-op Dairy's offload docks so that it looks more like the start of a factory yard than a maintained road. The grade is deceptive, too. Steep and hard-chined, it quickly ramps where the milk trucks have to maneuver, minding the slosh of their ballast against the tread grip on gravel. Turning off of 53 in Tom's Fairlane, you had to be mindful of your speed. Too fast and you'd spin in the deltas and washboard churned up by backing trucks, too slow and you'd have to down clutch into first and then coax the next quarter-mile until the hill settled near the cemetery, where contour might allow you to exhale and then slip with some ease into third.

I learned to drive a stick shift on the roads around Tom's farm, to read the stutter of a clutch and the slake of giving it gas enough to finish any given sentence. It helped to know the roads, too. Where the turns were banked and where they leveled enough to throw you, where the slow dips and hillocks of frost heave and culvert humps could be hit just so to give your guts a quick glimpse of weightlessness.

When I was sent off on errands on my own, I was given the keys to the Fairlane the same way I was told to take a borrowed Farmall M up to the Knob Pasture to cut clover. I was being given a machine that was vital. The driving of any machine was utilitarian and the strict economy of a small dairy farm demanded constant reminder that downfall lingered in the meanders: the frivolity of time spent jawing over a third cup of bakery-made coffee in Blair, the hubris of painting a second coat on the sides of buildings that didn't face the road, the sacrilege of Sunday spent in church during haying season when Monday called for rain.

A coulee is a small, narrowish valley that draws up to a pinch at one end. The aerial photos of this topography look arterial, then capillary, like the etchings of frost on a window where there is more breath than heat. Tom's farm was set midway from the effluvial mouth of Helstad Coulee, and where it dwindled near the base of three sandstone pillars the locals had named Chapultepec. Among farms settled by Scandinavians, naming one of the more visible landmarks after something as exotic as a Mexican castle suggests the whimsy of people isolated by the makings of their lives, and all the more so within a landscape that is slow to wake beneath the sodden quilts of winter and can burrow into dreary well past the latest of Easters.

Gas, give it more gas.

We're galumphing at a steep pitch, the Fairlane bucking like a pissed off goat.

Not so much clutch...more gas...no, the clutch...Jesus, can't you feel that?

OF COURSE I CAN. The car is now wildly oscillating in a comic peristalsis as if it were a stomach and Tom and I the lunch it wants to lose.

From somewhere acrid and metallic snorts an odd "spittoink" and then the Fairlane shirks an exasperated shudder and then. Just. Stops.

We are then rolling slowly backward down the narrow blacktop.

The hand break, Tom hisses patiently through clenched teeth, but before that sentiment can fully deflate, he yanks the break handle with a punctuated ratchet and glares with glazed incredulity. I'm suddenly foreign, mute, and as teachable as any half-cooked turnip.

There is balance in any act, driving, teaching, and being taught. And part of that balance has to do with anticipation. It's good to look ahead and lean into things, but you need to be ready to be pushed back, too. When I learned to drive a stick shift in those hills and valleys, Tom knew well enough to be hawkish and stern and to impart a particular impression about how things are and should be when done well. But he also knew enough to hand over the keys and say, *We need a dozen eggs and 2lbs of pork steak from the IGA in Blair, and Twesme's Feed should have the bailing twine I ordered last week.* And that would be that. I had a set of tasks and would be given the use of a common, though precious, machine.

Learning the pedals, to feel the proper catch of a belt or the spinning plates of a clutch, was to listen with your entire body and to never climb atop or inside a machine as much as take it on as an appendage. Tractors in this part of dairy country were necessary, but they were serious business. Growing up without a basement or a garage, with a father who couldn't bear to watch me wield anything sharper than a baseball bat, the lure of something as complex and deeply throated as a tractor was, well, powerful. But, frightening, too.

I've heard woodworkers and farmers say that injuries befall those who are too bold or too timid, too familiar or too naive. The taverns in Ettrick and Blair would be most full on the rainy days of haying season, but nearly any mid-afternoon you could watch a small collection of those missing fingers, hands, or most of an arm, playing cribbage or Euchre. Men with names like Emil and Leighton, Cyril, and Ray. If you had the temerity to ask, their stories would begin like this: October evening, I was clearing the last of the end rows when the corn picker clogged; or, we were off-loading grain when the auger shook hands with the sleeve of my chore coat; or, right before supper, lubing the PTO when she spat a cotter pin and bit me just like *that*.

Tractors tip, too. In the hillier sections of dairy farms a tractor can do two important things: it can help plant an extra 20 acres of feed, and it can tip over and pin you. That's what Glenn Jorgenson said and when I heard him say it, my veins were throbbing with adrenaline because I'd almost accomplished the latter while driving the M up a cow trail to begin the job of the former. I'd started easy up the grade at first with Glenn riding on a rod above a spring leaf, behind me and holding to the bouncing back of the seat, telling me what to do next. The M had a finicky clutch, and it'd slip under stress in low gear.

Goose the throttle...giver a little bit there.

And I gently nudged the throttle with my right palm.

Nah, giver like ya mean it...

So I did. And apparently I meant it just a little too much because the M's front end popped into the air like Roy-on-Trigger and before I knew it Glenn was leaping off the back and into a patch of raspberry bushes. His 200 lbs off the back were enough to bring the front wheels down. And I knew enough right then and there to kill the throttle and lock in both brakes. Glenn would be taking her up the rest of the way and I would be walking unless I wanted to listen to all the reasons why city kids shouldn't be allowed any nearer to a farm than a postcard he'd be all too willing to send.

Instead, this is the postcard I write some forty years after the fact:

Ridge cuts, second clover

Dusk. Rodding the throttle of a Farmall up the dozered cuts to the tops, I'm hauling a crimper three lengths back of Tom's sickle-barred Deere. His pass provides the cut while mine will split the green stems through knobby wringers and help the sun.

A day to dry in scatters, and then we'll rake and bail to the clank and bristle of cobbled gear: Tom's eyes etched to the haybiner, chugging out its line of bricks for me to catch by hand hook and knee-buck into nine-tie stacks; one wagon after the next, my feet learning to shift, bracing my weight against this contour; our faces flecked and stealing glances at a sky bunching to folds above the flats in the blue-black west.

Tonight, though the air's just heavy with the juice of busted grass, the ridge-top view of 15 miles in all-around: the entire county's green-gold carpet gone to rumpled waves of napped woods and the thread-bare spots where a farmer's trade is plied.

This is Tom's gift: the buckle and hum of the take-off axle, the smell of winter grease mixed with the mist off the clover, and all of this some tubercular spore to be captured by my lungs, some bright-ening contagion that might bloom there months, even years, later when I'm back in the city and lost to all of this.

Tom says, "Second clover by Solstice...." a sentence softly broadcast down the end rows to lie fallow in the stubble; how he means to say "fortune" without drawing fire; how he means, always, to be shaping the sounds which form the words to "home."

Watching the Sky

Andy Harper

In Clark County, Missouri, I grew up on the prairie. Those of us who grew up in Northeast Missouri, knew the fields, the eternal flatness, but also the hills which heaved themselves toward the clouds. Our early roads snaked through the sprawling undulations of a land that stretched on forever. Later roads were carved right out of the countryside, designed for speed, designed to put a limit on that earlier infinity we had once had a sense of, to bind it by signs and schedules, only to see those great roads flooded, closed, washed out, washed away, covered up, or, farther north, crumbled into the river.

As I say, we knew the fields and the flatness, the waving grasses and shining leaves that stretched on forever, with the faintest silhouette of trees in the distance. We knew the slightest climbing and dropping of land. We also knew the high hills and the deep hollows, where trees fell and, rotting, sprouted spongy grey mushrooms. But mostly, we knew the flat monotony of the plains. And yet it was not quite monotony that we experienced—on the contrary, our world changed day to day, hour to hour. I could look out my backdoor one day and see a world of blue snow and icy stillness; the next day, it would be a rolling blanket of soft mud, deep brown and rich with minerals but just as lifeless as the snow. Then, the tractors came through to turn the mud, to aerate it and transform the blank-page flatness and smoothness of it into clumped particles of topsoil, into a forest of dirt teeming with insect life and crawling with the fat worms my father would wrestle, squirming, onto the hooks of our fishing poles on the first warm days of spring. Then, the first leaves pushed themselves up out of the earth, so tiny and so frail. In a few short weeks, they were great stalks, taller than me, and a lush green, then they were golden, and then they were gone, and the earth grew hard again.

All that is a year, but, I tell you, the earth underwent a thousand changes over the course of a single day. If my home was characterized by flatness, then it is in the same manner as a canvas. The morning grass is shiny saffron in the rising sun, and it becomes plain and slender during the day. All the colors start out similarly illusory before taking on a journalistic straightforwardness in direct sun or a shadowy poetry under clouds. A richness of color is characteristic of twilight, the lushness of green and fullness of brown and glitter of gold. In the setting sun, all is silhouette, mysterious and naked. At night, the world is alive.

To some extent, I am writing as a child who enjoys making believe. On a grander scale, however, it is absolutely factual that our world took on many forms throughout the day, throughout the year, and throughout my lifetime, that on our great canvas of earth, no two moments could ever be the same. I have worked many days under the same sun and on the same land, and yet my memory is filled with thousands of visions, hundreds of feelings, and no two of them can be called in the least sense identical. It is important not to think of the flatness and uniformity of our geography as emptiness, because it is just the opposite—it is possessed of an unutterable fullness! And what is it full *of*, you ask? It is full—every hill and furrow, every creek and crevice and badger hole of it—it is full of the sky. And we, we were watchers of the sky.

When I came to Truman State University in the fall of 2008, Kirksville, Missouri, a town of 17,505 became the largest town I had ever inhabited. Wal-Mart stretched out at the north end of town, dominating the eastern horizon where Route 6 met Highway 63. Two McDonalds restaurants stood at opposite ends of the city limits, marking where 63 became Baltimore Street and where Baltimore Street again became 63. Those three and a half miles that lay between were flanked with an array of parks and eateries. To me, Kirksville was a big town with a lot going on, but I was in the minority. Many of the students in my dormitory hall complained of having nothing to do in Kirksville—that it was too small—but there was one thing about the place that, to my bewilderment, impressed every last one of them. It had never, thus far, occurred to me that people existed whose relationship to the sky could be so underdeveloped. It wasn't their fascination, which became evident on evening trips to state parks, but the apparent newness of it all to them. "Let's go out to Thousand Hills and look at the stars," someone would suggest. Freshmen stumbled across the Quadrangle on Thursday nights with their necks craned backward, their gazes swimming about the dizzying expanse stretched overhead.

A favorite hangout on many late autumn and early spring nights was a one-lane bridge over the train tracks off of Route K. We all called it "Train Bridge" and went there for our good, clean, late-night fun. We'd shut off our cars and walk up to the bridge, standing in the center on wide timbers, talking and waiting and gazing out at the double train tracks that ran under the bridge. Then, far off to the south, a light would appear at the edge of the distant dark trees, growing very slowly. Everyone would dart to the intermittent steel railing to watch the train's approach. It seemed to take forever, but then the tracks would begin to rumble, the wide railing to vibrate under palms. We turned to grin at each other, bracing ourselves for the long-anticipated moment of the train's passing. Finally, with a great whoosh of hot air and maybe even the blaring of the horn, the train would thunder by below wooden planks and disappear into the night behind, leaving its adrenaline-pumped audience to fall back once more in awe of the cosmos. The next train would come in two hours, and we were happy to fill that time with stargazing. Someone would take out an iPhone and use an app to identify constellations, or maybe we would all just point out the ones we already knew or watch for shooting stars and airplanes. Somehow, the majority of my classmates, who thought me deprived, had spent their whole lives deprived of the stars. While I had never known many of the places and activities that characterized their lives, the sky is tied to nearly all my memories.

The five acres of hay field cleared and set aside for our home were situated on the corner of Route 81 and old Schmid Road, a gravel road which has retained its nickname despite the fact that no one alive now can remember having known someone who was alive when the Schmids lived there. The land is all undulating corn, bean, and hay fields, with stands of trees separating one from the next. Three mulberry trees stood around an ancient well in our backyard, but other than them and a few Bradford pears decorating the front lawn, nothing stood between my brothers and me and our view of the sky. Our eyes were drawn to the clouds by day and the stars by night.

The sky has always held social importance for us. I had heard and seen pictures of folks gathering around fireplaces and patios, and my own family had gathered around televisions and bonfires; but my brothers and I had always gathered under the sky. Of course, everyone who gathers anywhere does so under the sky, but when my brothers and I came together in a calm moment, it was most often a late spring or early autumn afternoon on the soft grass and gentle slope of our backyard. Tractors and SUVs rumbled by on the highway, while my older brother munched on the wild green onions that pushed up through the landscaping rocks by the house.

One weekend, when I was ten and my little brother eight, we each had our best friend over for the night. At ten o'clock, our parents turned off the television and all the lights but for one over the kitchen sink and went to bed. In the silent darkness, mice could be heard scurrying about in the walls, the sink light buzzed slightly, and the stairs, striped with yellow tatters of the humming light, creaked and groaned below my tiptoes as I snuck back up from the kitchen.

This is when my bedroom transformed into the hull of a spaceship, the four of us gathered at my bedroom window gaping out at the moon and the planets and stars and speeding asteroids. As an enemy spaceship approached us dead ahead, I took to the control panel of my electric keyboard while someone cranked a Frisbee steering wheel hard to the left. We aimed our lasers on the enemy and fired. Then, we sped off across the galaxy, bound for home. Back on Earth, crickets chirped in union while bats flitted around the dusk-'til-dawn light. We watched as the moon slid across the surface of our swimming pool and onto the brown grass in the night, pointing to various shadows on the ground and telling spooky stories of "moon wolves" and "half-moon man." Eventually, all four of us ended up out on the back porch gawking up at the sky, still and silent.

Throughout my childhood, the country sky astonished the town children we had over for birthday parties and sleepovers. Later, in Kirksville, a friend from Saint Louis and I would drive out to a country cemetery tucked away and removed from the highway by thick trees; and as the sun set, our eyes were drawn almost magnetically upward toward our own neat square of blue-black sky, twinkling with white stars and framed by the tips and the tops of the tall, tall trees.

When I began studying meditation during my junior year at Truman, I visualized the fluffy white clouds that passed over the roof of my father's house, the green grass under my back, the hay waving in the field and, beyond that, the trees separating our field from the next. I could smell the hay and the grass and the earth that clung to their roots, and I could hear the crickets and the cows in the distance.

As a child, I used the same sky as a channel for a more primitive sort of meditation. Growing up with a southeast facing window in my bedroom wall and insomniac tendencies, I spent many post-curfew evenings gazing out at the night sky, the soft, deep blues and the yellow moon, the musk of dust fallen heavily over the sill. The scene inspired a sense of calm, perfect for quiet contemplation. My knees sunk into the musty carpet, my nose against the scratchy screen of the right-hand pane, the moon hung faithfully against the glass a mere inch above the window-lock. In the summer, I switched the lock into the up position and cranked the window open to feel the night air against my cheek, dusty through the web of the wire screen.

In addition to contributing to my mental health, these communions with the night sky inspired creativity throughout my childhood, and I often stayed up all night writing fiction or poetry. My wide-ruled notebook with the soccer ball on front lay open over the corner of the Harry Potter rug by my bed, and I stretched out on my stomach across the floor, my feet propped up against a dresser drawer nudged open. Here, I penned such literary pearls as "Attack of the Slime People," "Cat and Mouse: A Love Story," and "A Story of Soccer." One turbulent spring, as the right-hand pane of my window began to thaw, it cracked down the middle, scattering tiny crystals of glass across the carpet. Now, when I looked out, the moon appeared double in the glassy sky.

I also philosophized to the moon. Each night, when I couldn't sleep, I stole to the window, pulled up the blinds, and gazed out at the faithful yellow orb. This is where I did much of my thinking, where I asked myself the questions that swam around in my head all day, and where I produced the answers that together formed my sense of self. My view of the sky also became instrumental in my prayer life, as I often went to this window to pray. Closing my eyes made me dizzy, so I fixed them instead on the moon, a heavenly body after all, and spoke to it and through it, and it became my channel to God.

As captivating as such heavenly bodies could be, the most practical sky-oriented activity back home was cloud-watching. On the plains, we could see storms approaching for miles and twice even watched a tornado pass by across the field. While my younger brother held our whimpering dog on the floor of my older brother's basement bedroom, my older brother and I stood on the porch in a brisk April wind, studying the horizon. The freshly turned soil laid a rich brown across the flat land, while the trees around the pond swayed, gray-green, in the wind. To the northwest, across the highway and across the gravel road across the highway, in the distance, a long grey arm reached down out of the cumulonimbus stretched across the sky. My brother pointed, "Look," and I squinted to see. "See it touchin' down and then goin' back up?" To me, it appeared to be gliding slowly over the horizon, but when I focused, I saw it touch down and lift up in a manner that appeared calm and graceful from so far off. My younger brother, I believe, has never forgiven us for not calling him out of the basement.

Later, after my parents divorced, my younger brother and I moved into a trailer home in Wayland, Missouri, with our mother. Many evenings, we fixed our eyes raptly to the accumulating clouds, watching and listening for some sign that we should make the fifteen-minute drive to my grandparents' house to take shelter in their basement. We saw some beautiful storms in those days, and some beautiful sunrises too. The trailer court, like my father's property, and his father's, was situated on the edge of a hay field, and the proprietors had planted some spindly evergreens which, silhouetted against the rising sun, made up the view across Welsh Drive from my bedroom window.

My favorite weather phenomenon is fog. I distinctly recall the winding, hilly roads to the allegedly haunted former village of Dumas, Missouri, near midnight in a fog. At the tops of hills, we could not see past the hood of my SUV, and at the bottoms, we could not see that far. With friends in the passenger and back seats and Tom Waits's "Murder in the Red Barn" on my stereo, we recounted to each other the legend of the headless woman. It was 1892, and the train from Illinois had begun to shake as it crossed the bridge. Several passengers were thrown out of the windows and into the Mississippi River below, and one woman, through unknown circumstances, lost her head to the frothy waters. Her body was dropped at the tunnel at the town's entrance, and she searches each autumn night at 11:00 for her lost head.

And as we journeyed through the nothingness to meet her, up and down asphalt hills and round sharp gravel curves, we grew silent in awe of the great blackness into which we relentlessly hurtled. The town shrank away in the rearview mirror, and then so did the trees. Even the country homes thinned and stopped appearing on the edges of the fields. Everything disappeared until we were the one sound, the one light, the one breath, and the one movement in all the world. The blackness closed so tightly around us that we seemed to be shuttling through space itself, stars to the left and to the right and the Earth long since left behind. When we arrived at the tunnel, it was a deep black darkness of stone walls and standing water. The trees stood thick as the fog on either side of the gravel road, and a light shone faintly from the picture window of a house with too many "No Trespassing" signs. A big, black dog was approaching the car as a porch light came on at 10:55, and we chickened out. We returned to Kahoka to lie on a merry-go-round under the stars.

We were people who watched the sky. We gathered under the clouds, wished on the stars, prayed to the moon, and tuned in to the atmosphere for signs of danger. In the planting season, we awaited the rain; later, we feared it. Now, as I shoot up and down the Mississippi or the Des Moines, across Kansas or Illinois, down to Arkansas or up to Minnesota, I keep my eyes on the clouds, watching for trouble, for danger, for nightfall.

Poetry Introduction:
My Midwest, Or Whatever May Fall From The Sky

Mary Swander

My mother's family came to the Midwest from Ireland after the Potato Famine on coffin ships with people dying of typhus all around them and feces dropping in their faces from berths above their heads. My family members were considered the lucky ones. They landed in the US alive. They floated up the Mississippi River by steamboat and settled in Illinois, then pushed on into Iowa with the Homestead Act. The unlucky ones were buried at sea or crammed into filthy, flooded tenement basements in New York or Boston, sloshing through water up to their knees. By today's standards, my family members were desperately poor, but by Famine Irish standards, they were affluent. They had their health, the intelligence, and the resources to get themselves up the Mississippi River and out to the Midwest where there was free land to be taken from the Natives.

Cynicism aside, the open prairie, the wide expanses of rich, dark soil must have been overwhelming to these people who had lived like serfs to the British. In Ireland, they farmed so little tillable land that they created their own soil by spreading seaweed over the rocks to decompose. In Ireland, they were used to living in a coastal, moderate climate, in tight-knit semi-communal villages near small plots of potatoes they tilled with nothing more than a spade. In the Midwest, they had to learn how to till larger farms with different crops in temperature extremes in a landscape that resembled nothing they had ever known. But they did it, and they hung on through US famines and depressions, droughts and floods.

And these lucky Irish essentially became serfs again. The railroads recruited these immigrants to settle and clear the open Midwestern lands to keep their tracks safe from the Natives. Just as the Irish had fueled the British Empire, the US government used these farmers to provide their armies, to fuel the economy, and to feed their war troops. The urban Irish crawled out of their flooded tenements on the East coast and began assuming that they were the lucky ones. The unlucky ones were the hillbilly cousins who were banished to a land of flatness. The European mind valued oceans and mountains and could not accept any other geographical paradigm. Americans from both coasts took up the ancient city mouse mentality that the country mice were dumb, dull-witted rubes.

And the farmers often met these prejudices with radicalism. Midwesterners helped bring slaves up the river and find safe harbor through the Underground Railroad. They became leaders of women's suffrage. Midwesterners started the milk riots of the 1930s. Midwestern senators were some of the strongest voices against the Vietnam War. Midwesterners were some of the first to legalize gay marriage. And Midwesterners often met prejudices with prejudices of their own. Midwesterners started the Prohibition Movement. They joined the Ku Klux Klan. They invented "McCarthyism."

How do I write about the Midwest? I write with knowledge of the complexity of region: the opportunity it once presented and the history of exploitation that it has engendered. I write from the point of view of one whose very existence, very survival is embedded in this soil, but who also sees the great problems that erode and contaminate that dirt. I write from the perspective of one who was taught to work hard, no matter how hot or cold, rainy or snowy, no matter how tired or ill you may be. You endure whatever may fall from the sky onto your face—it could be worse—to reach a safer, better shore. I write from the point of view of one who loves the wide-open horizon, who feels claustrophobic in mountains and finds the Mississippi and Missouri rivers as enchanting and fascinating as oceans. As a Midwesterner, I automatically write from the perspective of the "other," one whose values and experiences have run counter to the mainstream. We live in a society where slurs against ethnic groups, religions, and gender have become taboo, but regional chauvinism is perfectly acceptable. I open the newspaper, turn on the radio or TV and these same folks who wouldn't dare use the "N" word, think nothing of denigrating Midwesterners or rural working class people. We're rednecks and hayseeds from the hinterlands, the backcountry, the backwoods, and the boondocks.

In my poetry, I also find myself writing counter to the mainstream. In a literary period where the experimental has become the conservative norm, I write outside the norm. I write in multiple genres. I write narrative poetry. Once in a while I even rhyme. I bring my poetry to the stage. I play the banjo before my poetry readings. I adapt my poetry books to puppet shows. What could be weirder? I'm often dismissed as a "regionalist." In today's literary world, this is a designation worse than death and its derogatory connotations only seem to apply to writers—most often women—who usually write from the landscape of the working class rural South or Midwest.

If I'm a regionalist, what the hey? My region has given me the room to go my own way. I find endless material here driving down the backwood roads. I find endless diversity. I've interviewed and written about the descendants of the Exodusters, ex-slaves who homesteaded Midwest farmland just as my ancestors did. I've written about Amish who were horribly persecuted in Europe and came en masse to the United States. I've written about Mexicans, Sudanese, and Hmong farmers who started out their American lives working in meatpacking plants and are now becoming our urban farmers.

The Midwest has given my poetry and writing depth, dimension, a sense of purpose and value. And surprise. Open to the delights of this landscape, I never know what new image will strike me. I've watched the restoration of prairie in many parcels throughout the area. I've watched the return of the use of cover crops. I've watched my no-till organic garden produce bountiful food year after year. I've watched the return of the bald eagle, falling from the heavens to nest in the maple tree outside my window.

I am, indeed, one of the lucky ones.

Mary Swander is Poet Laureate of the State of Iowa. Her latest book of poetry is *The Girls on the Roof.* Her two plays—*Farmscape* and *Vang*—are currently touring the United States. She is a Distinguished Professor of Liberal Arts and Sciences at Iowa State University.

At Joe and Lonna's Farm

Lindsay Tigue

Lonna shares her first impressions
of Iowa. How she wanted

to get under earth, how strange
to stand so tall on land, how very
far her eyes could see, how naked
she could feel without a hill

for shelter. *This place is impossible
stretch.* But she found

she never wants to leave. This is the year
I turn twenty-eight and I watch

alone from my porch as the nighttime heat
lightning flashes through sky to soundtracks
of passing freight. My actual thunder-
scaredy cat nuzzles his gray face

on my calf, reminds me of the man
who didn't love me back. This summer,

Lonna's husband Joe navigates
the creek by canoe. We pass

a rookery of herons. He points at birds
who appear to guard their leaves. *Here,*

it doesn't seem like Iowa, he says. Later, I sit
on the back of his flatbed, tearing

through plowed wildgrass. Branches
scrape across my back, sticks

get tangled in my hair. One day, we comb
the creek bank for shells and stones.

Isn't it marvelous Joe says, *what a glacier
can do?* In late summer, I drive out

to the farm most afternoons, once
the midday sun's begun to cool. I pull

purslaine from dirt alongside Lonna. We pluck
tomatoes from the vine. I watch

the chickens scatter for their weeds. Before
long, Lonna places warm eggs
into my palm. Some evenings,
we make jam, husking the ground

cherries, boiling and filling the jars. This
is the year my mind wanders

through hurt. Throughout the cold, quick spring
and the wet, hot summer, I walk through

how love left me in this
flatness. I find myself driving

toward warmth. I stand outside at night

feeling the broad and starry sky rest

atop me. How quiet,
yet marvelous, these epochs of unfreezing,

this roamed-out sense of mending,
this self believed already grown.

The Center of the Earth is a Little Off-Kilter

Lindsay Tigue

is what the newspaper says in regard to Ecuador's
Middle of the World, the equatorial park
whose monument to midpoint is hundreds of feet
from actual zero. But I like a middle that isn't
quite. For I'm in Chicago and, at home
in this Midwest, I can't sleep through the night.
The trains pass and stop right beyond my wall
and I wake flinching, dreaming they might
                 rush right through the brick and plaster.

But the end of my night turns into beginning
of morning and in half-sleep, my thoughts always
meander. When Rome fell the Middle Ages began
and measurements started to wander. How much
is a gill? A gallon?
                 Can you give me half a pounce?

I used to babysit a girl who pressed loose
the coarse skin around my elbow as I read to her
stories before bed. It was as if she could polish
me like stone, like she could knead
toward the center of my arm. She'd bend
my free limb like a doctor. She'd watch my joint
                 disappear into crater.

In middle school, I gave a presentation
on radiometric dating, the half-life of rocks,
the methods used to age this world. And when I wake
from nightmares about mass extinctions—
bees vanishing in the dark, I hear only the slow buzz
                    of my lights turning on.

At my parents' wedding anniversary, my dad
stood up at the table, toasted a glass.
He said, *I've known you*
                    more than half this life.

In Ecuador, tourists stand right on a yellow line
marking the not center. Take my picture. And when I notch
off days on my calendar, I think: we invented that, too.
I just can't tell you when morning began for I'm still
dreaming of elbows and bees. I'm just
                    waiting for reasons to measure.

How to Disappear in Michigan
Lindsay Tigue

"The cougar has been considered officially extinct in Michigan since 1906, although the animal has been spotted there with amazing frequency over the years."
　—National Wildlife Federation, 2003

In Kalkaska County at midnight, some creature lurks
and crawls. The quiet farm waits in the pause
before growl. The silence pools into land—

out toward holes where glaciers notched the fresh sea.
In that water, where we killed all grayling and cisco fish—
Blackfin, Longjaw, Deepwater, Shortnose—where we still

look for glimmers of schools; images, blurry,
swimming from hooks. But in Kalkaska, a beast
believed gone, bloodies a family dog behind a barn. We lose

chickens one by one, examining teeth marks on their necks.
New days mark new death. And in the early fog, we
discover claw-streaked tracks of pain scraped in a mule.

Some cat's shadow fleets through woods. There are ways
this story must go. And when we learn the missing hometown
girl—fourteen—was found in California, we cannot believe

somewhere she breathes. That she fought
to vanish. That she wished to run
away. We only want her back—wouldn't you

miss these inland waters, these waves persisting
in their creep toward shore? The image of a cat caught
slipping out of woods—we don't have to see it. We know

how it looks. We think we know what breathes. What's
breathing? We can see exhaled air at night. We know
what happens behind barns, inside bedrooms, under a sea.

If she does return, she will be just another face,
a hazy fact recalled from school. And we'll sleep
dreaming our own dark shapes to fear.

Huron

Lindsay Tigue

In Au Gres, kids still run
along the rocky shore of the limestone
point through mud-splash
and they throw sticks at a speedboat.
The sticks fall short,
way out from the hull.

Walrus bone and prehistoric
human remains were found near
this water. Once-plentiful sturgeon
tomahawked in lake shallows.

The settlers once found
large hard maples tapped
by Ojibwa for hundreds of years.

This was lumbering country
and for house-raising, people
came from miles around.
The fiddlers and callers
got people to dance.

They sent logs of old growth
down the river. The men
hunted bear for their stew.

The first switchboard in town
was made of bottles, old bones,
little scraps of iron.

Trillium

Melissa L. Sevigny

—for John

I hadn't a summer thought in mind
that day we met beside the brook,
the trees unleafed,
on my way to somewhere else.

You said, "Come look—" and took me to your find.
I spent more time than needed
on the stepping stones—my balance is good—
but the water there made me want to risk a splash,
so sweet a silver sash it draped
through scouring rush and brittle grass.

You found them yesterday.
I could see your track, straight up
among white oak and birch.
You said you hadn't been looking for flowers.
Who would?—this time of year
so strange, snow late in May
to make a fool of the few sunny days.

But there they were, white trillium
across the hill's bare crown,
silly somehow, the first of the spring—
out even before the wild violets had bloomed,
five or six dozen in the space of a shout,
and tipped three-petaled to the south,

gold at the center,
like the clappers of bells just waiting to ring.

Must be the sun, I said,
something about the way it catches here.
And you agreed. What else to say?
We went back to the brook
and broke the edge still rimmed in ice
with our boots in crossing back,
and I got in the car and drove away.

Garage Sale in Iowa

Melissa L. Sevigny

We looked for garage
sales each summer
on Saturday mornings,

arrived early enough
to get the best picks
from the clutter.

You could always
find the thing they didn't
want to lose—

calico squares for a quilt;
the toolbox of wrenches
worn shiny from use;

a two-volume dictionary,
the first paged open
to *grief/gratitude.*

Sometimes we'd spend
dimes from the grocery
money to ransom

the seller's peace of mind,
exchange a story:
the antique bookshelves

I wanted to fill,
the cherry wood scrap
you'd use to remake

a chisel's snapped handle.
All week I'd crave
the relief in their eyes—

garage sellers who knew
to post their signs early,
before the rising sun

brought unforgiving light.

Man Kneeling at a Rock

Sean Evans

A man walked to a rock
he thought was a good start
and knelt
in the Buffalo Grass
above an old wallow, soft
beneath the ball
of his knee

With hammer and chisel
the man looked across the wide sky
from this rock he'd found
to a high spot
where he thought there might be another
and another
that would satisfy him.

Nebraska Biome

Toni Easterson

Between Clayton and Springer
skies touch the ground
trapping me in a blue bowl.
In the distance freckles of cattle
appear and disappear;
now and then a cloud is pulled
along the horizon.
This land seems embroidered
with emptiness. God
must have been preoccupied.

Hoakie

Toni Easterson

Grandma Hoakie, who was not my grandmother,
cared for me on the afternoons
my mother played cards at the Masonic Temple.
While she watched me I watched her
from beneath the table in our breakfast nook.
Grandma Hoakie was a Menominee
who, in her words, did not have the wires
that carried talking, attached to her house.
My mother summoned her by hanging a
bandana in a bedroom window.
Grandma Hoakie, I was told, had raised ten
children. She wore skirts to her ankles
and shoes that laced, like my father's boots.
Her eyes held behind them the sorrow of
her people and her silence had the power
to push my mother's laughter from our house.

Hoarder

Heather D. Frankland

I collected your love declaration in this old mason jar
bought from a yard sale of neighbors I never met
until they were leaving.

I capped it tightly—your, "I love you,"
forgot about it for months until the cat almost knocked it over
stretching past plants to reach sunlight.

If only it could bloom into your tongue,
then your face, and your body.

If only, I could can you like garden tomatoes
or green beans, lima beans, peaches
store you in the kitchen cupboard
for the winter months when the sunlight
fades at five o'clock and I hide myself
in layers against the chill.

FF>>

Russell Jaffe

Your sons will say the same things again and again. Your daughters
        will say t
he same things again and again. Your sons will hold like detonators
        energy drinks,
assuaging the gravity of their final polemic: "This is who I am, I can't
        change that."
Your daughters could be the lipstick carrions looking to forward
        their careers on T
V shows you tape because they're on but cut off the endings because
        you just can't.
Your sons will ride #elevators above babbling cursive you said before
        bed was
romantic but that's its only defense. Your daughters will call the
        actions of the
similar indefensible. Your sons balk early and often. Your daughters
        will weep
outside Midwestern sports-themed nightclubs. Your sons will film
        themselves be
ing tasered by their friends.

Rock Island

Ryan Collins

An arch of the Centennial Bridge explodes
Into a murder of crows,

Fooled by the swing bridge to the west
To scatter their black masses &

Twist toward what they mistake
For south, thinking it will be warmer there.

Tension accumulates in my feet.
Pressure is applied, but not where the crows

Collect & dive a black violence against
Care, against relative direction or distracted

Motorists w/ hands at 10 & 12, feet on the gas
Darting across to somewhere warmer.

But how could anywhere so close be warmer?
Why slow down to watch as an arch

Of the Centennial Bridge explodes into
A cold black violence collecting

On the river, on every square inch of stone
& glass for a thousand miles in every

Direction, where not even the crows will fly.
A slow bridge slowing into winter,

A slow accumulation of tension in my feet.

Three Pastorals

Stephanie Schultz

I.
Pink flecks of cornhusks
hang in the air
for most of the fall season
as farmers release tractors and combines
into wild acres of earth.

II.
Pink flecks congregate
in crevices of city streets
lining curbs, clogging gutters
gently foreshadowing
a cold harshness that lies ahead.

III.
Pink flecks fade
into winter's first snowflakes
without anyone even noticing
the beauty of harvest season
and what it brings and leaves.

Bucolic

Stephanie Schultz

"I have never seen a sunrise," you said
sitting under a tree that midmorning.

I want to take you to my small farm town
and set you down in dirt with corn and beans

where we can see the plains for miles and miles
and feel the chill and dark of night behind

our backs as lines of pink, purple, yellow
stripe the blue horizon and rise to meet

in a great firmament so wide, so big
where day breaks dawn, where first lights take place.

A Sunset

Stephanie Schultz

Hidden Falls Park
Mississippi River
rocky shoreline
spindly trees
trunks like hands
fingers digging
in the beach
cool colors of water
a cooler breeze
an evening late
into summer
or early fall
speedboats
Padelfords
a dog a man a phone
a father
skipping rocks
models and
photographers
getting wet hair
a setting sun
a jet trail
flames in the sky

Eschelbach Farm House

Issa M. Lewis

under the thinnest of crescent moons   tractor paths furrowing the mud
of late spring   county roads   gravel shoulders crunching

one stoplight   one gas station   one highway exit
small town defined by crops   human geometry sprawling

lines blur   after thresher blades are barricaded in barns
grass high as the hip or more   sewing seeds of its own

this house was built by the Eschelbachs
Dean   his father   his grandfather

pull apart the floorboards   like years under your fingernails
you'll hear them whisper   you'll hear sheep bleating

as they clear stubbled autumn fields   you'll see
Ella Mae making pie in the kitchen   robin's-egg blue walls

creeping inward   like an old man's spine   bending towards center
or else expanding   no right angles in this place

dust settles on the woodwork   wallpaper fades   peels
the sheep were sold years ago   the fields became parking lots

cars for sale   a doctor's office   strokings and murmurings
of another world   stealing its way through the grass

like a cat   smooth-stepped   lush paws
flattening the ground for paving

Predicting Weather

Carol V. Davis

Even Aristotle believed in earthquake weather:
    Tremors caused by winds trapped in caves,
air breaking the surface. Cloud formations.
    An earthly stillness. Unseasonable warmth. Calm.

Today before dawn, here in Nebraska, fists of hail,
    the windows shaking, then rain slapping in waves.
Nothing unusual in these parts: thunder cursing,
the sky knocked about by lightning.

The first time the siren went off, I didn't know
what it was: a burglar alarm,
the water heater about to burst.
After the high-pitched wail, a man's firm but steady
voice announced (from where?):
    Severe weather. Tornado watch.

I suppose it's what you're used to. In Los Angeles
    when the glass shudders and rattles,
I stand under a doorway,
      grab the animals to prevent their bolting.
  Even so, when the cupboard doors swing open
     and the crockery takes flight
there's a moment of stunned beauty
    before the crash of porcelain on tile.

Like your parents

Jason Nicholas Vasser

While walking the arch grounds
as the stars blinked overhead,
beyond the smog of the city
and past all the clouds;

we caught a glimpse of Eads Bridge
and admired the beauty in its decay
hovering above the Mississippi current
during a beautiful fall.

You in that sweater we bought,
burnt sienna, looked perfect
against the leaves and
my hat, fresh from Levine's

carried a tilt you said
your father held in the Spring—
of when your parents met,
when they too necked while watching the water.

Swimming out of Season (And, Behold)

Susan Grimm

Maybe you've read my poem about the orange bathing suit. But
there are many ways to say the same thing.

At the outdoor pool the wind blows steadily out of the west making
a current as if this were a stream or a river replete with the
swim team that shivers on the edge.

For even a municipal pool can have big dreams, yearnings toward
dark forests and white water runs in a narrowed river bed.

A little like champagne along the legs. Not bad. And the clouds
moving like a frolicsome dream of silent buffaloes.

This goes with the seven lean years. Work hard. Get strong. Let
sorrow roll off your back.

"And it came to pass . . . that Pharaoh dreamed; and behold, he
stood by the river."

Exodus comes next. But my dream is backwards—or its prediction
or the months that it already took. The seven leanfleshed
cows have eaten up the good of the world.

Here's the meadow, stripped, and me, incomplete. I pick up the
bits of the world and press them to my cheeks and eyes. And
even though we are not pure, still, our longing opens like the
bell of the lily's throat.

November or Even If You Wear a Watch

Susan Grimm

Here's the danger—to love where you are. Peninsula of bacon and
woolen blankets, reassuring hiss of the furnace come on in the night.
The crazy flickering of light and leaves, bright stencil to the end.
(Not angora because I might be allergic.)

"Raindrops on roses"—I do love that. The white bush that only
bloomed once a year until they cut down all the trees and now the
abundance into November. Unto this.

A little more islanding every day. The wind blowing at any speed.
The attention your skin can pay with sweat and a sudden breeze.

Grape juice, that thick purple sweetness plumping the tongue. (Not
bee stung because.)

There's seeming and there's is. How time roots around like a hog and
inhales you whole. Big bruiser pretending never to end, pretending
the foot falls always the same.

Sometimes costumed with a cloak, like a vampire weary with his
own abundance, he forgets to line our face with his nails.

Bumper Crop

Susan Grimm

117 people live in Rome, Ohio, along the Ohio
River. This is in Adams County suggesting origination,
Rome suggesting might. Could I have driven through
on the way to the Serpent Mound, that lesser swerve
to the river, the mound like a sound wave in tonals
of green? They keep the air close there. This is not
to be confused with New Rome, alleged speed trap, or
the original Rome on the Italian boot, wolves howling
on the Palatine Hill. I was hounded there—at the bank
door, at the outdoor café—by the Rom in shades
of pink. I didn't cross the field where they were gathering.
Roam, forsooth, underlines me here, pressing my metal
flank, dragging my rubber tires down the road to Rome
township (Lawrence County—hanging a little lower
than the rest of the state). Rome apples, originally
Gillett's Seedlings, were introduced there in 1817.
Red Romes. Rome Beauties. In their orchards,
a kind of garden, we may pick and eat, although
you should be aware they're really best baked.

Cave of Light

Susan Grimm

—After Sandy, October 2012

Rain slick on the road in its sideways falling. Thresher song of the wind
and its harvest of leaves. I was trapped in the house my foot tapping
not taprooted to the sewer line like the tree outside. It thrashed
like a maraca. How could there be any leaves left? Let go, let go,
but it whipped like the head of a snake or a jack of 9-tails. There was a dry
rattle of windows in their long oblongs. At the mercy of the wind
which has no mercy. Across the street there were kitchen lights and tv
glows and the satisfied hum of the furnace. I was on the brown side,
every once in a while a trickle in the cave of night. The candles
made a little alcove. I could see my breath. The inwardness
of this kind of lighting like a chapel where you pray for the dead
the flames sliding sideways at the tip. I might have thought
about Plato's cave, our silhouettes banked together, made out of felt,
but I barked my shins, drank cold chicken soup instead. Up on the mantel
the candles doubled, reflected in that cold room where if I peeked over
someone else would be up from the chair, still hunched in her afghan, too.
I'd already forgotten the high yellow snarl of the waves on the Shoreway,
the water like a shaken rug or tasered glutinous bowl of goop. So many
things with open mouths. Waves closing over, me yawning, the cave
in the dark, the covers, under cover of night, coming over my head.

Echt

Susan Grimm

Walking up the stairs from the furnace
check or the emptied dryer, from the outside
door against whose panels nothing presses

like this. Going up the risers, slow, one by one,
the neck knotted up but erect. All day
your feet dance over it—toccata and muffled

carpet thunk. Root cellar. I had some dream
about that. Sod houses whose settlers
blew out their brains while outside the prairies

rolled away. The sense of something swimming
at your back through air or dirt—no matter. Something
wormlike, intent, the arms skinned back and lax.

Mother? Father? A darkness like the mouth's
wanting. Invisible thing surrounding or filling
with a slow dark cream. Mirror, twin, phallic love

post in a well of air with paint cans and nails. Let us
disguise with brushes, cobble up the holes. Stop
the bucket sloshing up from our own dark waters.

Des Moines lobe (12,000 ya)
// A storm passes (in the long run)

Claire Krüesel

You can't put your finger on it. Something swarming,
cold. So flat, so dry. Green rivers off a duck's back like
unread map: Iowa. You say you don't want to live here
but our fields already reach you, become you. We held

our breath longer, stand last in line to drown again. Storm
on your finger like a diamond, take it off before the dirt: inverse
of hurricane, volatility. Sweep out your fancy cheekbones before
they carve empty caves. Ours is a slow freeze. Sleet opinions,

scarecrow debris. Linens snap in wind but keep the sun. Iowa
farmhouses don't bother opening their mouths. Joinery without
nails, wood without name. The coasts import her long beams, frayed
where a swallow raised eggs, to root their homes to a place. Admit

you smell hay in the sun's sweet shadow. We practice cold feet.
We don't ask why. Ice will come again and so will the opposite
of drowning as the Mississippi rolls good-bye. Hello. Go to your
other places - we will be here when uphill flows down, when

your whitecap seas blind and you ask the weatherman to translate
water's lapping at your feet. We will be here—pitchfork; mud—
knowing right where we are at when the new storm swoops down
where the cables snake in, when the TV dials down its warm

snow to whisper over your shoulder—to report, it's your turn
in the alphabet: this time, history takes your silt-engraved name.

Adventitious Roots

Claire Krüesel

Always looking out, the rain-
scented sky of the plains in her
eyes, loose curls disobedient sun

yellow straw that just won't stay
bound tight: farm girl with a vision,
she left muddy boots back home,
drove
east
                         to learn Latin
names of the plants growing
roots where she'd started—*Zea*
mays color crayons of her hair—
blew
west
to study anatomy, slip on
a crisp white coat, nametag mentality,
scrubbed up like overalls, sterile prepared

the cadaver, bare, simple, splayed
open and spare of blood, so much
like all those sows she'd named and

cried for the spotted one. Bleach
got the blood out
but never the dirt.

I know where you are

Claire Krüesel

in the road you threw up
the paramedics said
black beans
cheese
softened shreds of a beige plane
I told your mother, "We always
had black bean quesadillas
in the dining hall." Mystery
solved. I always added olives
to mine.

I know you

I think you threw up
olives, too.

I wonder if someone
cleaned it up or if
a raccoon ate it—you
would've wanted it that way

they cut off your boxers

---

but you came back)

Iowa, your magnifying glass froze in your
pocket
shatter-resistant lens, I still have it
I imagine your eyes
on the other side

but I know where you are

Minnesota, the earth resistant like a real winter
in fact we sent you off under quite the snow
a big circle bulging out from the tent
everyone who loved you breathing
little clouds
we sang "You are my Sunshine"
it was dark and still snowing
hence the tent
you would've found it
homey

I know where you are

I know where you are

it's summer at a time of year
when everyone else you know has forgotten
about summer

you are examining an Egyptian butterfly
with an oversized magnifying glass
no circle big enough
for you

I know where you are

you are surrounded by exotic flowers
you've identified with a field guide
reading a thick book recently published
about our ancestors' genes
and people around you in turbans
are enjoying the sun in a way that's
practiced

I know where you are

in a photo on a dusty hard drive
put there before hard drives
got dusty

I know where you are

I thought I'd forget by now

I know where you are

I thought I'd write you to let you know
evolution is still real
and still "just" a theory
to some people (nobody
you and I know)

I know where you are

it is winter here and there's no snow
yet, and the same last year

in Minnesota then Iowa, you never knew
a winter without snow—even that winter
you went to Egypt, you came back

(there was a bombing there
the same day you arrived,

body heat
adding to entropy

I know where you are

the exact address
you'll be
even on holidays

I imagine where you are

not your body but
where your mind got stuck
in the helicopter ripping between white states
me speeding on the asphalt under you
when did you stop listening
when did the words stop
making sense

I imagine your mind mapping

the damage to your body
listening for clues from the voices
gnawing on data over you
trying to sate themselves
emotionally, like a hunger
for blood clotting factors

the ones I gave you for Christmas
red with butterflies
real enough
you could maybe identify them
with your field guide

I know where you are

always and finally
I can stop worrying
about you
about slushy roads and dark
crossways at the edge
of winter

I know what you feel

we talked about it once
when you're filling the bath and you
can't tell
if it's so hot it's cold or if
it really is
ice cold
you look at the faucet turned
to H but your body tells you
no, that's not true
it simply can't be
what I am experiencing

Heirloom

Janis Rodgers Soule

A buck walked here, his hooves pressed to wet sand,
like the brittle skin of my grandmother,
she who has become the spoiled milk in the fridge
the canned ham, piles of pine cones
her children have left at the back door.

In the half frozen creek bed, a shard from a green-
rimmed plate that belonged once to my great-
grandmother. The buck's antlers could be gnarled
wood, yet these are velvet and branching, they breathe
faster than any mammal bone. Calcified, they clear
snow to eat the vegetation beneath.

My grandmother planted a garden every spring,
before her fingers became stiff and white,
and all of her things, now ours.

Ode to a Walnut Tree

Janis Rodgers Soule

Walnut tree, flood-swept across the creek,
face resting in spindly purple grasses
and soft white clay- You peeled back
the earth squawking your wounds
like the storytelling of crows
risen up from the bank.
Your tender roots will shrivel
like a human heart detached
from its chest—

no more blood to the stem
no more minerals to the body.

Walnut tree, how deep did your roots
grow, tell us the story of your
mother—How far did she let you
fall from her lap, your oil-lobed body
in a mossy cradle, the hard, green
outside would keep you safe—
your native lungs and great vessels
sutured in place.

Heartland

Janis Rodgers Soule

My hair falls out
and collects on the carpet

like arthritic leaves
on the ground outside.

Quite legally, long plumes
of smoke reuse my body.

Heavy metals
snag in my lungs

and give voice to crows,
their smoked wings caught in my throat.

Trash is front loaded, fed
to gas, burned in each chamber

before smoke is cooled and humidifies,
injected with carbon and lime.

Lead and cadmium are trucked
from my heart, shipped to my blood.

This land does not nourish me
with its corn and soybeans,

the sound of the train I dread

lugging syrup and fat,

and hunger here in this barren
room like a cave without bats.

As the earth warms and crop yields
drop off in the Heartland

I will be fed
with wind and flood.

Midwestern Monsoon

Tony Quick

From your porch, cigarette clamped loose between fingers, see
Fireflies flicker, green glows spirit from one spot to the next
Competing quietly with the dominance of the blue black night.

Then gone

Gone, yes, like the memory of dreamt of dead loved ones
In the murky miasma of your waking hours.
Fading only to return in the ghost echoes of sleep.

Clouds crack open.
Rain races and rivets down on slick sidewalk
Dropping drumbeats, adorning asphalt with a wet wide sheet.

As it pours and white forks fire off,
Sizzling streaks slide wild, stream across air
Electric tumbleweeds roll along the blue-black hills

The train's bellow grounds you, reminds
Of the cigarette burned out in your grasp
You'll light another. And another.

Until the storm ceases, pulls back, opens to morning.
Sun resting yolk yellow on the long horizon.
Sky sepia, the hue of battered gold, peaceful except

The clouds curved still with the threat of torrent.

Boll Weevil

Xavier Cavazos

1.

king cotton
was eaten by me

was brought to his
knee by tiny me

now in evening
i move from tree

to weed to bankrupt
billfold

funny
aren't i

blackening these
southern fields

this emptied
space

this white
land

2.

if not for me   no need
for george washington

carver   no alternative
crop

to cotton
no peanut

to crack open
no shell

to
crunch

Collected genus species by George Washington Carver for Dr. Louis Pammel, Carver's mentor & professor

Xavier Cavazos

1.

Cypripedium Candidum

the blossom
droops

like a hung
head

the
body

slender
& lean

root
digg-

ing
deep

into

2.

Erythronium Americanum

rich & shady
dog-tooth-violets

long
stems

hold up the
moon with song

sways while you
sleep   signs

when you wake
dark-bottoms

blown
by wind

brought
by ship

1895 Bomb Yearbook

Xavier Cavazos

—Iowa State University

quartermaster
george washington

carver   you are standing
so erect in this student army

training corps photo
quartermaster   the highest rank

for any student   sealed & stamped
approval from the department

of military science & tactics
you are wearing two white gloves

& holding a cadets helmet
with an eagle emblem

on it   quartermaster
your uniform

the standard united states
officer's fatigue   soaring

george   you are
soaring

Carver Dreaming 1898

Xavier Cavazos

dreamt i was one of the 10th cavalry men
black as an infantry gun barrel

scarier than roosevelt's rough riders
ripping up the plains

bare-backing the comanche like
a spell   the kiowa   the kiowa-apache

the arapaho & southern cheyenne
dreamt i was a dark-tropical-soldier

a real-live-spanish-regiment
fighter   bastard of the civil

war   1776's four-score
& seven years

was never for us
the beloved 10th

like geronimo
we keep fighting

on   dreamt i swam
to cuba   took shelter under san juan

hill   ate tropical fruit   sewed
a blanket   killed a few spanish soldiers

became a hero
& crossed long divided

racial-country-lines
prayed to my master

up in heaven
i dreamt i was

a soldier

Ode to Farm & Fleet

Jennifer Fandel

For I love our rich scent of tractor tires
mixed with the dark, dyed canvas stink of
stiff-legged Lee and Wrangler jeans and
the metallic tinge of fertilizer. Perusing
your roomy, well-swept aisles

brimming with everything a girl could need—

wrench sets, cast iron pots, animal feed, chain link— I
can believe I'm so much more than a buyer

of windshield wipers, work boots, a turkey fryer,

burnt peanut candy, and June's *Field & Stream.*

I drive home through a countryside gone in one blink, a
land divided and strung by wires,

and I think on how there's no way to get back

to the fields of wheat and the drowse of chafe

New Palestine, Indiana

Julia Anna Morrison

I expected the trees to have been longer
since you let go

or stretched more graphically apart

The Atlantic looks slightly flat again after our dream-week in
New Palestine

discolored on the left side where the east bleached the
sail-ropes

I came to adjust to the length of the odd-numbered trees
Three points were slit off

It isn't that I don't outhear you this morning

I think that it was hailing
remotely or are there hail-marks

I am prepared—
the trees are far apart

Effects

Julia Anna Morrison

Outside, I photograph hailstorm effects occurring in the wrong
month. Just one more whirl of the clear color and I'll come in.

We wasted the bluish light from the morning. Yes, I grew a
heart. I can't tell with which I am loving you.

The marks on your body don't really alarm me. See
what the storm did to this field. Nothing.

I wish I couldn't feel like that wind over and over.

Your pain was knowing I was in pain since we were little. Though
you've never cut yourself on it, thank you for imagining that the trees
are almost glass.

In case you miss me, I left this tree and the reflective weather around the
tree to you.

March

Julia Anna Morrison

I hardly notice, almost blank, but I do see it.

It smells differently than winter, like air, and I don't sleep well near
       flowers. Nothing
happened that I can think of in March. Yes, I could use a different
       shovel. This one is red,
for planting. What do I do if the flowers are blurry.

What do I do if I see him. He's supposed to be in another river, it's
       the water I saw him in; I
loved him finally—I told it, dumbly.

It's March, the semi-flowers are turning, my wrist hurts. Soon I will
       wear a swimming suit
and look ugly.

Some days are longer depending on the length the tree is out.

Geography

Khadija Anderson

When I was young my mother told tales
of pussy willows and cattails
Cardinals red as maraschino cherries
and shoveling snow up to her thighs
in her childhood Chicago

I only knew obstinate terrain
blistering cement under bare feet
peacocks exploding from rooftops
Luis running unpaved roads of the varrio

Here Larks were cigarettes
an ornament for skinny boys with tousled hair
standing with hands in pockets
on their mothers' porches
their mothers who also came from the cold

Animals Were Looking at Me

Jeff Tigchelaar

One neat thing about where I live in Kansas
is that you can turn north off Sixth
just past the Walmart and the strip malls,
go about half a mile, round a bend, take a left,
turn into the dirt lot with the Martin Park sign,
get out and walk a quarter-mile on the path, and all of a sudden
you come out on this rural road
and you're totally in the country, which
you can tell because animals
are looking right at you: geese, a goat,
a white horse with some sort of jacket,
a little donkey,
an alpaca.

It's the strangest
kind of eye contact

and it's impossibly quiet

but then a leashless pit bull comes charging
and only stops when called
by its owner from the window of a trailer
and soon you'll begin—I'll begin—breathing again

and the dog, dejected, will amble home
and I'll unfreeze and keep walking,
the horse having now turned its back,
the alpaca now rolling on the ground,
no longer interested in me.

Middle March

Su Hwang

I drove from the West, past
The perpetual March of the salt flats
Where the desert butts the Great Lake,
Deep into the windswept interior
Beyond the slate rocks of southern
Wyoming toward the outer banks
Of Superior, I make
My new home, here at last

Among the stock and keep,
Petrified oceans of rolled bales of hay,
Abiding a creed to live simply off
The land in accordance with the sun,
Rising in its wake, moving to the sway—
The muted thunder of a million
Husks until the cloak of spit
And tar brings such sweet sleep,

For dreaming is a silly whim
Conjured by the weak, as the heart works
In the well-tilled fields, soil imparted
To skin, bone, and the holy garden
Crop of men, unflinching and certain,
I am here now among them,
Galled hands resting on hips
Taking it all in—a hymn.

Home Sweet Home
Su Hwang

The soft tick-ticking of spray, the purr
Of a John Deere tractor draws near

Tracing the horizon with a finger
The sky is even bigger than you

Remember, a hulking mass of
Cumulous wonder and yet there

Is something numinous at its core,
This place, this otherwise silent place

Where the fields speak in whispers
Ear to ear like little girls passing secrets.

Home, Iowa

Su Hwang

He wanted to be a fireman because he loved the sound of sirens
and how it sliced through all that was barren. Then a detective he
thought, like Sherlock Holmes when The Hound of the Baskervilles
played in town. Never a farmer though—never the vocation of his
father or his father's father.

But he was a good boy and woke at first light to help in the mired
fields, buckets and galoshes suckling the mud as the mist of morning
coated his eyelashes, giving him the look of crying. I'm going to be
an archeologist, he announced on his tenth harvest moon. Where in
God's name did you hear about such things? His mother asked, her
gaze fixed to a point beyond the flume.

Could they not see what was etched into the maize? The teeth
of Bengal tigers, cobblestone alleys in Rome, the finest jewels
embedded deep beneath ancient tombs—something new each time
he peeled the head, sheath by sheath—an atlas revealed behind the
silks.

Come now, boy. His father finally spoke, wiping his mouth with his
sleeve as he heaved his only son by the throat. Time to feed them
pigs.

One Kitchen One Afternoon

Christopher Citro

Most of our young at some point leave,
and who can blame them? And those that don't
we end up wishing would. What future's
there in pancake breakfasts and next year
the frackers may come? I've news
for you, they're here already and precious
little any of us can do. Two wells already in
just to the south, the deepest so far just
past the hill there. Rents have doubled. Our bank
got robbed last week by a man in a mask
on a bicycle. He pedaled across the bridge
into town, and when he was done, pedaled out.
Undrinkable water can't hardly be made worse.
Town used to smell of cut lumber.
She jokes about being able to set it alight
then fills a mug and tries for real.
And we could all sure use the money.
A look of concentration folds her forehead
as she lowers a match to clear water.

Whatchamacallit

Christopher Citro

I don't eat candy bars, being that I'm thirty-eight.
While Krogering I pass over the candy aisle
as if it's a long, brightly-colored blind spot.
I used to eat them when I was a kid, especially
in the movie theater at the mall up the road—
the little suckers glowing in their case like beige bricks
next to the luminous popcorn machine in the lobby
lit only in pools by black tubes from the ceiling.
I saw Superman there, the one with Christopher Reeve
who ended his life paralyzed from a fall off a horse.
At the end when he was flying through the air
in a rush to save Lois Lane, my mother yelled
"Go Superman, go!" so loudly I tried sliding
from my seat to crawl free from the theater.
This was also where I made out for the first time.
The girl kept sticking her tongue down my throat,
and I kept trying to see if Michael J. Fox would make it
back from the past to save his parents (or himself—
I forget which). Michael J. Fox has Parkinson's now.
The movie theater closed when a multiplex went in
up the road from the mall. Plus the owner got busted,
projectionists selling cocaine to football players.
A friend of mine helped. The last time I saw him
he tried to show me *Henry: Portrait of a Serial Killer*,
and I crawled out of his basement two minutes in.
The mall got chopped in half by new owners:
one side a parking lot now, the other a strip mall.

I don't recognize it on the rare occasions I fly
back to Whatchamacallitsville, Ohio.
I try not to even look as I pass by.

Translation

April J. Larson

In minus twenty-five degrees
snow swirling like white sand

a license plate LITWLF
meaning a Leech Lake Band

of Ojibwe family
given name Littlewolf

bordered in red and black, little wolf
Ma 'iingan in fading tongue

Cutbank

Kristin Stoner

The body of a doe hangs
in a fallen tree over a thalweg,
a stiff pelt too long on the line,
open-mouthed, empty-eyed,
teacup hooves pointed down,
in accusation of the water.

It's a wonder how something so still
was a flurry of panic not long ago.
Slipped, perhaps, on a steep slope,
giving over to danger for thirst.
Or worse, trying to cross for food,
or worse, for fear.

She can be imagined a gold myth
emerging from a shade of green,
young crop, the earth magic black
beneath her, then, soon, a limp corpse
carried and winding past small lives
of flatheads and river eels.

These dog days expose spring's casualties,
the havoc of river's brown rush,
a tree pulled down to the cutbank,
now just a tangle of brittle branches,
now just another dead goddess
waiting the slow turn to silt.

Severe Weather

Kristin Stoner

continues throughout central Iowa.

    river swells
    levee failures
    evacuations

Heavy with river mud, we sink
into dark, larvae-ridden waters,
too weighted to climb on roofs,
too hopeless to search for higher ground.

    reservoir control
    engineers
    embankment dams

We smell the empty lake,
the rotting carcasses of carp and crappie.

    contaminated drinking water
    unseasonable downpours
    five hundred year flood

We suffer the isolation of a nowhere place.
Each town too affected to help the next.
Each farm an island.

            power outages
            flash floods
            spillway spills

We know water over road drownings,
hear:

            Presidential Disaster Declaration
            USDA Rural Development
            Model for Recovery

Meanwhile,

elbow-deep in basement sewage,
we cut carpet into manageable pieces,
scrub at black polka-dotted mold,
pile pieces of our lives on street corners for pickup.

The Deserter

Kristin Stoner

He harvested me in Omaha
with dirty fingernails
and an earthy grin.

I ached
for serenity,
open sky,
open soil,
fertility,

somewhere I could see the storm
before it reached me.

But a farm is an island,
the fields a sea,
and the rows of crop
looked every day
more and more
like bars.

Kwansaba For a Deer That I Helped My Uncle Butcher

Jeremiah Driver

I believe in your blood that now
stains my hands; no longer warm but
cold and sticky. What a fever you
must have been, rushing through fields, over
ditches and cooling your ghost, your guts—
blood, in the calm waters of a
brook. In your death we have met.

Pollen

Sandra Marchetti

Droplets. Clumping molecules.
Leaves' breaths
on the backs of cars
that only through water were—
and then were only ever
particular ghosts—
a neon peridot.

The pollen falls around,
pushes back
through nostrils,
sifts in lashes,
lands in beds
under eyelids.

We pull our eyelids
at their sheeted corners,
as if to press the eye all the more
toward the bloom,
the dusty after-center of nature's
first derivation.

god-stem

Sandra Marchetti

I come to see the tree
on fire:
dark art,
buoyed god—
round as a bush.

It is temporal rush,
green less each hour.
The rising skirts
whistle up,

wheel air
under the tree;
leaves
crisp to coals
burnt off their branches.

I see a little pink
beneath it,

some flagging
applications of summer

lead toward the virtue
of the fire—

the triangular
strength.

Messages

Carly Sachs

The universe is always leaving messages—
Someone's hand on your thigh while you listen to the radio,
My mother believes the touch of wind is her father
From the other world telling her it's ok.

Before yoga class in the park someone spelled I love you in flowers
And I want to believe it's for me, my inner voice speaking
to my outer doubter, the way I had cut class and interlaced my
          fingers
around my grandfather's when he was in the hospital.

That's where my mother found us after work silent together
in the language underneath the language.
How do you translate a breath or a kiss or name the sensation
we call loss, how the sound trails off quietly the way dusk embraces

the trees along the highway. Everything dark, passing,
But I want you still, the way you were when you were sober,
Before the garage had the holes you made in it, before my heart
was worn thin like cotton, before the skin of fear could peek
          through.

When the deer gather in the yard, I watch them looking in at me
as if they were either looking past me into the beyond of the future,
or stunningly lost, bereft as a window, blank as page or plate waiting
to hold whatever arrives.

Berry Bender

Carly Sachs

Nostalgia is pickling or pressing,
to hold what cannot be held, to remain
as if memory. The frame rather than
the photograph, or the photograph
rather than the frame.

There is nothing like strawberry picking
for a broken heart, thinks Ramona.
She can have her berries and pick them too
which makes her think she's getting away
with something.

Squatting in the dirt is like spooning with the earth.
The way things used to be is a phrase she finds herself saying.
She wants to know the land like the beloved's skin,
the way the house used to move with the noise of him.

A berry forms like a tear, or the pucker
before the kiss. To make jam, you have to add
sugar. She wonders what the pectin is
that will get her heart to harden and set again.

Real Butter

Carly Sachs

A refrigerator tells a story. When you invite me over,
I like to open the door, the fleeting world within a fleeting world.

The bookshelf of the body. The condiments that cement
your future. What you consume, consumes you.

A refrigerator is not a zen garden or minimalist sculpture
Or graveyard for half-full mustards and mayonnaise.

Take-out containers say you're not here or you don't like
to dirty your hands. I look for local cheese, milk

that comes in jars and homemade jam.
I want a good party, a gathering of just enough.

Ginger and tamari. Local eggs and arugula. Maybe cornichons
or at least kosher dills. A French Bleu, a sauvignon blanc.

And everyone these days seems to have a thing for the Greek
yogurt. Meet me with your figs and heirloom tomatoes,

I want to say, have you tried their Stout
or met Anders, the cheese maker at the farmer's market.

But I'll be happy if there's real butter
and cream for my morning coffee.

In some languages hunger and desire
share the same root. The beginning of the narrative,

a refrigerator is a map
or snapshot taken.

The place of longing
and belonging.

To the right you'll see

Trevor Ketner

cornrows stacked like ziggurats
up the hills, each row
a prayer in leaves and swelling grain.

our lady of blank stone, a monolith
in hands and limbs reaching over a graveyard
pocked with pink silk and plastic flowers.

the place where I keep thinking
mountains should be, so they appear,
the flickering silhouette of a memory
across a knee-high corn horizon.

A Wood in Nebraska

Trevor Ketner

What silent monsters are these,
their teeth tangled in the ground,
their hair green mimics of clouds?

We'd cut them down where I am from
to craft altars of their bones,
carve flowers into their dismembered limbs,
but here they let them loom along

the highway where the unfaced
bodies of all the dead, pet cats lie
to sleep in the ancient, cereal rows.

Their crackled pelts clothe arthritis
and clad their thoughts in texture.
Their thoughts are on ways to properly
worship the sun. They grow themselves

a too-silent armada of green admirals,
entire fleets anchored in swollen fields,
their masts their own unshaken spines.

Missing, Nearly

Trevor Ketner

When the Russian olives forged themselves
silver in the wind, my father blared the horn

of the red, family SUV heralding the blur
of the road's delineation. He commemorated

the side panels of the eighteen-wheeler
as they trembled themselves very nearly

into our imagining of what could happen
to the driver side mirror. *Objects are closer*

than they appear. I saw the Russian olives
in my father's eyes and knew it to be true.

He had leaves for lashes and I plucked each,
each the same, to make a wish, a cobbling

of words; each poem the flash of a titanic
machine, breathing smoke and trembling.

Bodies of Water

Martin Ott

I grew up on Lake Huron,
wind scent inside everything
vespers to some aching shore.

The years brought the churn
of too-cold water to surface,
raised dunes from the waves.

We all read about vessels lost,
rough waves the size of living.
I navigated far, I lost myself,

my reinvention of dry riverbed
along a false trail of stone eggs,
other men's kingdoms, the salt

never able to rub away the lake.
I became a myth that I launched
every so often, from coral reefs

to the glaciers of the invaders
I carry in my blood and deep
recesses no one but me could

drown in. I was impossible.
It was impossible to foresee.
The lake flowed in your wake,

was always there, in the fingers
of the tributaries we came to be,
the bodies we joined incessantly.

Samantha's Wedding:
Spring 2006 Winneconne, Wisconsin

Katherine Ann Davis

I fly back from DC for curiosity,
and for our clique's latest wedding.
Dye my hair black for no reason.

Seven sex jokes from the pastor
all the girls have used.
I have no one left to roll my eyes with.

Of course the reception is where
three of the girls tend bar.
Of course we are women now.

The bride asks us to take pictures,
hands us disposable cameras.
I point the lens back at myself.

When she tosses her flowers, I go
down the street to the schoolyard swings.
Ten years since I've sneaked vodka in Sprite.

Through the willows the stars were always brightest.
On New Year's we'd mix soap
and blow bubbles that froze to our wands.

Tonight it isn't so cold. I walk barefoot across the lawn.
By the sidewalk a lone clump of daffodils
springs up from the grass.

Japanese Maple in Indiana

Katherine Ann Davis

It's *impossible to avoid*, you say.
You touch my elbow to guide us
through the courtyard, to the trucks
we have filled
by separating our things into boxes.

The fading sunlight is broken
by late-fall leaves; dipping low,
the sun adds layers to our shadows.
Only the leaves of the maple remain.
For it: a circle cut from the concrete,
a pile of mulch to nourish the roots
punctuated at the center by a trunk
that splits its bark
as it twists into itself.
We never were able to straighten it.

You lean into me to avoid its twigs,
its sharp pointed leaves, thin and tinged red
curling downward over more rigid parts.
But, against one another,
they gently lie
and hardly rustle.

Orchard

Joe Betz

—Bloomington, IN

1.

On the bench I read,
mouth full of apple,
poets with dead fathers
should not write them
in or out of poems,
that an image of wasps
leaving a broken peach
left rotting on concrete steps
connotes so much pain,
and it's always pain,
that even descriptive suicides
shuck their skin
into the pathetic ditch.

2.

In the orchard, the bees
fly near their hive, the starts
from last year's strawberry patch
lift white blossoms below peach
and apple trees. Four years old,
espalier training limbs to wire
like a yearly tailored smock,

buds promising fruit
that if left alone
might grow fat and fall

of its own volition, become part
of the soil, darkened by ants in waves.

3.
And wasps, too, might be there,
but only because the sweet rot
calls their congregation,
and you'll notice they sing louder leaving
than arriving, their swoop before
skeptical and lovesick, as if they weren't
sure how to act before clenching mouthfuls,
in love with fall, the wrong idea of harvest.

Stuck in the Middle West You

Michelle Menting

We all hide wings on these plains of grasses, it seems: everyone
ready for flight. We spread. We glide. Listen, this isn't a metaphor
for flying or fear of taking off with nowhere to go. These lakes of
corn, isles of switchgrass, rocks of buffalo—what if this breadth of
ground is more than cropland for longing? What if this is finally
clear: you belong here, like I do. We'll stretch calm over the prairie,
spend cowboy nights beneath

> its frameless sky and stay warm in the folds of sleeping bags
> like corn encased in husks. We'll stay full just palming remnants
> of apple seeds. We'll look up and wonder when others will learn
> it's silly: there are clowns to the left of us, jokers to our right.

Bildungsroman

Michelle Menting

In 8th grade biology, our teacher leads us
down the path, takes us through the woods
to learn about chlorophyll and change.
We pass the leaves—the crinkled, the fallen,
whatever remains of green and clinging—
and he lectures on switchgrass instead,
how it hugs the shorelines of ponds and bog thickets.
We study its stems: their shape, their sides
so quick, so capable of slicing.
My hands aren't nimble in the chill of autumn.
The blades, they slip from tips of my fingers,
and an edge of grass fillets the length of my thumb—
transforms it into a one-gilled minnow.
I wonder at this cut, this slash, this fish-lung
gaping at my knuckle. I poke at pinkness:
two folds of skin that refuse to bleed,
and I fall behind the rest of the class, wander
alone among the oak and pine into a moraine.
There I try spooning a fallen elm tree,
one that crashed not long ago.
Now when a breeze pushes its way through,
it bullies only dead branches.
But the sparse hairs on my arms,
how they fray, how they thread.

Villa Park, Illinois

Kenneth Pobo

In "The Garden Village" we grow
practical plants like tomatoes and beans,
normal roses and zinnias. I want

orchids and palms. When I move
away, I get them—they promptly
die. My parents sell the little

white house, the rectangle-shaped yard
with a Chinese Elm that an ice
storm split in half—they come

to Pennyslvania to be near me,
never see Illinois again.
Some plants get yanked up,

left to wither when the gardener
goes inside for a peanutbutter
and jelly sandwich. Illinois,

something I fly over on the way
to requirements in a distant place.
The roots, still vital,

I haven't left Illinois at all—30 years
and it is home. Vanished.
The orchid I didn't recognize.

Blue Grass and Awnings

Kenneth Pobo

Diego's Bar has a fascinating blue
glass top. My martini catches the sky
as I drink. The early Bee Gees,

songs from *First and Horizontal,*
put me in a good mood, the sixties
on a stool nearby. A stranger

voices strong opinions, asks:
Is *Illinois west of Pennsylvania?*
He laughs. I could tell him

our flat Illinois hearts hold
powerful rivers. Our minds grow
great corn—the Midwest is often

the butt of the joke. We overturn
punch lines. Our counties have syllables
that weave and wiggle: Sangamon,

Jo Daviess, Grundy, Vermilion. Clouds
drop weary butts on plastic
white chairs under droopy awnings.

He pities me, I guess. It's fine.
Illinois is my spine—it showed me
how to stand up.

Lightning Bugs
Elizabeth Schultz

They are lights trembling
in the liminal space
between day and night.

They flash in the grass,
a dash, a pulsing dot, a code
they interpret unerringly.

They flicker above the clover's
pearly heads, the female longing
toward the male's signal.

Captured in jars, they become
lanterns to shine about
until the gleam goes out.

Gone from cities, Japanese
department stores release them
on rooftops for children to chase.

In Kansas, they are stars
sprinkled across the lawn.
But no metaphor jars them.

Fire flies.

Toward Winter

Elizabeth Schultz

Beyond the bird bath,
and barren ash tree,
beyond the rose trellis's
tangle of thorns,
the peony leaves are
drooping yellow, and
young maples, in a row
against the back fence,
are pale red, the color
of blood, watered down.

Home Turf in the Midwest

Salvatore Marici

The steward sows
native grasses
and wildflowers seeds
in 1.5 acres
designed and maintained
to resemble Astroturf.

Skycald on her two-story cedar deck,
she hums songs songbirds sing.
Her feet and arms mimic
the hummingbirds' wings flap
of figure eights.

Neighbors twist outside faucets.
Water leaves garden hoses
rains lawn chemicals into earth.
Weekends, they shake their heads
at her weeds as they drive
John Deere tractors back and forth.
Then they park their toys into garages
and go inside conditioned air.

At dusk, she shawls
her shoulders,
hears crickets chatter
and sees fireflies blink orange
between sideoats gramas
and aromatic asters.

The Merge:
Chicago Near North Side 1920s and 30s

Salvatore Marici

The unified fragrance of tomatoes,
garlic, basil, and meatballs
sneaks out opened windows

Lingers on front porches
of three story brick buildings
where men born in Sicily
sit with their young children
on Sunday afternoons.

On the steps,
fathers teach first-borns
in English
with accented vowels attached
to wave the American flag.

The Height and Fall of Little Sicily

Salvatore Marici

A few days before Memorial Day
during 1920's in the Chicago Near North Side
men's shoulders support and their steps sway
a platform where a wood Mother Mary stands.
When back at Saint Philip's church steps
Father Luigi sprinkles holy water.
Parishioners clip dollar bills to the wire aura
purchased permission to kiss the statue.
White robes drape two girls wearing cardboard wings.
Callused hands pull ropes harnessed to their backs.
The angels recite Latin three stories high over
grills scaring black stripes on green peppers' skin,
fennel sausages dripping fat
and the barrels of wine and beer
the neighborhood's Don provides.
Shops and corners scream, "rat a tat" no one sees.
A cluster of girls in plaid skirts and white blouses walk.
Boys in black trousers, white shirts, and black ties follow.
In one-room grocery stores, twine suspends
pear shape provolone and hard salami from ceilings.
Feet squeak floor planks where wood barrels
filled with black and green olives sit.
Vinegar stains the outside curves. On sidewalks
eggplants and apples display on shelves.
Bakeries sell cannoli and cookie sheets
of white bread splattered with chunks
of tomatoes, mozzarella, and splashes of olive oil.

Puffs of risen yeast and flour harden into crust
steam into the streets.
Men climb boxcars from California,
taste and choose red grapes they press, pour juice
into five-gallon clay containers in kitchens.
Tenants pay rent to Grandpa with dried fruit
the government allocated and Grandma rehydrates,
then bakes. She gives pies to the renters.
The city demolishes those homes
during and after World War II.
Cabrini-Green constructed over foundations
like ruins in Sicily. Saint Philip closes.

That Smallest of the Great Lakes

Morgan Harlow

I remember stopping by Lake Erie
near Vermilion, Ohio
the exact spot unclear
as if I were a giantess
peering into a looking glass
on the world
from that small craggy beach
at the roots of cottonwood and willows.

Michigan Pt. 1

Esteban Colon

Needles erupt
      green from trees, bark
      calling down a dipping Earth, by
low
hanging branches framing
      rainbow leaves,
raining
light upon a soft carpet of grass, waiting
to tickle cheeks, watch
diving worms,
           drink
deeply the water rolling into the pond below
before
galloping feet move
             dirt/mud, running
into imagination
            where
plastic and dead sticks become the
instruments of war,
            bodies
too small for military garb arguing over
who got shot, who
got the jump on whom,
            brains
filling clips,
          roaring the thunder of falling shells.

Michigan Pt. 2

Esteban Colon

Needles find holes,
closing pores like the ears
                              of disagreeing sisters
every
tree dropping the
          salted rain of Willows
as
eyes
resurrect the ammunition their children could
only imagine,
screaming
past crumpled leaves, their
mother deep in winter
while words and
                    touch
become the thunder
                    of falling shells.

A Father's Lament

Fred MacVaugh

Cornfields buried knee-deep in snow,
A winter-long monotony of weight.
Only movement, walnut-black water
As clear as a bruise against glistening skin.

All summer, sharp-toothed chiselers
Clear cut the crops, gnawed and hauled
Into stream stalk and creek-side sapling.
Today, in early thaw, the runoff soil settles

In snowmelt dammed by toppled timber.
Before irrigation, in drought, these dams
Were godsends. Not today. Fucking beaver.
They've leveled crops and profits, buried land.

Like my boys, I had a dream once. They left for lives
Far removed from harder rain and heartache.
With higher water and floods today, many sell;
Fewer salvage lives, fewer farm again.
Like earth, once gone, they've gone for good.

Northwest Minnesota in January

Nathaniel Lee Hansen

"Hey, No Mosquitoes," brags the sign
beside the fire station tonight.

Wind chill at minus forty-five—
air raw as a scratched skeeter bite.

Horoscope

Laura Apol

LIBRA: In a past incarnation, it's possible that you were
imprisoned or burned at the stake for expressing your beliefs.
That might help explain why you're sometimes reluctant to
speak your mind with total candor in this life.

Never mind the others—
for me, the horoscope is true.
I remember those flames.
I've spent half this life avoiding their return.

Those flames lit my childhood.
The stake was the kitchen chair, where
after a fight my brother and I were set, knee to knee,
forced to smile until our anger was done.
My anger never was done, but I was always
the first released.

Those flames blazed through my adolescence.
The stake was the passenger seat, where
I fawned and deferred
so boys who collected guns
and washed windows at the Gas and Oil on Main
would ask me out again.

Those flames raged through my marriage.
The stake was everywhere:
dinner table, kitchen sink,
back yard, double garage.

I was a dutiful wife,
keeping cupboards filled, laundry baskets empty,
kneading bread in silence
though my resistance rose.

In church, at holiday parties,
with the playgroup in the park:
I said I believed what I couldn't,
said I voted for Reagan when I didn't,
was silent when it came to wars, poverty, choice
bit my lip through jokes about Jews, gays,
liberals and blondes,

never heard my own anger
crackling around me, never noticed
that the blood in my mouth
tasted like ash.

Reorienting

Nancy Cook

We lived north of it all, if all
are the people and appendages, crops
and customs of this farming country. If it
equals the state of Ohio, we lived north of it all,
the back of our small town braced against the edge
of Lake Erie, a broad expanse of gray and green. We lived
in view of the sunrise, the sunset, a foreign country directly across
but not in our sight. We lived where visiting arctic winds could assault

the red brick walls of our homes, the ones leaning north
toward Draco's distant light, where once, from the driveway, below
the kitchen window, Mary Ann called for me through heavy leaded panes
storm-windowed against the cold, chinked open two inches to
      welcome the spring

that hadn't arrived, but would crawl in soon
from the south. I rushed out the door in anticipation
of something, the cheery tulips, the pale-petaled bloodroot, animals in heat, blazing azaleas that flourished in spite
of the climate's inhospitality, and I left behind the muted blues
of the carpet in the den, the Catholic school uniform skirt tossed on
the closet floor, my mother's tired voice, the somber basement echoes

from the classical clarinet my father played this, as every,
Saturday morning. We ran down the drive, Mary Ann and I, two friends,
at twelve, not accustomed to the breasts that floated with us as we escaped

with unguarded joy, not yet familiar with the sapient
gait of caution. Behind us, the sun was newly risen, higher
in the sky at this early hour than it had been just the week before,
a shade warmer, too, turning our jacket fleece from black into navy blue,
and maybe we knew even then that Mary Ann's brother, wearing the
gray-green
drab of the Seabees, was lost somewhere north of the DMZ in a
country braced against

the edge of its other half and madness. It stopped
us cold, this sun on our backs, higher than it had been just
the week before, breaking through the leaded panes of our winter
selves, catching up with the pink blossoming tips of our new breasts,

and warning that we were
not quite ready
to face it all.

Ox and Lamb

Lou Amyx

—Journal Page Marked 29 June 1851

think if you could not make one more step

already the men
have beaten two of our oxen

to their deaths
the wheezing creatures fall

yoked to their brothers hooves split like oysters

mired to their shoulders in this murderous bog

sixteen teams
lurch forward one wagon

then back
for another wagon

hope
is four miles today

home
four miles is an hour's walk

what drives these men to torture and leave

the killed beasts of their god-given dominion

these women
to offer so many children

all rot the same
in rock and mud and numbing rain

Love on the Plains

Dometa Brothers

Outside the darkened Iowa sky is thick with rain.
Violet, violent heat traces sheets of energy from darkened sky
to darkened earth.

Somewhere beneath is the vague frightening blackness
of the river, shrunken back
from its banks, brief illuminations of fireflies.
Switchgrass, bluestem, and the honey locust quiver
under the weight of sky.

Inside we are carved earth and the breath of life.
Your mouth tastes like mine, and the shadow of light
hints at the trace of long form.

Beyond the strange doubleness of limbs
the air folds across our forms
—a complete space. There is living in the earth,
in the air. We are potential and kinetic energy.

In heavy doubled darkness,
bearing the weight of the horizontal sky,
swallowing traces of light,
the blossoms descend from the honey locust tree.

More

Dometa Brothers

I am half sick of brown bird beauty
and all that is austere.
I want, I want to fall
more. Just more
of everything. But most of all
to see hear taste touch move more.

I am dying for a cosmogony of senses

—some articulated accent of red tulip,
caterpillar hair soft folds barely concealing
some guiled sweet gatherer's sip.

No more bare beauty. I want none of it.
Which is just what there is
to have

to have some unashamed
mystic divine something
something grand beyond grand
and
some stars—some unnamed constellations scattered—a dew
from heaven's dark firmament—competing.

Competing. Yes! Competing pageantry.

I want a riot.

Cascades of everything! Let there be
bowers burdened with burgundy roses
falling
to soaked earth heavy with the smells
of rain, roses, smoldering skies
like
the filaments of green blue gold
spun from the aureole,
reflected in your sea glass colored eyes.

A mind maddening reflection,
an infinite regress
multiple, mobiacal, madness

I want

To mark the movement, all
movement, from the hush of your
eyelashes breathing life
into the mound of my cheek, falls
To
the thrumming, pulsing movement
of my heart, your blood,
our undiluted souls incandescent—
in the bump pulse of a wrist
more cataracts without, within

I want to fall
—find reason—
to reach and rend
something remarkable—

Remarkable. Something, some muse

I want
to open—to unfold—
a thousand plaited satin ribbon
like
the tightly furled lilac fuse
bursting.

White

Dometa Brothers

The snow swirls down through moonlight, streetlight, windowlight
settling in opalescent folds between hills,

drifts up along the trees—rising
climbing the darkened bark's crevices.

On this white world a stain is impossible.

Put down your papers. Leave your desk.
I'll gather your whiteness in my sun-dark arms as

the water-spun flowers of night fall, float, fly
animated—each a silvered slivered melting jewel.

Look here at the window above you:

The flowers recreate themselves on glass—
Transparency wedded to transparency—illumined in the firelight

of our room. I'll trace the seed of your soul
under the translucent skin of your collarbone.

Settle here in the sheet's white folds while

the wind builds
and the cloud-dark moon sets
more and more and yet more crystal

bud drops to fill the vale.
Undulating drifts
round an uncertain center.
swell and slope paper white 'gainst storm
darkened earth.

There

—arrange the blanket—

sink against the crook of my arm.
Outside the storm subsides.

The wind eddies; the first light shines
through annealed bride-blossomed-windows.

Layovers

Andrew Payton

The last leg of every flight
is fall. I watch a crow step
from lamppost with a confidence
I envy when suicidal—

the *I know I'll make it, just go*—

He unfolds his wings,
glides to the bloodied head of rabbit.
A Chicago snowstorm obstructs
my westbound return—

a system divides
the country in two:
my native East,
        my adopted Midwest.

In Virginia, I press my hand
to terminal glass. Swallows
over baggage carts disappear
into hangars. At dinner

a friend speaks of the mantis shrimp
with barbed spears for limbs
so strong no aquarium contains
it within such simple glass.

In winter, steam from the coal plant
catches in sycamores, sculpts
ice over pedestrians. The corn fields
give their bodies to the war.

Can you sense it? That far-off terror?
The too-quiet, the babies in strollers,
the thick-limbed parents. The hellos
I don't begin to believe.

The hammer to the window?
The rush of conditioned air?

Preparations

Andrew Payton

I swim to the other side of the river
and learn how those people live.
I watch the dough rise on their porches
and taste the water from their wells.

Driving in a snowstorm across Iowa
we pass forty seven wrecks—we know
because we count. We smile and joke
and try to feel okay about our dying.

When we read the news we fill the tub
with water and whet our blades. I count steps
from door to river. We memorize the sound
of sliding bolts and loading chambers.

Onions blossom and walnuts fill their arms
with fruit. Though the tank is full of gasoline,
we have nowhere to drive. These city deer
are tame; they look us humans in the eye.

If the Creek Finally Runs

Andrew Payton

Every day while I wait for the bus a man
passes pressing a small dog to his chest
beneath his coat. Clearly, not every day,
only when it rains, which is seldom now
since the creek's drying up and we measure
its progress in disappearing. That stone,
this stone, no stone. But now the creek
fills in and the man holds his dog to chest
and tucks his chin to the wind and despite
these patterns of creek and no creek,
I don't think the fish will return. The bus
arrives on time and I see the same hands
bracing their bars against the rocking
but reading different magazines. Conversation
is the same—what he did and how that hurt
or what dress for the wedding. But the bus
is not yet here and the man with the dog
doesn't say hello, for rain is too serious
a thing to waste time on hello. The creek
passes under the bridge under the wheels
of the bus and I see that it's a skeleton
of its former self today, and maybe one day
the rhythms will stop or speed up or maybe
find another drummer, and the man's dog
will die or maybe the man will die, and they'll
get a new bus or change the route, or maybe
the creek gets tired of where it's going

and who it meets once it gets there and one day
we wake up to find it's crested a different hill,
carved a different gully and it won't be me
standing on the corner, hanging over the railing,
thinking always man with dog and bus on time
and always creek and always when I look at my hands
there are hands and when I draw breath something
is there to draw and so I asked the man
what kind of dog fits inside a coat and he said
I have some place to be.

The Unplanted Field
Andrew Payton

Last night we forgot to close the gate
and this morning wake to find six deer
grazing winter vetch in the upper field—

we try to herd them back to the woods,
rattling hoes against the fence, hooting,
and stomping our boots to the ground,

but the deer panic, and the fence too high
to jump, ram their muzzles bloody on wire
and pine logs. Five find the exit,

but one doe rams so many times she snaps
her neck. We haven't a gun, and so death
spreads over hours, and while seeding onions

we watch in the corner of our vision
the animal pedaling the air, asking her legs
to remove her from this pain, this slow drugging.

We leave her to the weekend, and Monday
the vultures or coyotes have not yet come
to scavenge, only the flies, which consume first

the eyes and anus. I slap her rot-ballooned flank
and listen to the hollow. I imagine a knife
slitting the hide, letting the pressure free.

Letting her breathe, and after such terrible sleep.
We say we'll take care of it—get out the tractor,
drag her to the irrigation ditch—but this is the ground

to keep her, mine are the hands that built the fence.

Special Thanks

Without a wide array of good-natured folks devoting their time, effort, and encouragement, *Prairie Gold: An Anthology of the American Heartland* could not exist. Among these fine people, we must first and foremost extend our thanks to our publisher, Steve Semken and Ice Cube Press. Independent book publishers provide new, creative authors and editors with the support necessary for that ever-important first publication. Without your encouragement and cheerful effervescence, Steve, this anthology would be nothing more than an idea. You have our utmost thanks and gratitude.

We would also like to extend our thanks to several other individuals for their gracious gift of time and talent toward the anthology: Dean Bakopoulos, Mary Swander, and Debra Marquart for lending their expertise, craft, and love of the Midwest in writing the introductions to each section of *Prairie Gold*; Elizabeth Stranahan, our consulting editor and publicity coordinator, for providing a second pair of eyes and hands in editing and marketing; and Jamie Campbell, *Prairie Gold*'s cover designer and graphic artist, for patiently providing dozens of mock ups of the physical look of the book. Thanks to Kelly Slivka, Chloe Clark, Elizabeth Giorgi, Samantha Futhey, Dana Thomann, and Corrina Carter for copy editing support. Thanks as well to Iowa State University's English Department, particularly the faculty in Creative Writing and Environment and English Literature, who have been great mentors to us all.

Finally, we want to offer a huge expression of gratitude for our many authors that submitted their wonderful, moving, and emotional work. Without their creativity in representing personal perspectives on the Midwest, *Prairie Gold* could not stand as a unique collection of Midwestern literature.

Prairie Gold editors: left to right: Stefanie Brook Trout, Lance M. Sacknoff, and Xavier Cavazos.

Prairie Gold EDITORS

Lance M. Sacknoff earned his BA in English Writing at the University of Pittsburgh. He recently earned an MA in English with a specialization in Literature at Iowa State University. Since arriving in Iowa, Lance acted as a technical editor on a manuscript by Paul L. Errington, a Midwestern biologist and conservationist influential in the field of predator-prey dynamics and a colleague of Aldo Leopold. Lance's own scholarship focuses on environmental criticism with specific attention to human-environmental communication and ecosemiotics. *Prairie Gold* marks Lance's first effort in compiling a Midwestern anthology.

Xavier Cavazos is the author of *Barbarian at the Gate*, selected and introduced by Thomas Sayers Ellis as part of the Poetry Society of America's New American Poets Chapbook Series. His debut collection of poetry, *Diamond Grove Slave Tree*, is forthcoming from Ice Cube Press in 2015. Cavazos has taught writing and composition at Iowa State University and currently teaches in the Writing Specialization Program at Central Washington University.

Stefanie Brook Trout has always called the Midwest home. She currently lives and writes in Ames, Iowa, where she is a candidate in Iowa State University's Master of Fine Arts program in Creative Writing and Environment. At ISU, Stefanie is an undergraduate English instructor, the nonfiction editor for *Flyway: Journal of Writing and Environment*, the MFA Student Coordinator for the Everett Casey Nature Center and Reserve, and a member of AgArts, an organization that explores the intersection of agriculture and the arts. Stefanie holds degrees from the University of Michigan in Ann Arbor and Marian University in Indianapolis.

Contributors

✦ **Fiction:**

Jason Lee Brown "The Original Redskin": Jason is the author of the novel *Mattoon and the Mad Gasser* and the poetry chapbook *Blue Collar Fathers*. He is Series Editor of *New Stories from The Midwest*, a semi-annual best-of anthology. "The Original Redskin" is part of his recently finished collection of stories set in central Illinois.

Michelle Donahue "Growing Corn": Michelle grew up in sunny Southern California and is currently lost in the corn mazes of Iowa. She is a current MFA student in Creative Writing & Environment at Iowa State where she is the managing editor of *Flyway*. Her work has appeared or is forthcoming in *Whiskey Island, Redactions, Front Porch Journal, Paper Darts*. You can find her at michelledonahue1.wordpress.com

Matthew Fogarty "In the Milo": Born and raised in the square-mile sub-urbs of Detroit, Matthew lives and writes in Columbia, where he is fiction editor of *Yemassee*. He also edits *Cartagena*, a literary journal. His fiction has appeared or is forthcoming in *Passages North, FRiGG, Fourteen Hills*, and *Midwestern Gothic*. He can be found at www.matthewfogarty.com

Barbara Harroun "Trapeze": Barbara is associate faculty at Western Illinois University where she teaches basic and creative writing. She has an MFA from Purdue University. Her work has appeared in *Buffalo Carp, Sycamore Review*, back-to-back issues of *Another Chicago Magazine*, and *Friends Journal*. She lives with her family in Macomb, Illinois. She's deeply rooted in and still enamored by the Midwest.

T.C. Jones "Across Ohio": T.C. is a graduate of the University of Pittsburgh. His writing has appeared in the *Monarch Review, The New Yinzer, Gadfly Magazine*, and won the TAR award for fiction in *The April Reader*. He is finishing a collection of short stories examining Rust Belt culture and currently directs *Jam2Jam*, a quarterly literary and art series. He lives in the Lawrenceville neighborhood of Pittsburgh with his fiancé.

Rachel Lopez "Carlie's Ride": Rachel's fiction and poetry have appeared in *Reed Magazine, Inkwell Journal,* and *Hint Fiction.* Though originally from the east coast, the streets of Des Moines course through her veins, and one foot is eternally planted in that humble, dirty, hopeful, electric Midwest city. Lopez teaches English at Iowa State University.

Stephanie A. Marcellus "Heartland": Stephanie lives in rural Nebraska and writes short stories and poetry. Her work has recently appeared in *Alligator Juniper* and *The Blue Bear Review.* She received her MFA in creative writing from Colorado State University and is an assistant professor of English at Wayne State College.

Jim O'Loughlin "Something Other Than Garbage": Jim teaches English in the Department of Languages & Literatures at the University of Northern Iowa. He is the host of the long-running Final Thursday Reading Series in Cedar Falls. Find out more at: www.finalthursdaypress.com.

Molly Rideout "The Great River Road": Molly is a fiction writer and essayist with a love for the rural Midwest. She is the Co-Director of Grin City Collective, an artist residency and collaborative located on a 320-acre farm near Grinnell, Iowa. She wrote "The Great River Road" in 2010 while studying at Grinnell College.

Sheila Thorne "Tracks": Sheila now lives in Berkeley, California, but grew up in a Chicago suburb. Her fiction has been published in *Nimrod, Louisiana Literature, Natural Bridge, Prick of the Spindle, Clockhouse Review,* as well as in the anthology *Texas Told'em* (Ink Brush Press, 2010).

Leni Yost "The Weaving": Leni was a newspaper writer and now works as a freelance writer and author. She earned degrees in English from the University of Iowa, a master's in English from Arizona State University, an MFA in creative writing from Arizona State, and has been published in leading literary journals.

Meghan Brown "Dakota Good Enough": Meghan is a nonfiction writer and anthrozoologist who studies animal-related subcultures and animal protection reform. A native of Colorado, she is proud to make North Dakota her honorary second homeland. She will complete her Master of Fine Arts in creative writing and environment at Iowa State University in 2015.

D. Gilson "A Need to Know Basis": D. holds an MFA from Chatham University and is a PhD student in American Literature & Culture at The George Washington University. His chapbooks include *Catch & Release*, winner of the Robin Becker Prize from Seven Kitchens, and *Brit Lit* (Sibling Rivalry, 2013). His book *Crush*, with Will Stockton, was published in 2014 from Punctum Books.

Andy Harper "Watching the Sky": Andy is a creative nonfiction writer in the University of Nebraska MFA program and holds a BA in English from Truman State University. "Watching the Sky" is taken from his current project, a place-based memoir in essays. He enjoys hiking and travel.

Zachary Hawkins "Field Stones": Zachary is a sixth generation farmer in Wabash County, Indiana. His writing has appeared in *The Wapsipincon Almanac* and *Flyway: Journal of Writing and Environment*. He makes music as one-half of the folk duo Jayber Crow.

Will Jennings "Learning Shift": Will's essays have appeared in *Water~Stone Review, River Teeth Journal, Fugue, The Southern Humanities Review, The Examined Life Journal, ICON magazine*, and have twice been nominated for a Pushcart Prize. He is a past recipient of the Brenda Ueland Prose Prize. He teaches Rhetoric and Sustainability Studies at the University of Iowa and lives part-time in rural, mid-coast Maine.

Catherine Lanser "Maintenance": Catherine has lived in Madison, Wisconsin, for nearly 20 years. Her narrative nonfiction has appeared in the anthologies *Stories of Strength, Classic Christmas, Chick Ink, Christmas Traditions: True Stories that Celebrate the Spirit of the Season*, and *Being a Grownup: A User's Manual for the Real World*.

John Linstrom "Fuckaroo!": John is Director of the Liberty Hyde Bailey Museum in South Haven, Michigan. His work has appeared in *Valparaiso Poetry Review* and *The Reed*. He adapted "Fuckaroo!" from his current book project, *Havening*, which pits his life against that of fellow South Havenite and agrarian philosopher Liberty Hyde Bailey.

Marc Nieson "Lost and Found": Marc is a graduate of the Iowa Writers' Workshop. "Lost and Found" is excerpted from *Schoolhouse: A Memoir in 13 Lessons*. His fiction has earned a Raymond Carver Short Story Award and a Pushcart Prize nomination. He teaches at Chatham University, and is working on a new novel, *Houdini's Heirs*.

Paula Sergi "Lucky" & "Small Town News": Paula holds a BSN from the University of Wisconsin, Madison, and an MFA in creative writing from Vermont College. The Wisconsin Academy of Sciences, Arts, and Letters selected her as their cultural ambassador to Hessen, Germany. She received a Wisconsin Arts Board Artist Fellowship and is the author of three poetry chapbooks and co-editor of three anthologies.

Sarah Elizabeth Turner "Cold Feet": A Wisconsin native, Sarah has an MFA in creative writing from Hamline University, St. Paul, Minnesota. Her work has appeared in *Rock, Paper, Scissors; She Bear Literary; Versus;* and *Sleet*. She writes mostly creative nonfiction and can be found blogging at *Sarah in Small Doses* (sarahinsmalldoses.wordpress.com) or doing improv.

Benjamin Vogt "Mnisota": Benjamin is the author of the poetry collection *Afterimage*. His work has appeared in *ISLE, Orion, The Sun*, and been nominated for a Pushcart Prize. He has a PhD from the University of Nebraska-Lincoln and blogs about writing and the prairie life at *The Deep Middle* (deepmiddle.blogspot.com).

◆ **Poetry:**

Khadija Anderson "Geography": Khadija returned in 2008 to her native Los Angeles after 18 years of exile in Seattle. Khadija's poetry has been published in print and online, and she was nominated for a 2009 Pushcart Prize. Khadija's first book of poetry *History of Butoh* was published in 2012.

Lou Amyx "Ox and Lamb": Lou began writing with the production of two plays by the Edward Albee New Playwrights Workshop. Her poetry has been published in print and on the web since 2009. A chapbook, *The Bracelet*, is available from Finishing Line Press. Lou was recently appointed managing editor at *Blue Lyra Review*.

Laura Apol "Horoscope": Laura is the author of *Crossing the Ladder of Sun* (2004, winner of the Oklahoma Book Award for poetry), and *Falling into Grace* (1998). She has just completed her third collection, *Requiem, Rwanda*, drawn from her work using writing to facilitate healing among survivors of the 1994 genocide.

Joe Betz "Orchard": Joe lives with his wife in Bloomington, Indiana, where he is an instructor of English at Ivy Tech Community College-Bloomington. Previous work appears in places such as *Hayden's Ferry Review* and *Anti-*. He is a graduate of the University of Missouri-St. Louis MFA program and can be followed on Twitter @Joe_Betz_

Dometa Brothers "Love on the Plains", "More", "White": Dometa is Assistant Professor of British Literature at Iowa State University (dometa@ iastate.edu). Her research focuses on poetry and the history of science and mathematics as relates to the development of the Romantic poetic imagination. She has published a number of essays and book chapters on science and literature.

Christopher Citro "One Kitchen One Afternoon", "Whatchamacallit": Christopher lives in Syracuse, New York, and his poetry appears or is forthcoming in *Prairie Schooner, Ninth Letter, Subtropics, Third Coast, Cream City Review, The Hollins Critic, Verse Daily,* and *Elsewhere*. His creative nonfiction is forthcoming in *Colorado Review*. He received his MFA in poetry from Indiana University in 2013.

Ryan Collins "Rock Island": Ryan is the author of three chapbooks, most recently *Dear Twin Falls* (H_NGM_N, 2013). His poems have appeared in *American Letters & Commentary; Asymptote; Black Clock; Columbia Poetry Review; DIAGRAM; Forklift, Ohio; Handsome; iO: A Journal of New American Poetry; PEN Poetry Series; Spork; and Transom* He is Executive Director of the Midwest Writing Center in Davenport, Iowa.

Esteban Colon "Michigan Pt. 1", "Michigan Pt. 2": Esteban is an enthusiastic consumer of beauty and a published poet, *Things I Learned the Hard Way* (Plain View Press), from the south suburbs of Chicago. He is an experiential educator and an avid distributor of hugs.

Nancy Cook "Reorienting": Nancy grew up in Cleveland, Ohio, and now lives in St Paul, Minnesota, where she tries to maintain some balance of her parent, lawyer, teacher, and writer selves. She runs the "Witness Project," a series of community workshops that enable the development and dissemination of stories of, by, and for populations under-served by the justice system.

Carol V. Davis "Predicting Weather": Carol is the author of *Between Storms* (Truman State University Press, 2012). She won the 2007 T.S. Eliot Prize for *Into the Arms of Pushkin: Poems of St. Petersburg.* Twice a Fulbright scholar, her poetry was read at the Library of Congress. She teaches at Santa Monica College.

Katherine Ann Davis "Samantha's Wedding: Spring 2006 Winneconne, Wisconsin", "Japanese Maple in Indiana",: Originally from Wisconsin, Katherine Ann received her MFA from the University of Maryland and is currently a PhD candidate at the University of Tennessee, where she is fiction editor for *Grist: The Journal for Writers* and is working on a novel about a failed collector.

Jeremiah Driver "Kwansaba For a Deer That I Helped My Uncle Butcher": Jeremiah is an MFA candidate in writing at Sarah Lawrence College in Bronxville, New York. He is the Assistant Poetry Editor for *LUMINA* and teaches in Queens, New York. He grew up in Illinois where he worked and graduated from Southern Illinois University, Edwardsville.

Toni Easterson "Hoakie", "Nebraska Biome": Born in Eau Claire, Wisconsin, Toni graduated from Gustavus Adolphus College. For many years she lived in Connecticut, where she studied writing at Wesleyan University. She returned to Minnesota to discover she had missed this land and the people who call the Midwest home.

Sean Evans "Man Kneeling at a Rock": Sean earned an MFA from Iowa State University where he was the Pearl Hogrefe Fellow. A devoted environmentalist, Evans poetry is lyrical and sparse. Evans poems confront themes of addiction, love, death, and wildness, with a tough eloquence that is honest and never easy.

Jennifer Fandel "Ode to Farm & Fleet": Jennifer's poetry has recently appeared in *Measure, RHINO, The Baltimore Review, Calyx, Architrave Press Editions, Midwestern Gothic,* and *A Face to Meet the Faces: An Anthology of Contemporary Persona Poetry.* She grew up in northwest Wisconsin and now makes St. Louis, Missouri, her home.

Heather D. Frankland "Hoarder": Heather is originally from Indiana. She received her MPH and MFA from New Mexico State University. Currently, she teaches composition at Pierce College in Washington State. She has been published in *Lingerpost, ROAR, damselfly press,* and *New Purlieu Review.*

Susan Grimm "Swimming out of Season (And, Behold)", "November or Even If You Wear a Watch", "Bumper Crop", "Cave of Light", "Echt": Susan's book of poems, *Lake Erie Blue,* was published in 2004. She won the Copper Nickel Poetry Prize (2010) and the Hayden Carruth Poetry Prize (2011). Her chapbook *Roughed Up by the Sun's Mothering Tongue* was published in 2011.

Nathaniel Lee Hansen "Northwest Minnesota in January": Nathaniel's writing has appeared in *The Cresset, Midwestern Gothic, Bluestem, The Evansville Review,* and *South Dakota Review.* His chapbook, *Four Seasons West of the 95th Meridian,* was published by Spoon River Poetry Press, February, 2014.

Morgan Harlow "The Smallest of the Great Lakes": Morgan is the author of *Midwest Ritual Burning* (Eyewear Publishing, 2012). She studied English literature, journalism, and film at the University of Wisconsin-Madison and earned an MFA at George Mason University. Her poems and other writing have appeared in *Blackbox Manifold*, *Tusculum Review*, *Washington Square*, and *The Moth*.

Su Hwang "Middle March", "Home Sweet Home", "Home, Iowa": Su is a writer and life enthusiast. Born in Seoul, South Korea, she grew up in New York but has lived in the San Francisco bay area on and off since 1999. Su is currently living in Minneapolis where she is learning to love the 10,000 lakes as an MFA Candidate in Poetry at the University of Minnesota.

Russell Jaffe "FF>>": Russell lives in Iowa City, Iowa, and is the Co-Editor of the poetry chapbook press *Strange Cage* (strangecage.org). He also curates the press' reading series. He is the author of the collection *This Super Doom I Aver* (Poets Democracy, '13) and collects 8-tracks.

Trevor Ketner "To the right you'll see", "A Wood in Nebraska", "Missing, Nearly": Trevor is an MFA candidate in poetry at the University of Minnesota. His work can be found online at *Pif Magazine* and *Fjords Review* and in print in *The Conium Review*, *Fourteen Magazine*, and *The Round*. His collection *Butterfly Pinned* was shortlisted for an Atty Award.

Claire Krüesel "Des Moines lobe (12,000 ya) // A storm passes (in the long run)", "Adventitious Roots", "I know where you are": Minnesota native and Ames, Iowa, resident Claire views the world through shifting perspectives of scale: via Biochemistry training, singing in choir (stories in each brief moment), and memories of objects and place. Now a graduate student in Iowa State University's MFA program in Creative Writing & Environment, Claire connects with the community by teaching yoga and playing in local bands.

April J. Larson "Translation": April lives and writes in Northern Minnesota not far from the headwaters of the Mississippi in Itasca State Park. She is in the last year of an MFA Program with Spalding University, Louisville, Kentucky. She enjoys studying languages and music, and teaches Spanish and therapeutic Soma yoga. She is currently preparing a chapbook of poetry for publication as well as researching the ancient Persian ghazal form of poetry.

Issa M. Lewis "Eschelbach Farm House": Issa holds an MFA in poetry from New England College and teaches composition at Davenport University. She is the 2013 recipient of the Lucille Clifton Poetry Prize and has previously appeared in *Prairie Wolf Review*, *Backbone Review*, *Looseleaf Tea*, *Extract(s)*, *Scapegoat Review*, *Pearl*, *Naugatuck River Review*, and *Switched-On Gutenberg*.

Fred MacVaugh "A Father's Lament": Fred is a museum technician at Fort Union Trading Post National Historic Site. His poetry appears or is forthcoming in *13th Floor Magazine*, *Plainsongs*, *South Dakota Review*, *Treehouse*, and *Watershed*. He has an MFA from Iowa State University and serves as an editor for *Newfound* and *Hothouse Magazine*.

Sandra Marchetti "Pollen", "god-stem": Sandra's first full-length collection of poems, *Confluence*, will be published as part of Gold Wake Press' 2015 Print Series. Her volume *The Canopy*, (Midwest Writing Center Press) won the 2011 Mississippi Valley Chapbook Contest. Sandra's poems have appeared, or are forthcoming in *Subtropics*, *THRUSH*, *Nashville Review*, *Ohio State's The Journal*, *Gargoyle*, and *Phoebe*. https://facebook.com/sandywritingservices

Salvatore Marici "Home Turf in the Midwest", "The Merge: Chicago Near North Side 1920's and 30's", "The Height and Fall of Little Sicily": Salvatore's poetry has appeared in *Circle Magazine*, *Slow Trains*, *Descant*, and *Toasted Cheese*. He was the 2010 Midwest Writing Center Poet-in-Residence. He has a chapbook, *Mortals, Nature and their Spirits* (Ice Cube Press). His first full book of poetry is *Swish Swirl & Sniff* (2014).

Michelle Menting "Stuck in the Middle West You", "Bildungsroman": Michelle has published poetry and prose in *The MacGuffin, Bellingham Review, Superstition Review, Midwestern Gothic, Ascent,* and *PANK.* Her chapbook, *Myth of Solitude,* was recently released from Imaginary Friend Press. Originally from the upper Great Lakes region, she currently lives in the Great Plains.

Julia Anna Morrison "New Palestine, Indiana", "Effects", "March": Julia, raised in Alpharetta, Georgia, is a graduate of the University of Iowa Writers' Workshop. She has received fellowships from the University of Iowa and her work has recently appeared in *Redivider* and *Gulf Coast.* Currently, she writes and teaches in Iowa City.

Martin Ott "Bodies of Water": Martin is the author of the novel *Interrogator's Notebook* (Story Merchant Books), and 3 books of poetry: *Underdays* (Notre Dame University Press, 2015), *Captive* (De Novo Prize winner, C&R Press) and *Poets' Guide to America,* co-written with John F. Buckley. He blogs at writeliving.wordpress.com

Andrew Payton "Layovers", "Preparations", "If the Creek Finally Runs", "The Unplanted Field": Andrew is a Maryland native and MFA candidate in Creative Writing and Environment at Iowa State University. His poetry has been published in *Notre Dame Review, Fourth River,* and *Natural Bridge.* He won the 2013 James Hearst Poetry Prize at *North American Review.*

Kenneth Pobo "Villa Park, Illinois", "Blue Glass and Awnings": Kenneth's chapbook *Save My Place* was published in 2012 (Finishing Line Press). Forthcoming from Eastern Point Press is a new chapbook called *Placemats.* He grew up in Villa Park, Illinois. He teaches creative writing and English at Widener University in Pennsylvania

Tony Quick "Midwestern Monsoon": Tony is an east coast fiction writer and poet. He holds a bachelor's degree in English literature from St. Mary's College of Maryland and served as fiction editor for Iowa State University's literary magazine, *Flyway: Journal of Writing and Environment* in 2013.

Carly Sachs "Messages", "Berry Bender", "Real Butter": Carly teaches writing and yoga in Kent, Ohio. She is the author of *The Steam Sequence* and the editor of the anthology, *The Why and Later*. Her poetry has been included in *The Best American Poetry*, *The Bloomsbury Anthology of Contemporary Jewish American Poetry*, *Bourbon for Blood*, and *The Incredible Sestina Anthology*.

Elizabeth Schultz "Toward Winter", "Lightning Bugs": Retired from the Kansas University English Department, Elizabeth is a dedicated advocate for the arts and the environment. She has published two scholarly books, two books of poetry, a memoir, a collection of short stories, and a collection of essays.

Stephanie Schultz "Three Pastorals", "Bucolic", "A Sunset": Stephanie is a marathon runner in St. Paul, Minnesota, where she is also pursuing an MFA in creative writing from Hamline University. Her work has appeared in *Rock, Paper, Scissors*; *Paddlefish*; *Diverse Voices Quarterly*; *Blast Furnace*; *tcmevents.org*; *talk.brooksrunning.com*; and *Lifting the Sky: Southwestern Haiku and Haiga*.

Melissa L. Sevigny "Trillium", "Garage Sale in Iowa": Melissa grew up in Tucson, Arizona. She has a bachelor's in environmental science, an MFA in environmental writing, and has worked in the fields of planetary science, water policy, and sustainable agriculture. Her first book, *Mythical River*, is forthcoming from the University of Iowa Press.

Janis Rodgers Soule "Heirloom", "Ode to a Walnut Tree", "Heartland": Janis is a poet, essayist, and anthropologist living in San Diego, California. She recently obtained her MFA in Creative Writing and Environment from Iowa State University. Her latest work can be found in *Conjunctions* and *Poecology*.

Kristin Stoner "Cutbank", "Severe Weather", "The Deserter": Kristin received her MFA in poetry from Antioch University, Los Angeles, in 2008 and is currently an English department lecturer at Iowa State University. Some of her recent publications include *Natural Bridge*, *Review Americana*, and *Rose Red Review*. Kristin lives in Des Moines, Iowa.

Jeff Tigchelaar "Animals Were Looking at Me": Jeff Tigchelaar's poems appear or are forthcoming in *Pleiades, LIT, Hobart, The Offending Adam, Court Green, Fugue, CutBank, Gertrude,* and *A Ritual to Read Together: Poems in Conversation with William Stafford* (Woodley Press). His blog, *Stay-at-Home Pop Culture,* is published by *XYZ Magazine* in Topeka, Kansas.

Lindsay Tigue "At Joe and Lonna's Farm", "The Center of the Earth is a Little Off-Kilter", "How to Disappear in Michigan", "Huron": Lindsay's writing has been published in *Prairie Schooner, Indiana Review, Passages North,* and *Rattle.* She was a Tennessee Williams Scholar at the Sewanee Writer's Conference. Her poetry collection, *System of Ghosts,* was a finalist in the 2013 Noemi Press Book Award.

Jason Nicholas Vasser "Like your parents": Jason is an MFA in creative writing student at the University of Missouri–St. Louis. As a member of Alpha Phi Alpha Fraternity Inc. he's active in the community, currently serving as Coordinator for UMSLs Writers in the Schools Program.

The Ice Cube Press began publishing in 1993 to focus on how to live with the natural world and to better understand how people can best live together in the communities they share and inhabit. Using the literary arts to explore life and experiences in the heartland of the United States we have been recognized by a number of well-known writers including: Gary Snyder, Gene Logsdon, Wes Jackson, Patricia Hampl, Greg Brown, Jim Harrison, Annie Dillard, Ken Burns, Kathleen Norris, Janisse Ray, Craig Lesley, Alison Deming, Richard Rhodes, Michael Pollan, and Barry Lopez. We've published a number of well-known authors including: Mary Swander, Jim Heynen, Mary Pipher, Bill Holm, Connie Mutel, John T. Price, Carol Bly, Marvin Bell, Debra Marquart, Ted Kooser, Stephanie Mills, Bill McKibben, Craig Lesley, and Paul Gruchow. We have won several publishing awards over the last twenty-plus years. Check out our books at our web site, join our facebook group, follow us on twitter, visit booksellers, museum shops, or any place you can find good books and discover why we continue striving to, "hear the other side."

Ice Cube Press, LLC (est. 1993)
205 N. Front Street
North Liberty, Iowa 52317-9302
steve@icecubepress.com
twitter @icecubepress
www.icecubepress.com

to Laura Lee & Fenna Marie
who relish the seasons, gardens,
clouds, people, and all forms of
living here in the middle.